THE FOUNDATIONS OF LITERACY

The Foundations of Literacy

Don Holdaway

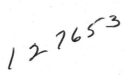

Ashton Scholastic
Sydney Auckland New York Toronto London

Holdaway, Don.
  Foundations of Literacy.

  Index
  Bibliography
  ISBN 0 86896 014 4

  1. Reading (Elementary). I. Title.

372.414

First published in 1979 by Ashton Scholastic P.O. Box 579, Gosford, N.S.W.

The text of this book was set in Trump Medieval, designed by Georg Trump (Schriftgießerei Weber, Stuttgart), with Antique Olive (Fonderie Olive, Marseille) for the headings.

Filmsetting by The Typographers, Sydney.

6 5 4 3 2   1 2 3/8

Printed in Australia

Distributed in the U.S.A.
by
HEINEMANN EDUCATIONAL BOOKS, Inc.
4 Front Street
Exeter, New Hampshire   03833

Contents

Preface

This is fundamentally a book by a teacher for teachers. Many years ago as a young sole-charge teacher I faced a school of New Zealand Maori children in Wairau Pa, Marlborough—at that time, a depressed rural community. They taught me some hard lessons which at first I undervalued. They taught me that literacy could be developed out of song and chant; that the pre-verbal expression of art could flower into language; and that fascination in stories led more directly to reading and writing than my competently prepared lessons in word recognition. They were kind and forgiving—as all *teachers* should be—setting me on a career of child-watching and child-admiration.

This book, with all its faults in scholarship and dispassion, attempts to embody the learning which arose from those early lessons in the fundamentals of education—it is a child-watcher's guide to literacy. The watching may have been wrongly directed from time to time (who teaches us to watch?) but it led irrevocably towards respect for the learning potential of young children.

After five exhausting years of learning and humility and joy with these children I came under the influence of three very important people in New Zealand education—Dr. Beeby, the then Director of Education; Ruth Trevor, the first informed student of reading teaching in the country; and Myrtle Simpson, creator of the *Ready to Read* series. There is no way in which I could objectively evaluate their influence on me as a teacher—I was simply fortunate to be there.

As a clinician for five years, teaching failing children to read and write, my respect for children's potential grew. Although I operated the only such clinic in a large city, there was no child I met who did not want to read and who did not have the ability to do so. This led me to think, to read, and to observe even more closely. Increasingly, my experience of teaching, operating within a child-orientated reading of the research, confirmed my belief in the potential of young learners—and failers—to teach *themselves* within a properly supportive environment. Formative influences during this period included the emancipating work of Sylvia Ashton-Warner and Jeanette Veatch; and the often brilliant formulations of the great American eclectics, especially Paul McKee and Constance McCullough.

About this time I came across the early work of two Americans who had survived the crippling obfuscations of educational thinking in their own country. The first, Ken Goodman, writing his early articles in *The Reading Teacher* around 1964 stimulated an intensively cognitive interest in what I understood through my own work with children. The second, Bill Martin, provided a wealth of children's literature and a sustaining spirit of fellow-feeling which drove me back into the ordinary classroom with conviction and zeal.

During the sixties Auckland became a fully-fledged modern city with a new type of inner-city school—known for decades in other large cities of the Western world—characterized by poverty and a rapid influx of migrant people.

There were two sources of this great migration into the city: people from many different islands of the Pacific basin, largely of Polynesian culture, moved to New Zealand in search of opportunity—bringing cultural riches with them; and the indigenous Maori people—the beloved *tangata whenua*—emerged from their rural isolation, misinformed, to seek what the cities offered.

Compared with the great cities overseas Auckland's problems may have been small, but they presented the educational system with an awakening that was unprecedented. In 1967 Mr. Eric Horsfall, then District Senior Inspector of Schools, set up a study group to find solutions to the literacy problems in the new type of school which had arisen in the inner city and in the brand new housing estate suburbs.

Talent from the whole range of the establishment—from the university to the classroom—was enlisted in a quite unique educational adventure that spanned ten years. The programmes, techniques, and styles of teaching which arose came to be loosely bound together under the term *shared-book-experience*. The generative ideas included a determination to apply genuine developmental principles to the problem (and a willingness to research such principles); the enrichment of a basic *language-experience* methodology by the enjoyment of a rich literature in story, chant, and song; techniques required to bring such a rich, open literature into the competence of young, uninitiated learners; and a frontal attack on the problem of competition and other aversion-producing influences within the school environment.

Auckland was fortunate at that time in having the input of fine developmental research in literacy-learning, stemming from the work of Dr Marie Clay of the University of Auckland. For all those fruitful years the results of her exemplary research, her fertile mind, and her selfless commitment to the needs of children and ordinary teachers sustained the action research in classrooms. Her work has now received due international acclaim: in those early years, however, we had a very special feeling about the top-quality, generative ideas which were in the air because of her work. Perhaps of greatest importance in terms of her early influence on classrooms was the stress she placed on child-watching or monitoring (with an intelligible technique ready-made for teachers to use), and the notion of self-correction as vital to literacy-learning, which sustained a proper faith in children's ability to teach themselves. She also redirected instruction away from external, sequential controls towards the fostering of self-regulation and what she called the 'self-improving system' of operating. I trust that the fact that she is the most quoted authority in this text is sufficient compensation for this inadequate acknowledgement of her contribution.

New Zealanders, a race of islanders at the antipodes, have always felt inferior about their own initiatives (in many instances quite properly) and have therefore been a studiously well-read and widely-travelled people. Ideas from international movements in linguistics, second-language teaching, learning theory, open education, and multi-cultural teaching interacted with committed and creative classroom traditions to formulate new, yet responsible and informed approaches.

The New Zealand Department of Education encouraged and supported these movements, providing opportunities for grass-roots research and development and providing the resources for massive in-service re-education of teachers through the E.R.I.C. programme. Perhaps only in a country of the size of New Zealand could such a set of facilitating conditions be created and sustained through all parts of the system in a spirit of fraternity and genuine commitment to children. Yet, even there, the experience was unique and exemplary. As a hierarchy, the Department officers from top to bottom broke through all the stereotypes of obstructionism, delay, red-tape, and faction in a quite remarkable support of the system which they administered. Much must be acknowledged to the leadership of the Director of Education, Mr. Bill Renwick, without distracting in any way from the informed good-will of his team.

The freedom I enjoyed to work fruitfully in this project was sustained by my colleagues of the Auckland Teachers College. The Principal, Duncan McGhie, facilitated my engagements beyond the College and provided constant encouragement.

This book is the product of those years of colleagueship and co-operation. To mention other names from among that huge group of participants would be invidious. I am deeply grateful to them all, but particularly grateful to the talented young teachers who welcomed me into their classrooms and returned *their* skill to the whole enterprize.

As a vital personal note in the middle of this history—the advance organizer of an obituary—I should acclaim the influence of my own children. It is not so much the special paternal feeling as the unparalleled opportunities for observation—the changing of nappies and the regretted belt under the earhole—which make one's own children one's best teachers. To them who will handle a changing world better than I was ever trained to do, I owe a debt of joy and knowledge too accurate to be embodied in any mere book.

The group of people who bonded themselves together in common concern in Auckland expressed their fraternal enterprize by membership in the International Reading Association. Annual national conferences began in Auckland in 1969 and underpinned the Auckland enthusiasm by national and international initiatives. Throughout New Zealand, the organization grew healthily from local concerns and the regular local meetings, dealing with the problems of their children and teachers, formed the foundation of a national community.

One acknowledgement I would like to make is to the late John Sinclair, Principal of Jean Batten Primary School during the period of crucial trialling of many of the ideas presented in this book. A man of remarkable ability and courage—and humility—as a facilitator and reformer out of covert scholarship and concern, he continued to strive when he ought to have rested. He knew no other way of living, and so he died.

In the preparation of the manuscript I have to thank an able friend, Alvin Smith. And for invaluable comment I am indebted to Barbara Watson and Geof Ward among many who have responded in helpful ways. The peculiarities of style which place this work in some strange *genre* between an academic treatise and a novel, between a work of philosophy and everyman's guide to literacy; between a sermon and a celebration, I take all the blame. Finally, to the *benign* influences of Bacchus and Eros, I give my due.

Don Holdaway
Gosford, N.S.W.
October, 1978

1
An Open Approach to Literacy

Learning to read and to write ought to be one of the most joyful and successful of human undertakings. Notoriously, it is not so. By contrast, most developmental tasks such as learning to walk or to talk are learned almost universally with deep personal satisfaction. What explanation can we give for the continuing difficulties experienced by so many children in learning the tasks of literacy? Are reading and writing intrinsically more difficult even than learning to talk? Are they artificial and unnatural in relationship to other developmental tasks? Are the methods of teaching inefficient even after so many generations of experience and research? Is the school environment unsuited in identifiable ways to the literacy undertaking?

Why another book about literacy?

This book is an enquiry into such questions as these. It is also an attempt to explore solutions both at the level of theory and in honest engagement with the realities of practice. It sets out to be an exploration of what is really possible, rather than just another academic exercise in an endless debate without issue. It is a challenge thrown out in a serious and responsible way—a reaction against the sterile debate of false issues and an invitation to focus on central questions that are too often evaded. Others have made the same plea before or are making it from a variety of standpoints today. In this sense this book supports a tradition of sanity and deep concern for the children who need not fail. The book makes its ultimate appeal to good sense and experience in the world, and is arranged neither as an academic critique nor as a set of prescriptions for the classroom. Rather, it is hoped that it will suit the needs of those who are determined to try out ideas for themselves, to think deeply and to be convinced slowly; those who are prepared to read more widely when in doubt; and those who wish to influence outcomes from an informed conviction which they have tested in their own experience. The exploration takes us from simple and fundamental issues through more complex and debatable ones. Each section moves from hypothesis, through theory and testing, to classroom implications and suggestions for teaching. Ideally, the adventure should be undertaken in a slow, open-minded, questioning, manner allowing the opportunity for working with the ideas in real situations, or at least for personalizing the ideas by rigorous comparison and reflection.

Why is there a problem?

Even in the most advanced societies schools have failed to achieve the 19th Century dream of a universally literate society. The dream may have been unrealistic or the goal even undesirable, but nothing in the educational world can match the resources of every kind that have been poured into this effort and, more recently, into the remediation of its countless failures. Should we not have sufficient clues from the broad span of research in learning, in human development, in linguistics, and in sociology to draw sound conclusions about this failure and its proper resolution? The most complex of human skills are learned in natural environments without the support of highly trained professionals. Have we been overlooking some vital issue because of the sanctity of conventional schooling or because of the fallacies of academic analysis?

What is called for is an extremely open-minded enquiry which takes nothing for granted from the vast accumulation of habits, assumptions, experience and research which surround the subject like an impenetrable jungle. If we continue to make literacy a criterion for basic human dignity in our society, we cannot tolerate the failure with its poignantly modern forms of misery and maladjustment. Instead of setting up expensive and wasteful remedial programmes with a whole new establishment to support them in their inescapable effects of grinding the indignity deeper, we should either find a *preventive* solution or excuse a large proportion of children from school attendance. The present status of the problem, as already endlessly researched and largely unsolved, suggests that no assumption should be sacrosanct in our attempt to understand the matter.

Some important features of the enquiry

In the broadest terms, what sort of process or processes are we concerned with in reading and writing? If we are to be responsible in the enquiry, to what areas of knowledge must we turn? What map should we lay down if we are to explore the terrain thoroughly? What criteria should we set up as touchstones to progressive evaluation of our progress?

A basic set of considerations would include at least the following:

1. Literacy is a matter of language

A traditional error of thinking about reading and writing was to see them as discrete subjects isolated from the world of language and spoken culture and then to teach them as if they had no relationship to listening and speaking. Although lip-service has been given to remedying this mistake in recent years, the habit of regarding reading, writing, spelling and written expression as separate subjects is so deeply entrenched that they continue to be taught in little relationship to each other or to oral language. It is inconceivable that children could learn to talk quite separately from learning to listen, yet in school we continue to contrive barriers between related aspects of language.

The last thirty years has seen a revolution of knowledge in linguistics and in language acquisition. Some attempts have been made to apply those new linguistic insights to literacy, but except in the case of a few able psycho-linguists and sociolinguists whose work we will consider later, such attempts have in the main only served to increase the general confusion and provide further fuel for the factional and perennial debate about opposing methods. Modern knowledge about the nature of language and language acquisition *has* much to offer in clarifying the reasons for instructional failure, but this contribution must be seen as something quite separate from the specifically *educational* prejudices of individual linguists.

Modern linguistics is concerned with the scientific study of language. There are three major branches of linguistic study:

Semantics: The study of meaning in language.
Grammar: The study of syntax and morphology.
Phonology: The study of sound systems of language.

There has been a tendency for modern linguistic study to avoid semantic questions because of their complexity and to concentrate research on the more amenable problems of syntax and phonology (Bruner 1975, pp.61–2). Although we have neglected syntactic questions in the teaching of reading and writing, it would seem that we have neglected semantic questions even more. Semantic theory is a lively and growing area of linguistic study, and it would be a pity if the application of insights from linguistic science generally to the concerns of mastering literacy continued to reflect the timidity of many modern linguists over questions of meaning. However, it is in the continuing study of the acquisition of spoken language that the most pertinent contributions are likely to be found (Britton 1970, pp.33–96). Such studies are concerned with the *learning* of *all* aspects of spoken language, and as observed in *real* settings rather than in the distorting experimental frameworks that we have become used to in educational research.[1]

By concentrating in the past on the exclusiveness of literacy tasks even from each other we have undervalued the fundamental processes of all language and even created activities such as 'word calling' which are basically non-linguistic in nature and are practised only in schooling. During our enquiry we need to remember that anything that can be said of human language and language learning has some vital bearing upon the processes of literacy.

2. Literacy has many human dimensions

Language is the most complex of human activities, engaging the organism simultaneously at every level of experience. Muscular and sensory processes operate automatically at speeds well beyond conscious control yet remain sensitive to deliberate intervention for problem-solving or for correction and confirmation. In perception, sensory information is processed sub-consciously from its raw form into meaningful units. In expression, thoughts are translated into articulation or into written symbols by encoding processes too complex for complete analysis. Language fails in its intention if cognitive processes are not active and dominant, while these same processes activate predictive alertness. Cognitive activities also govern feedback, and so guide, control and correct in the total orchestrated performance. Some part of the intention or effect of language is always emotional in nature no matter what the primary function—which may in itself be concerned with feeling. Finally, the whole concert of activity proceeds at such a startling pace that only a fraction is under conscious control: the greatest burden of work is carried out in a delicately structured automatic performance by little understood processes in the nervous system.

In carrying out any language activity, then, the human organism is engaged globally, and malfunction in any area may seriously impair learning. The extent to which language is dependent on deeply automated systems and on delicate control systems has been largely overlooked in the teaching of reading and writing. We tend to teach as if the child should have conscious control of every response—which is impossible—rather than teach in such a way as to facilitate the rapid development of smoothly operating automatic systems

(Smith 1971, pp.23–26). Furthermore, by constantly intervening in corrective ways we tend to inhibit the development of those vital feedback systems which sustain healthy functioning. These are topics to which we must return again and again throughout our enquiry.

Language has other human dimensions of equal importance to those we have considered. The way a person functions linguistically is such an integral part of self that it cannot be separated from the health and well-being of the person. Full human status in our society cannot be attained in the absence of functional literacy. Unlike special talents, literacy is required not to be better than others but simply to be *like* them—to be fully human. Experience of failure or inadequacy in language, even for short periods during learning, may undermine personal confidence and well-being in frightening ways. Remedial intervention poses such risks to self-esteem that it is difficult to implement a programme without predominantly negative effects—even on learning. Thus any theory or practice of literacy teaching which fails to take into account the deep and powerful implications of language in the whole personality fails at a most fundamental level.

Communication is only one aspect of the multi-functional nature of language.[2] Language is such an integral part of experience that *every* human purpose or function has a linguistic correlative—as soon as a new human need or preoccupation arises, an appropriate language form is created to represent it. One of the reasons for ease in oral language acquisition is clearly the wide range of powerful functions to which language is put by young children—its versatility is immensely rewarding, bringing powers that must seem almost magical to the infant learner. Literacy skills, on the other hand, tend to be taught using language for a narrow range of purposes instead of exploiting its functional richness. (Halliday 1973, pp.7–20). An effective learning environment for the acquisition of literacy should be alive with activity which is felt to be deeply purposeful in all the ways of human meaning. For these reasons it will be necessary to explore the *functions* of language in detail.

3. Literacy is developmental

Developmental learning is the type of learning engaged in by infants before they enter school and by school children outside the instructional environment. It occurs with a minimum of instruction as a 'natural' part of ordinary development but may include the learning of such culturally conditioned tasks as doing up buttons, lacing shoes, or riding a bicycle. It is perhaps 'natural' in a *different* sense that schools should set up very different conditions for learning the tasks that they are commissioned to teach, including reading and writing. There are many reasons for this. Teaching literacy skills is the peculiar function of schools but, because of their distance from the real activities of living, because of their institutional framework, and so on, schools find it difficult to provide the conditions for developmental learning. Literacy has always rated of prime educational importance, and all the techniques of formal, institutional instruction have been focussed on it. Paradoxically, when the school meticulously leaves no stone unturned to *teach* literacy skills thoroughly, it leaves no room for children to *learn* those skills with the same efficient use of their faculties as they bring to bear on comparable tasks outside the school.

Developmental learning is highly individual and non-competitive; it is short on teaching and long on learning; it is self-regulated rather than adult-regulated; it goes hand in hand with the fulfilment of real life purposes; it emulates the behaviour of people who model the skill in natural use.[3] Could reading and writing be learned in similar ways? The very idea gives us as teachers a sense of insecurity—it is almost as if this type of learning, so manifestly efficient, threatens our professional functions. It also raises some uncomfortable questions, such as, 'How do we go about "modelling reading and writing in natural use" in the classroom?'

4. Literacy is learned

The history of ideas in the acquisition of literacy is a history of competing methodologies focussing on teaching or instruction rather than on learning. In the past fifty years we have seen a revolution in knowledge about the nature of learning, yet in the vast literature on the teaching of reading, so voluminous that the dedicated student is threatened with verbal suffocation, there is seldom a mention of this knowledge. For instance, in the massive and influential study by Jeanne Chall, *Learning to Read: The Great Debate* (1967) or even in the 600 pages of the Bullock Report, *A Language for Life* (1975), only passing mention is made of how reading is actually *learned*.

We must not allow our pre-occupation with the humanities to prejudice us against this new knowledge. The modern behavioural scientist is concerned with observable behaviour, and how behaviour can be shaped. It may be true that this non-mentalist bias has obscured many important issues in language learning.[4] Such a point of view has been expressed cogently by such different people as Frank Smith (1975), Carl Rogers (1969), and Susanne Langer (1967). But this must never be taken as a justification for dismissing as irrelevant the most universal insights arising from behavioural research in learning. Some of these important insights are that punishment and fear are impediments to the sorts of learnings with which literacy is concerned; that reward and significance and meaning—whether or not we use the term 'reinforcement'—are in fact essential in learning; and that to be ignored or bored—neither rewarded nor punished, extrinsically or intrinsically—destroys motivation and limits the extent to which new skill can be put to use. Common sense stands squarely behind most of these insights, and there is no room for factionalism here.

It is often the most fundamental and universal insights that are *not* applied, and no amount of precision or refinement in syllabus design or in instructional technique can compensate for such a failure. Understanding the importance of these basic universals of learning could be compared with making sure that the baby's mouth is open before attempting to get food into it. The nature of the food and the ability of the baby's complex digestive system to handle it are refined matters, which we may not understand well and hence should research and argue. But if the mouth is *not* open, or will not *be* opened, or even if the food is spat out, the baby's metabolism will suffer regardless of how scientifically accurate is our choice of diet to suit baby's digestive idiosyncrasies. Carrying the analogy a little further, it would seem that much argument about educational matters calmly accepts the tightly closed mouth of the baby or the regurgitated food on the floor, and opts for pre-digestion of the food and administration intravenously. The technology is complex, modern, and almost miraculous, but in its application it is abysmally stupid and wasteful. It will be our contention that the most powerful rewards in learning reading and writing are intrinsic and meaning-centred, and that self-regulation in actual reading and writing is more important than extrinsically applied contingencies—or even than instruction of any kind. But this does not remove the need to ensure that both the instructional environment and instructional intervention should embody these basic principles. The majority of schools fail to achieve this for a majority of children the majority of the time.

When we do in fact apply the most basic things we know about learning to the actual performance of our schools, we see that the results we are getting are precisely those we should expect. From the point of view of reinforcement contingencies alone, learning theory would predict that if literacy is taught in an environment in which competition decides the nature and levels of individual rewards for learning, an over-reinforced elite will excel (slanting use away from understanding towards performance); a large minority subjected to intensive punitive feedback will fail (with appalling effects on mental health); and a majority, treated to years of indifference and low levels of reinforcement, will use literacy as little as possible outside the instructional setting. And this would be the likely outcome even when a comparatively efficient 'method' of teaching had been applied. Why then do we complain and engage in wasteful public debate when the system is functioning in precisely the way we should expect?

There is a great deal of agreement among learning theorists about fundamental questions, but for a variety of strange reasons both society and the schools have failed to be convinced. Some fear determinism, the vicious mind-teaching of behaviour modification, as if efficient teaching could be anything else. The paradox of this objection is that the more efficient teaching becomes the more offensive it becomes. So thinkers of this kind opt deliberately for the gross inefficiency of our present system at the same time as they complain about it. Nobody thinks to question the right of children to have a choice not to learn to walk or talk—the most determined learning that there is in the world. We all expect our children to walk and talk and would be deeply distressed if they failed—in that sense we are all determined to have determinism.

The objectors would insist at this point that children learn *these* skills 'naturally'—no manipulation, no jelly beans. They should really observe the behaviour of parents with their massive handouts of parental affection when baby tries to walk or talk—the cuddle and the 'Clever girl!' are worth 100 jelly beans each. Learning 'naturally' is learning with ideal reinforcement contingencies when there is usually immediate reward for approximation in the right direction.

One of the most fundamental and irrefutable principles of learning concerns the negative relationship that exists between productive learning and punishment. (By 'productive learning' we mean 'learning that is to issue in confident use of what is learned.') Punishment issues in aversion—narrowly towards the behaviour being punished but broadly towards the 'subject' or activity generally, towards the teacher, and towards the context or environment in which the punishment occurs. Thus, if a child is embarrassed by making a 'mistake' in oral reading, he will avoid that type of mistake narrowly to the extent that he can distinguish what type of mistake it was. But since he was trying to do the right thing anyway, the punishment is likely to make him avoid oral reading because *any* response may be unsafe. But of even greater importance, the learned aversion is likely to spread to reading generally, to whoever may have ridiculed him, and to the environment of the reading lesson. Furthermore, the aversion is likely to influence him *deeply* in the protective functioning of his autonomic nervous system, especially if the experience is repeated often. He may then respond to reading compulsively by creating defense mechanisms, by developing a tendency to shift into emotional blockage when facing difficulties, or even by becoming neurotic in a variety of ways. For all these reasons punishment does not produce 'learning that is to issue in confident use of what is learned'.

Despite these clarities, and notwithstanding significant reforms, instruction in literacy becomes a most punitive and aversive experience for a large proportion of school children. It does so largely because of failure to apply the most basic things known about the conditions of learning. It must be admitted that this failure is largely forced on teachers and our enquiry must attempt to discover in what ways and for what reasons. We need to take greater account of indirect forms of punishment in relationship to literacy learning and of those conditions under which guilt and despair become associated with the undertaking.[5]

It is time, as many of our most active researchers would agree, that we concerned ourselves more seriously with the processes by which literacy is actually learned rather than with arid argument and research about competing methods of teaching. Our first responsibility is to observe with proper humility and open-mindedness how children making healthy development in literacy actually operate, and to what extent basic insights about learning apply to the acquisition of language and of literacy. The challenge then would be to replicate healthy learning conditions for all children—to modify our teaching and the nature of the school environment in support of such conditions rather than to allow the institutional convenience of schools and preconceived notions of teaching to impose their own conditions.

5. Literacy is a cultural matter

A disproportionate share of the failure to transmit the skills of literacy falls on children from cultural backgrounds at variance with the culture of those who have traditionally influenced the language of schooling.[6] And it would be true to say that our schools now represent a special sub-culture, embodying attitudes and values—and even a special type of language—to be found nowhere in the open society beyond. The alienation felt by many children in confrontation with the sub-culture of the school presents many problems for which there are no easy answers, and it presents a special problem for literacy learning. Of all *spoken* dialects, that favoured by the school approximates most closely to the dialect of books. Becoming literate is greatly facilitated by a natural familiarity with and love of book language—ideally the learner *identifies* himself with the dialect of books and lays personal claim to it. The alien, formal dialect favoured by the school and the associated system of values and attitudes which some children fear, constitute a barrier between them and the special dialect of book language which they need to accept if they are to be gladly literate. The dialect of books frightens them unnecessarily because they have learned to fear the dialect of the school.

Culture is a sticky word but one for which we have no adequate alternative. The patterns of acquired belief, assumption, attitude, prejudice, dialect and behaviour through which we meet our common human needs throw up such striking differences between groups of people that fundamental identities of need and value are obscured. Literature at its best, and children's literature in particular, transcends the surface distinctions of cultural difference and embodies universal human concerns. A fine literature can form the bridge across cultural difference to literate language. Teaching methods and materials in the last generation have tended increasingly to exclude true literature from the literacy undertaking in the interests of controlled vocabulary or phonetic sequences. If the human richness and joy of a fine literature could be moved across into the centre of literacy teaching, many of the problems of cultural dissonance might be minimized.

6. Literacy is a complex matter

The five points considered above make it abundantly clear that we are dealing with one of the most complex phenomena in experience: the processes of literacy are complex; the acquisition of literacy skills entails the most complex forms of learning; the institution of schooling presents complex impediments to learning; and the cultural determinants of literacy in school and community are complex. We should therefore not expect simple answers nor complete answers to the questions we pose, and we should prepare ourselves for the complexities that lie ahead. Certainly our endeavours cannot be guided by a single golden rule framed and hung on the classroom wall.

What are the special traps in studying or talking about something as complex as reading and writing behaviour? When we deal with simple matters familiar to the senses, we can be literal and be understood without ambiguity. We can learn to label a foot with the verbal marker 'foot' and agree about the shape and function of different feet, and even use the term in special ways such as in the sense of a measure, indicating this clearly by the context. When we come to talk about more complex matters not available in sensory perception, literal forms of discourse become limited. Even such an apparently simple concept as 'love' cannot be described with the same type of clarity as 'foot'. How do we communicate with each other about our inner feelings, about what we believe or value, about why a particular work of art pleases? How do we communicate about abstract or complex matters such as the quality of mercy, the nature of the atom, or the language learning of young children?

Talking about complex matters

To understand something is to account for it in terms of a lower order of complexity than the unintelligible something itself—we must move from the known to the unknown, the homely and familiar to the abstruse, the concrete to the abstract. It is a matter of reorganizing what we know to account for what we don't. This entails operating metaphorically in one way or another—taking something familiar in experience and using it analogically as a picture or model to order the chaos into intelligible patterns. Even our common vocabulary about thinking is full of metaphors—under-standing, in-sight, re-present, de-scribe, spec-ulate, imagine. This display of images from seeing and picturing is in itself an interesting comment on the way we comprehend.

When we use a metaphor we point to important likenesses, openly admitting that the comparison is not one of identity—we imply unlikenesses as well. When we compare the structure of the atom to the solar system, we imply a number of appropriate associations—such as the fact that most of the system is made up of empty space and there is a relationship of force between the nucleus and the orbital electrons which accounts for their motion. We also imply certain inappropriate comparisons, such as that the electrons are of unequal mass, and their orbits are moving in the same direction. Despite the weaknesses of the analogy, it proves a powerful intellectual aid, and we are not really confused by the ambiguities. The control of how the metaphor is to be interpreted, what are the appropriate and inappropriate associations, requires a special type of judgement made on the basis of the wider context. Analogies, models and theories are complex metaphors and their proper use entails awareness of the appropriate *and* inappropriate senses of the comparison.

We may think that it is better to escape the inbuilt ambiguity of metaphorical modes by sticking to the facts and speaking literally, but this can get us into even worse difficulties. Firstly, in literal discourse only one thing can be dealt with at a time, which means that complex wholes must be divided into component parts. In this process we can dissect the whole inappropriately; undervalue, overlook or overvalue parts; and most importantly lose sight of how the parts fit together into a functioning whole. The first thing that is lost in the process of division is the notion of function or the way something operates. The idea of reading as a set of separate skills, for instance, has been open to all of these fallacies. A whole is more than the sum of its parts, and often that 'more than' includes the really important things. We need a metaphor or a model to deal with this problem.[7]

When we appear to be dealing literally with the parts of a complex whole an *unstated* model is implied, and this can be much more dangerous than an open acknowledgement of the nature of the model in the first place. If our discussion of reading is dominated by the idea of vocabulary and various types of word recognition, or our notion of language is dominated by the idea of words, we imply unfortunate models of functioning and impose them on teaching without realizing clearly that we are doing so. We may even carry out immaculate research on the assumption that recognizing vocabulary is the crucial problem of reading or that understanding the meanings of words is the crucial problem of language, but if the implied model of functioning is erroneous, the application of the research is likely to be misguided. In both of these cases important parts of the whole have been overlooked, and the implied model, that language is simply the manipulation of words, overlooks syntax, sentence meaning, and total process. We may emerge in serious dispute about conflicting research without realizing that the unstated models, if exposed, would indicate that the question at issue was trivial or even plainly mischievous. A question we must learn to ask more often is, 'What is the underlying model here?'

Throughout our enquiry we will be dealing with models of many kinds—models for learning, models for teaching, and models for language processes. If we are always explicit about the models involved, we at least avoid the pitfalls of believing that they are not there.

Models can be tested, provided that they are explicit. The value of a model may be readily measured by its predictive power—its ability to forecast that certain observable facts will arise as outcomes of its application. This is the way in which the firm structures of physical science were built up. Our enquiry will be successful to the extent that the models we construct to understand the learning of reading and writing not only *appear* to account for the observed facts but also have this predictive power which invites and facilitates ratification. In particular, they should work in the real world of the classroom.

Learning spoken language: towards a first model

There is no more successful example of language learning than that provided by mastery of native language during infancy. Since time before history, regardless of race, class, or educational background, families have succeeded in transmitting their native language to their infants—or their infants have succeeded in learning the language within a natural environment of language use. The efficiency with which spoken language is learned is beyond question: it presents a body of evidence which dwarfs that of modern research into insignificance. What possible evidence could research present which would have the effect of questioning the effectiveness of those processes by which infants learn language? We would be arrogant in the extreme if we were to disregard such processes in our search for models for language learning.

Many experts would protest, however, that acquiring spoken language during childhood is a special case—it arises from some inbred, human capacity predisposing the human infant to acquire language from simple exposure, and it is hardly to be called 'learning' in any usual sense. They would say that it is a fallacy to apply principles we see operating in early language acquisition to the learning of literacy skills which, by comparison, are artificial and unnatural—and must therefore be *taught*.[8]

Our answers to this objection should be clear and forthright. First, the onus of proof that acquiring spoken language is *not* like other forms of learning lies with the protestors, and nowhere have they achieved this. If we find that all the conditions necessary for efficient learning in other fields are in fact present in early language acquisition, we would require very special evidence to exclude language acquisition from that general process. Secondly, we cannot be justified in dismissing the relevance of early language acquisition for literacy learning unless we have assured ourselves by extensive and rigid trials that literacy cannot be acquired in the same manner. Such trials have never been conducted, but there is a wealth of evidence which we will study later indicating that literacy skills develop in the same 'natural' way as spoken language when the conditions for learning are comparable.

It is not difficult to understand why many linguists consider that mastery of the spoken language comes about without learning in the normal sense. Any form of language learning in the school setting—including learning a second language—presents difficulties to some children, despite careful instruction. But most children learn to speak with such ease and rapidity at such a tender age, and with so little direct 'teaching', that a special explanation beyond the ordinary seems called for. How, it may be asked, can any infant learn to talk without instruction unless some special mechanism is at work? Perhaps Wordsworth was right and, hidden in those 'clouds of glory' that the infant trails behind him at birth, lies the secret of speech.

From the point of view of classroom instruction, let's look briefly at some features of infant language learning. Mothers make use of the close proximity they enjoy with their infants by talking to them as if they could understand—and in a fundamental sense they do in fact understand. It is true that good teachers would model appropriate behaviour like this, but if they received only the crude responses that the baby gives to the mother, would they be looking for a hypotheses to explain the disappointing achievement—intellectual handicap, deafness, minimal brain injury?

Mother, and sometimes father and others in the family, persist as if nothing were wrong. They reinforce the baby's babbling and even mimic it. Furthermore, they seem to *enjoy* doing so. This would be going too far for most teachers—it would be difficult to find instances of this kind of behaviour within the school environment. All the family now start modelling a small range of central words with a special, slow and affectionate intonation—'Mum-my', 'Dad-dy', (or even Dad-da', and in some strange families, even 'din-dins'). The response for some months, unless we have an extremely sensitive ear for intonation, is disappointing. But the family is not disappointed.

Mother is likely to hear and recognize the first real approximations to the modelled words that the infant utters, and she may keep this to herself—or rather, between her and the infant—as a private joy that nobody else could yet understand or accept, or she may report it to the family and induce baby to show off the new competence. But it may happen in another way. Dad may have become used to the babbling infant as a sort of pet that you talk to like your dog—not quite human because there is no 'real' communication. Then one day he hears baby utter something like 'Jar-jar'. The effect is electric. He lifts up the infant in an extravagant display of pride and affection and yells, 'She's saying "Daddy"!'

Now, one thing is certain: the infant is *not* saying 'Daddy', she is saying 'Jar-jar'. It is hard to imagine a teacher rewarding a child for such a gross error—and certainly not so extravagantly. One of the things we have been cautioned against as teachers is implanting errors by accepting incorrect responses. Surely we can expect nothing but disaster from the behaviour of this typical family. Yet the process continues along the same lines, only at a sensationally accelerating pace. With rewards such as these so readily at her disposal, baby soon begins playing this language game avidly and by some mysterious means gets better at it every day. Perhaps there *is* some hidden mechanism at work.

Language acquisition and learning theory

We have just recalled the way in which adults behave towards an infant learning to speak. How does this behaviour relate to what the learning theorists tell us about the principles of learning? In the most general terms, they say that, if you want a response to be learned, you should reinforce or reward almost every approximation towards the desired response made by the learner, and you should do so immediately after the response.[9] Now this is precisely what parents do—they reward their infants with adult attention, approval, and affection (among the most powerful of reinforcers) immediately they make a linguistic attempt remotely recognizable as an approximation to the word being patterned. A yell of 'lala' from the cot will bring mother or father miraculously with the bottle, or an imperious 'bloo' will have father light another match to be blown out. Things happen for baby within a split second of making any sort of language noise.

If we wished to identify clear examples of learning theory in action, we could find no better instances than are thrown up universally in the homes of language learning infants. Far from being an exception to normal learning, early language acquisition provides almost perfect exemplification of effective reinforcement contingencies operating in a manifestly successful learning system. There is a great deal more to the matter which we must consider as we proceed, such as the ability of infants to intuit the grammatical rules of their language without tuition, but at the most basic level, the case against normal learning in early language acquisition looks very thin.

Suppose we turn the tables and consider for a moment what might happen if some mother decided to teach her infant to talk in what she chose to call a 'scientific and rationally structured manner' modelled on the way she was taught to read. First she analyses the language (making all the mistakes of abstraction which we studied earlier) into its forty or so phonemes, and grades them in difficulty of enunciation. Her theory is that by teaching each of these phonemes in a clear and systematic way she will make it possible for the baby to blend them into words, first of two, then of three phonemes. Imagine the sounds that would issue from that household—including the protests of the baby. There is no need to work the example through in detail: the matter is so obviously ridiculous that it is difficult to take it seriously.

The developmental model

There seems a strong case for looking at initial language learning as a suggestive model—perhaps the basic model—for literacy learning.[10] What are the major characteristics of such a model? Firstly, it is a special case of developmental learning—the conditions are similar to those prevailing when an infant learns to distinguish the three-dimensional world in visual perception, learns to crawl and walk, and much later, learns to relate to peers, to ride a bicycle, or to think in 'concrete operational' terms. We are not really dealing with a distinctively different *type* of learning even though the language *task* is distinctively different from other developmental tasks—as most of them are distinctively different from each other. (Some of the perceptual and cognitive tasks, however, have much in common with language processes, and we will need to study this relationship later in the enquiry.) The model we are looking at, then, is the model of developmental learning.

The mastery of developmental tasks takes place with such apparent ease and with so little consciously planned teaching, that we are inclined to call such learning 'natural' in distinction from the learning of skills which require—or appear to require—intensive instruction. But there is evidence that this distinction is not as absolute as may at first appear. Developmental learning is highly motivated, consistently purposeful, globally activating, powerfully reinforced both intrinsically and extrinsically, and meaningfully related to other aspects of development. If the learning of spelling or mathematics were supported by such conditions, it too would begin to look more 'natural'.

Furthermore, the way in which supportive adults are induced by affection and common sense to intervene in the development of their children proves upon close examination to embody the most sound principles of teaching. Rather than providing verbal instructions about how a skill should be carried out, the parent sets up an emulative model of the skill in operation and induces activity in the child which approximates towards use of the skill. The first attempts of the child are to *do* something that is *like* the skill he wishes to emulate. This activity is then 'shaped' or refined by immediate rewards, both intrinsic and extrinsic, for targeting approximations. The shaping is supported by ready assistance provided on demand, and by good-natured tolerance and almost inexhaustible patience for inappropriate responses. From this point of view, so-called 'natural' learning is in fact supported by higher quality *teaching intervention* than is normally the case in the school setting.

Developmental learning has other characteristics which we will study later in greater depth. Briefly, it tends to be regulated and paced by the learner in response to inner controls of a highly sensitive nature that could neither be understood, nor replicated, by the guiding adult on the outside. This regulation system may decree, for instance, a period of regression to a lower stage—something which would seldom be predicted or required by the progress-oriented adult.

Developmental learning is supported by intrinsic reinforcement cycles even more powerfully than by the extrinsic patterns of reward that we noticed in association with learning speech.[11] Just as the infant learning to grasp and manipulate a rattle is rewarded immediately by auditory sensations and is thereby induced to persist with the activity through a series of modifications, the child experimenting with oral language is rewarded in an immediate and cyclic fashion by auditory sensations which he can compare with models implanted earlier, and so continue targeting approximations even in the absence of the extrinsically reinforcing adult. 'Mistakes' or bad approximations seldom bring painful experience—rather, they bring that absence of pleasurable concomitant experience (the sound of the rattle) which induces modification. The next try, then, attempts a return to successful control. Such reward structures support massive repetition which rapidly passes control of the skill to complex, automatic systems below the level of consciousness. To put the matter very simply, the child's own system acts as an amazingly sensitive teaching machine.

In summary, then, developmental learning, of which the acquisition of spoken language is a special case, would seem to have the following major characteristics:

The learning begins with immersion in an environment in which the skill is being used in purposeful ways. Readiness is timed by the internal 'clock' of the learner.

The environment is an emulative rather than an instructional one, providing lively examples of the skill in action, and inducing targeting activity which is persistently shaped by modelling and by reinforcement.

Reinforcement contingencies, both intrinsic and extrinsic, approach the ideal of immediate rewards for almost every approximation regardless of the distance of the initial response from the perfect 'correct' response.

Bad approximations—those moving away from the desired response— are not reinforced.

What aspect of the task will be practised, at what pace, and for how long is determined largely by the learner. Practice occurs whether or not the adult is attending, and tends to continue until essential aspects of the task are under comfortable, automatic control.

The environment is secure and supportive, providing help on call and being absolutely free from any threat associated with the learning of the task.

Development tends to proceed continuously in an orderly sequence marked by considerable differences from individual to individual.

The final sanction for taking this model seriously for reading and writing would be an honest and rigorous trial of the model in this application. In the school environment this is likely to prove more difficult than may at first appear. As we proceed with out investigation we will consider the implications of the model applied to literacy skills both outside and within the school. Before doing so, it may be helpful to view the teaching of literacy from a historical viewpoint and to see how our past and current practices measure up to the developmental model represented in the acquisition of spoken language.

2
Historical Viewpoints and Current Practices

Literacy has been so central a function of schooling that major aspects of this one undertaking have tended to be regarded as separate subjects and have developed methodologies of their own, often in philosophical conflict with each other. Thus, it has been typical to see separate programmes in reading, writing, spelling, and composition or written expression operating in quite unrelated compartments, with reading taking pride of place. In spoken-language learning no-one would consider separating listening from speaking (although when 'oracy' recently became an important concern of the schools, this is precisely what tended to happen).

Even more distant from classroom practice is the notion that since thinking, expressing, and experiencing are centrally related to language, the literacy programme should be closely linked to other subjects, and to the related arts in particular. Here again, no such artificial barriers are set up in the pre-school, developmental environment in which spoken language is mastered.

Methodologies for teaching the different aspects of literacy have tended to develop along narrow, pragmatic lines dictated by classroom expediency and justified by success in achieving limited goals. The limitation of goals tended to spring from examination or evaluation measures imposed by authority figures in the institutional framework. Little thought was given to how children actually learn language skills, and teaching methodologies were developed for *each* subject as if a quite different type of learning was involved. Emphasis was on the perceptual and performance skills which could be readily measured and were superficially different in each 'subject', while common central features of language, such as understanding and expressing meanings, tended to be overlooked.

Slow progress towards universal education kept alive the false expectation that by attending school all children would learn to read and write. Even when the problems of the dull, the poor, and the plainly 'bad' children were sorted out as justifiable exceptions, it gradually became apparent that the schools were failing to fulfil the dream in far too many cases. What else could be wrong but the methods of teaching?

The failure of the schools was met with frustrated concern and heated public debate about what they should be doing. Methodologies changed radically from time to time as educational dreamers and opportunists provoked anxiety and capitalized on the ever-vocal disaffection. The search for the perfect method was mounted—a search that was to continue for three generations. As method followed method, the statistics of success and failure remained remarkably constant, yet everyone declared that things were different when *they* went to school—and so reaction set in demanding a return to methods which in their day had failed. The swinging pendulum became an all too accurate symbol of educational thinking and an indictment on the common sense of a people and a profession. Meanwhile, children everywhere learned to talk.

Method or madness

Reading has enjoyed an unassailable pre-eminence in schooling in the modern age and there is no difficulty in understanding why—it is the only doorway to Western, linear culture—the very symbol of education. Reading as a school subject has thus become essential in the fantasy experience of even the most lowly modern parent. The ordinary parent is *deeply* concerned with only one aspect of schooling—'teach my children to read and you can do anything else you like with them'. It is impossible to understand the continuing melodrama of factionally competing methods without becoming aware of the peculiar power that reading represents in the minds of modern people. Anyone who cannot spell, write legibly or figure accurately can expect a degree of sympathetic indulgence, but failure in reading has been fantasized into a modern sin.

As might be expected, succeeding methodologies have each emphasized something vital in the full story of literacy learning. After all, each major method has been successful for about the same proportion of children, while at the same time producing its own crop of failures. And it is to their successes that teachers point in justification of the method being used—the failures can always be explained in terms of factors in the children or beyond the school such as laziness, low intelligence, cultural deprivation, broken homes, lack of basics, or whatever the fashion in educational ideas suggests.

Although each methodology has emphasized some vital insight about the learning process, often in response to an important, prevailing psychological theory narrowly interpreted, such insights have been readily put aside as the next reform has taken hold. Over and over again, in the ardour of oversimplified reaction, the baby has been thrown out with the bathwater. In almost every conflict of reading method it would be true to say that both sides had been right in insisting that their insights were crucial, but both sides had been abysmally wrong in insisting that the insights of the other side were totally mistaken. Both sides have usually been culpable also in focussing on low level, perceptual skills and in failing to see the matter of literacy whole and in relationship to other disciplines. All the characteristic mistakes of abstraction and factionalism have compounded the debate in tragically irrational ways.

Thankfully, the home, where the infant learns to speak, is not an arena for factions or public debate. Violent shifts in method have never been a characteristic of the oral-language development of infants. Furthermore, the rich, developmental-learning environment provided in the home embodies the many apparently contradictory factors vital to language learning, and does not overemphasize one at the expense of another. (We should acknowledge, however, that there are enormous differences between homes in the adequacy with which they enrich the language environment of young children, and return to a closer study of such differences later in our investigation.)

Extreme polarities of method developed as the pendulum swung. First there was the opposition between the teaching of alphabet names and the teaching of letter sounds, both of which are necessary to teaching reading in a way that is intelligible to young children. Next there was the polarity between phonics and whole-word perception, both of which again, properly understood as aspects of how the reader functions, are essential to proper processing. This type of opposition became refined by academics into analytic-versus-synthetic approaches—whether we start from the smallest elements and build into larger ones or the reverse. This formulation has a nice respectable sound about it, even though in its factional setting it is a cover for stupidity of the first order.

In spoken-language acquisition we see some of these same apparent oppositions as features of healthy functioning. In the listening/speaking complex, infants operate both analytically and synthetically from the beginning, sorting meaningful words from larger utterances and *simultaneously* struggling with the precise articulatory details at the phonemic level. Spoken-language acquisition is characterized by 'integrated function'. This is so sensible and *right*, both in the growth of speech and the growth of reading that it is difficult to understand why so much energy has been wasted on such artificial problems in the 'great debate' about methods of teaching reading. Perhaps Jeanne Chall's famous locution, 'Reading: The Great Debate', should be changed to 'Reading: The False Debate', for there is little of greatness about it.

With the work of Arthur Gates in the thirties a new battle was mounted between oral and silent reading, between word accuracy and 'comprehension'. This argument did at least bring meaning into the picture squarely for the first time, and it could be said that if the fine research and speculation of Gates had not been factionalized, reading may have been placed on a sound basis. However, the vogue for ten 'comprehension questions' into which Gates's work tended to be boiled down, became a destructive influence itself. Meaning had again become separated from the integrity of the reading process—which is one in which comprehension takes place at the centre of the activity and not at its periphery.

More recently, following the monumental analysis of Jeanne Chall (1967), the polarity has been between what she called 'code emphasis' versus 'meaning emphasis'. Each of these traditional polarities represents an extreme over-simplification of the reading process. The really important question is, 'How do these apparently contradictory aspects of learning to read fit into the total picture?'

In his remarkable work of 1908, *The Psychology and Pedagogy of Reading*, E.B. Huey had already analysed the true issues of the 'great debate' and exposed the errors of a perception-oriented approach to reading. After seventy years we still face essentially the same debate. It is clear that the sources of unreason lie deep in the assumptions about learning and teaching which our culture of schooling cherishes.

The teaching of handwriting, spelling and written expression have never generated a comparable debate nor been induced into the violent swings of method that have characterized reading. The problem has more often been one of neglect and sterility centred around the same general philosophical mistakes as were made with reading—the isolation of related skills in subject compartments, and the concentration of teaching effort on superficial, perceptual and mechanical aspects rather than on integrated function.

The production of written language is a hazardous process in a corrective instructional environment such as a school. Letters have to be correctly formed by immature muscles, words have to be correctly spelled in defiance of any rational system, grammatical structures have to be correctly formed, and if you are lucky, communicable meanings have to be encoded. It is little wonder that many children escape the dangers of the corrective environment by producing as little written language as the school will allow.

Here again, the developmental model contrasts strongly with the instructional model as implied by actual teaching. If we were to expect immediate correctness and perfection of articulation from children learning to speak, the learning of spoken language would be almost as hazardous and its production as sparse. Infants would tend to say as little as possible for fear of correction or embarrassment. They wouldn't need to be as apprehensive of the competitive environment as school children must be, but they would certainly be silent more often than they are.

A thumbnail sketch of reading methods

There has always been a tendency, as we have already noticed, to look upon reading as a matter of recognizing words—what we have called a 'perceptual and mechanical focus'. Early methodologies provoked dissention at this level and there is, therefore, not a great deal to be gained from a detailed historical study. In the following simplified account of methods of the past century, we will attempt to identify the vital insights embedded in the dispute.

Alphabetic versus Phonetic

In the alphabetic approach children were taught to recognize the letters and be able to name them—the approach started with detailed visual discrimination. When a child came upon a word which he didn't recognize, he was required to spell out the word letter by letter and then attempt to pronounce it. An advantage of this approach not seen later was that the reader was given the opportunity for some sort of processing—he had a second or two to consider before committing himself to a response. During that valuable time he was required to observe all the letter detail and to do so in a strict left-to-right order. This may not have been the most appropriate thing to ask him to do with his time, but it was probably as helpful as 'sounding out' the letters without knowing which of its possible sounds each letter might be representing. Two valuable things stand out: the helpfulness of having a vocabulary with which to identify and talk about letters; and the importance of allowing processing-time for problem-solving in word recognition.

In the phonetic approach children were taught the sound associations of the letters (difficult for a five year old since some letters like 'a' have as many as nine common sound associations—at, ate, all, ark, away, head, wash, oar, ear). On meeting a strange word the reader was expected to 'sound out' the letters and 'blend' them in such a way as to approximate to the sound of the word. Later he was expected to apply the rules of syllabification (which only editors and printers seem able to interpret, and then by some rather dishonest conventions apparently to be learned by exposure). It is obvious that the possible letter-sound associations of a word can be helpful and vital clues in efficient word-recognition if used as *part* of a proper strategy—but what is the strategy? Certainly nothing like 'blending', which is one of the most intrinsically difficult tasks even for a mature adult reader. Tragically for children, it was not until the late forties that any attempt was made to study strategies and to teach them. Later we will explore why it is necessary for children to have a grasp of both letter-names and possible sound-representations if they are to make sense of instruction in reading. On the negative side, both of these methods detracted attention from the nature of reading as the creation of meanings. They grotesquely emphasized oral accuracy and in so doing reduced a receptive language-activity to a mere performance skill.

A major form of reading disability arises from this crucial distortion—what might be called the 'performance syndrome', in which children read for someone else and finally opt out of conscious attempts to understand or control the task. They can only perform when plugged in to another 'computer' which does the correcting, and when the contact is broken, the activity, for what it is worth, ceases. A wide range of characteristic disabilities, which we will study later, arise from the performance syndrome. *We need to remember that reading, although active and creative in making meanings, is a receptive, thinking skill like listening, and not an expressive performance skill like speaking.*

Phonetic versus whole word or 'look-and-say'

Following the remarkable discoveries of the Gestalt psychologists in the first quarter of the century, it was realized that in the great majority of cases word recognition involves the immediate perception of whole words. Mature readers seldom stop to analyse the letter-detail of any word, and even the learning reader doesn't really begin to read in any true sense until he recognizes 'at sight' the majority of words in a passage. (The work of the Gestalt psychologists, concerned with the perception of form and configuration, helped to rectify the synthetic bias of Western thinking, which had come to see all systems as starting from parts which were then built into wholes.)[2]

The look-and-say approach emphasized the teaching of whole words, or at least insisted that whole words should be taught to beginning readers and only later should any form of word analysis be introduced. However, little research was undertaken to determine what features or details of words are significant to children in recognizing or discriminating words—it was assumed too easily that shape or 'word form' (almost identical for many common words) triggered recognition.[3] Two unfortunate practices became set during the reign of the look-and-say approach: new words were taught in isolation from a meaningful context before reading took place; and the concept of 'controlled vocabulary' changed the character of books for reading instruction in ways which distorted and impoverished the language quite grossly.

The debate which raged (and continues to rage in some quarters) between these opposing approaches was seldom reflected in absolute terms within actual classrooms—teachers tend to have more sense than to become extremists. However, great harm was done as proponents of both approaches began to influence publishers to produce 'readers' which lacked literary worth or interest, and destroyed natural language-use—whether they were phonetic readers or look-and-say readers.

Whole word versus sentence

In the middle of the look-and-say era thinking and research became more refined in some quarters, leading to techniques which still play a dominant part in modern instruction. One such movement was that arising from the insight that the smallest meaningful unit of language is the sentence, and that real reading must begin there, since only when meaning has been created has reading occurred. This methodology also stressed the importance of context clues in word solving and helped to reorient learning towards natural language-processes.

Taken to an extreme, however, the sentence method neglected vital features in the development of visual discrimination and basic directional habits. It brought disrepute to the movement towards meaning and natural language by applying a narrow set of insights in blind faith rather than from an informed basis of research and practice. In the hands of unskilled teachers it degenerated rapidly into another look-and-say approach as teachers strove for security by teaching isolated words to ensure that children could 'really' recognize them. There was still the underlying assumption that the real test of reading was whether or not a child could recognize word items out of context. It must be admitted that authority figures in the system had more to do with enforcing this criterion than teachers, who as so often happened were forced into compliance in defence of their jobs.

Most importantly, perhaps, in a competitive structure which measured success and controlled advancement by movement through a series of 'readers', children and over-anxious parents soon learned the knack of fooling the teacher by learning each book by heart. This practice undermined the sentence approach even more than the whole-word approach.

Book approaches versus language-experience

Almost a generation had passed since 'readers' contained natural stories which had not been mangled to serve some instructional purpose—it was almost as if children were being forced to learn to read a different language from the one they spoke so well. Language-experience methods arose in reaction to this sorry state of affairs. It was realized that a major insight for the beginning reader must be that written language is talk written down. By developing reading materials from the children's own language about matters of which they had real experience it was hoped that a bridge would be built between familiar language and printed symbols. This approach also brought reading and the production of written language together for the first time in natural and helpful ways. Especially when teamed up with the sentence approach, language-experience brought an air of sanity into literacy teaching.[4]

However, practical difficulties tended to undermine the effectiveness of the approach: great demands were placed on teachers to prepare reading materials dictated by individuals or by groups of children, and it was difficult to provide for adequate repetition—as was done in a mechanical fashion by 'controlled vocabulary' readers—or to monitor the progress of children in clear and systematic ways. Transfer to book material was often undertaken too soon and without adequate preparation of children for the strangeness of the language they encountered in the readers then available in most classrooms.

More importantly, the language-experience approaches overlooked a number of crucial differences between written and spoken language. Oral language tends to occur in, and be supported by, the sensory and social situation in which it takes place, and its ambiguities are clarified by that situation—and by voice intonation, facial expression, and gesture. Written language lacks this situational support and has therefore developed conventions to avoid ambiguity which are so distinctive as to make it a special dialect. Furthermore, conversational language tends to deal with the trivial and the ordinary and usually lacks memorable content. Written language, on the other hand, is difficult or expensive to produce, and normally records memorable matters in as memorable a way as possible. A diet of ordinary conversational language in reading can be very boring and unsatisfying. If the labours of learning to deal with written language are to be thought worthwhile by the learners, they must be rewarded by very special meanings and satisfactions such as those stemming from exciting stories or patterned language. Endless instant 'stories' about going to the shop or visiting a fire station make dull reading or writing, and may deeply misinform children about the proper purposes and rewards of literacy.

Language-experience techniques, however, do properly comprise an important part of any sound, modern literacy programme, and we will return to them repeatedly in the practical aspects of our study. An important recent development of the approach, *Breakthrough to Literacy*, is dealt with below.

The eclectic approach

As the limitations of different methods became slowly apparent, and as research indicated that different methods tend to suit different children, sensible people began to avoid dependence on a single method and use a combination of approaches loosely tied together without too much regard for an encompassing theory. Such practice came to be called the eclectic approach (meaning that practices were borrowed freely from a number of different sources) and an attempt was made to create more balanced programmes to meet differing individual needs.

Although such approaches marked a significant breakthrough in practice, and embodied a proper humility about current ignorance of the real processes of literacy learning, they inevitably lacked consistency and coherence. Things were done pragmatically without a clear idea of *why* they were being done. The organizational complexities of such programmes often led to little better than a hopeful chaos in which both children and teachers were deeply confused. Researchers continued to concentrate on the arid comparison of different methods and combinations of method, perpetuating the mistake of emphasizing instructional techniques rather than learning strategies.

During the fifties a determined effort was made in the United States to solve the literacy problem in the schools once and for all. Teams of very experienced and talented academics worked with publishers in creating 'basal' reading programmes supported by massive guidance to teachers in the shape of manuals and resource books of an extremely detailed nature—almost offensively prescriptive of every word the teacher should utter. These basal programmes reflected the best of informed opinion from many sources, presenting eclectic approaches in a coherent and systematic bundle. Brave attempts were made to rationalize conflicting theories and present packages which were balanced and responsible. Many of these programmes and the materials which supported them contained very fine things, and clearly improved the standard of reading instruction, but none of them came near to overcoming the inherent jumble-sale confusion of eclecticism. Towering figures, wise and committed, emerged—among them Gray, McKee, Russell, Dolch and Monroe—still worthy of study, but confined within a limiting tradition.[5]

At the end of the sixties the great American experiment had clearly failed, despite a level of support both economically and academically that no other country could conceivably mount. America seems to have returned to the crudities of pendulum thinking. Despite the fact that among them are strong voices speaking from a clear vision of what might be,[6] they are being stampeded by the recurrent public outcry into a back-to-basics movement without anyone having clarified just *what* the basics are.

Some important methodological experiments

In the past twenty years there have been a number of attempts at radical solutions to the literacy problem. Each has advanced our knowledge and range of technique in important ways—even if negatively. For reasons we must explore, none has significantly altered the level of success and failure in the enterprise. Among the more influential of these movements are the following:

The organic vocabulary—Sylvia Ashton-Warner

Working in the look-and-say era, but with insight far in advance of current belief, a quite remarkable figure emerged in outback New Zealand. Sylvia Ashton-Warner, committed to teaching new entrants in a rural Maori school, brought her exceptional sensitivity as a novelist and artist to bear on the problems of leading non-European, rural children into literacy. Her work received little recognition in her home country—except among a responsive few—and it was not until the publication of her two novels, *Spinster* (1958) and *Teacher* (1965), that her ideas gained the recognition they deserved.

Basically, her insight was that reading should be motivated by the deepest springs of meaning in the human heart. Working from the tradition of look-and-say and language-experience, she provided her children on request with those words which most powerfully engaged them, words from the centre of their deepest fantasies—kiss, fight, beer, hit, Mum, aeroplane, fast car, blood, skeleton. These were once-seen-never-forgotten words which established an initial vocabulary for both reading and writing. In addition she broke down subject barriers over the whole curriculum and integrated all the arts both for their own sake and in the service of literacy. Placed in a context of modern linguistic insight, and broken free from the factional limitations of the time, Sylvia Ashton-Warner's insights are a joy to saddened hearts.

Reading through writing—Grace Fernald

Grace Fernald was a person of remarkable commitment to those children who were suffering because of what schooling had failed to do for them. She thought creatively about their plight and experimented fearlessly to find new entry points for reading following initial failure of the visually-orientated approaches of the normal classroom.

Starting from the simple securities of language-experience procedures, she explored the latent powers of sensory channels other than the visual, pioneering the use of tactile and kinaesthetic modes in literacy learning (Fernald 1943). She realized that perception is a matter of meanings seeking expression through any sensory channel that is open, and through her success with children displaying exceptional problems, she broke down the dependence of traditional procedures on visual modes. For the first time in educational settings, language began to appear as the multi-sensory, multi-functional activity that it is.

Sound practice in ordinary classrooms now encompasses the use of tactile and kinaesthetic procedures in the teaching of reading and spelling. The acceptance of multi-modal involvement in literacy learning helps to remove traditional barriers between the teaching of literacy skills and the globally active functioning that characterizes developmental learning.

Individualized Reading—Jeanette Veatch

In an era dominated by basic-reading series and sequential programmes, and graded texts and workbooks, it was something of a crusade to suggest that children could learn to read using a wide range of trade books which they selected for themselves and read at their own pace, and it was something of a disaster that the educational climate was so unfavourable to such a sane and simple idea. Jeanette Veatch pioneered the techniques of individualized reading and fought the reading establishment with tremendous energy and skill.

It could be said that her approach to learning to read was the first clear statement of developmental principles in reading growth that was worked out in detail and tested rigorously in classrooms. She had an incisive and zestful way with words and her books on the teaching of reading through individualized procedures remain classics in the field (Veatch 1959, 1966, 1968). Her sensitivity to children, her common sense about the reading process, and her skill as a teacher justified the unbounded confidence she displayed in developmental learning before research had turned strongly in that direction. Individualized reading procedures provide a practical starting-point in a developmental approach to literacy learning—they establish a beach-head in the realm of the possible. Our study of these procedures and our use of them in the classroom may foster the extension of developmental modes within the school structure.[7]

The Initial Teaching Alphabet (i.t.a.)

Sir James Pitman, the descendant of a long family line of orthographic specialists, despaired at the reluctance of the establishment to consider a rational revision of English spelling. As the next best thing, in the interests of confused children, and as a possible way of educating a generation towards reform, he devised an alphabet for the initial teaching of literacy. A brilliant orthographic compromise, the Initial Teaching Alphabet could be used to spell words in a phonetically consistent way without markedly altering the shape, or *gestalt*, of most English words, and retained the major letter-to-sound associations of traditional orthography. He drew on his resources as a major educational publisher and an influential lobbyist to see that a significant range of books would be printed in the revised alphabet.

A formidable experimental structure was set up under the experienced leadership of John Downing and with the support of the English educational establishment. The idea was that children would learn to read and write in the i.t.a. medium and then make a change to traditional orthography after two or three years. Cynics predicted that the scheme would fail as children made the transition, and that their ability to learn traditional spelling would be seriously impaired. In fact, neither of these predictions was accurate, and this tended to show that once the *strategies* of literacy had been mastered and children had become familiar with the nature of the tasks, impediments such as phonetic irregularity could be taken in their stride (Downing 1967).

Of much greater significance was the release of expressive energy by children through the medium—most experimental settings displayed a great increase in the quantity and range of written expression produced. The fact that any reasonable spelling was accepted by teachers, and the consistent way in which written words could be created by children, seemed to release them from the fear of mistakes into a desire to write, similar in its scope to the desire of infants to experiment with speech. This is the only setting in which the principle of approximation has been tolerated for spelling, and it has confirmed what should have been expected from an application of the developmental model.

Deep-seated prejudices probably inhibited these teachers from taking the same tolerant view of approximation in reading behaviour, and may have been partially responsible for the failure of the approach to show significantly better long-term effects on reading. Other factors may include the bad match between the use of print in the real world (traditional orthography) and its use in instruction (i.t.a.); the application of the medium in methodologically archaic styles of phonics or look-and-say; and the inhibiting effect of such traditional assumptions about schooling as intensive correction and competition.

From the extensive research generated by the experiment no-one can doubt that, from the orthographic point of view, the approach works. Thus its very efficiency as an orthography, combined with its failure to achieve significant long-term improvement, alerts us to the conclusion that orthographic irregularity is not central to the difficulties inherent in our ways of teaching literacy —that we need to look elsewhere for the major inhibiting forces which distort the literacy undertaking.

Breakthrough to Literacy

The most recent attempt at a radical reformulation of the literacy undertaking, and the only one which has attempted to face up squarely to language implications, arose from the application of recent linguistic theory in England. Deeply indebted to the language-experience tradition, *Breakthrough to Literacy* highlights the importance of creating written language from the earliest stages (Mackay, Thompson, and Schaub 1970).

The techniques and supporting materials make it possible for the beginner to express personal meanings in written language at the same time as he learns to read. The major impediments to written expression—handwriting and spelling—are bypassed in the first instance by providing a convenient file of printed word cards that may be manipulated into meaningful sentences in a 'Sentence Maker', and later copied into a personal reading book. Letters may also be manipulated to make words at a later stage of development. Grammatical understandings are facilitated by the use of affixes to modify base words rather than treating each derivative as a separate word.

An unfortunate limitation is the delay in the use of upper case letters, but this feature may not prove to be as essential to the system as the originators believed. Early books in the accompanying series are printed in lower case letters only. Any deviation from standard conventions of print as experienced in favourite books, names, labels, and TV commercials limits the opportunities to practise literacy in developmental ways. The instructional gains of tampering with the conventions as used in normal living are unlikely to compensate for the losses in natural experience of print from the earliest stages.

In experimental situations in Australia and New Zealand *Breakthrough to Literacy* has proved a significant success, although the results hardly warrant the claim of a breakthrough. Introduced into ordinary classrooms it presents great difficulties of an organizational nature and is not easy for teachers to understand fully. At best it provides the basis for a greatly facilitated language-experience programme, displaying the distinctive strengths and limitations of that approach. In combination with other techniques that will be discussed later in our enquiry, it has proved an exciting approach for children, generating a great increase in personal writing. At worst it decays into a new look-and-say approach, requiring the building of an extensive sight vocabulary before the system begins to deliver results in written expression and reading.

The insights embodied in the *Breakthrough to Literacy* materials deserve our serious consideration and we will return to them on several occasions.

Neglected sisters—handwriting, spelling, and written expression

Learning to produce conventionally acceptable written language presents the greatest combination of difficulties of any language task. While it is doubtful whether reading need be significantly more difficult to learn than listening, it is probably true that the combined challenges of handwriting, spelling, and written expression are significantly more difficult than learning to speak.

Refined muscular control of the hand and arm, together with hand-eye co-ordination, present special problems even in non-linguistic tasks. The irrationalities of spelling are, of course, notorious and need not be laboured—as someone has said, the trouble with modern English spelling is that it does not spell modern English. (Whitehall 1951, p.134).

The distinctive difficulty of written expression in comparison with speaking is not quite so obvious—it is largely a factor of pace. Linguistic expression takes the form of sentences, and production requires the ability to encompass the whole sentence *in the mind* from beginning to end during the execution. If the processes of production are very slow or are interrupted by extraneous cognitive and emotive problems such as the spelling of a word, it becomes difficult to develop the middle or end of a sentence in continuity from the beginning. At first sight there is some justification for the traditional solution of dividing the tasks of producing written language into three distinct 'subjects'.

Handwriting

Modern approaches to the teaching of handwriting to beginners are not too distant from the copy-book approach—except that the copy tends to be on a blackboard or in a workbook, or the caption on children's art expression. During the first two or three years at school children have been expected to master a print-script of separate letters—a style that must be abandoned or unlearned later in favour of a cursive script often very distant in letter form from printing. A tidy perpendicular form of printing has usually been preferred, despite the fact that a true perpendicular line is intrinsically difficult to achieve and maintain in a regular way. For some years a sloped printscript, capable of natural joining or running together, has been taught in New Zealand schools, and this seems a most sensible reform.

In practice it is fairly clear that two problems stand out as impediments to mastering handwriting.The first, as with any potentially boring and laborious task, centres around motivation and reward. By separating the learning of handwriting from its natural setting in purposeful expression, insoluble problems of motivation arise for the majority of children.

The second problem centres around questions of progression and approximation. What does writing look like in its earliest form and through what stages does it pass before becoming an acceptable, conventional script? The developmental answer to that, as displayed in such books as Marie Clay's detailed account, *What Did I Write!* (Clay 1975), is very different from the progression embodied in traditional school practice. In actual developmental studies we see a natural and continuous progression from scribble-like forms of play writing, through a very complex series of approximations and experiments each displaying the mastery of some new convention, towards goals which imply an understanding of the conventions of print rather than a simple ability to form acceptable letter shapes. The traditional progression tends to neglect the interlocking insights about how print embodies linguistic meanings, and instead moves directly towards acceptable letter form.

For those children who are unable to make the link for themselves between the apparently meaningless exercises in calligraphy to the fascinating purposes of embodying meanings in print, the traditional separation of 'printing' from proper language activity presents enormous problems of attention and perseverence. The extrinsic rewards offered on a narrow basis for approxima-tions to 'neatness' not only fail as appropriate reinforcement but may actually misinform or confuse young children about the purposes of the task, and in doing so cut them off from the sources of *intrinsic* motivation which are quite adequate to sustain practice and development at an efficiently high level.

Furthermore, as Marie Clay has demonstrated with detailed clarity, there are close links between beginning writing and beginning reading. In her own words:

> For a preliminary period creative writing activities appear to be an important complement to a reading programme.In the child's early contact with written language, writing behaviours seem to play the role of organizers of reading behaviours (1975 p.3).

This is a subject which we will need to consider in much greater detail as we proceed, but at this point in our brief historical survey, it is sufficient to note the traditional fallacy of treating handwriting narrowly as a predominantly visual and motor skill rather than as a centrally cognitive and generative task embodying insight into the conventions of print.

Spelling: Lief wosnt ment too bee eesy!

It seems rather unrealistic to talk about historical methods of teaching spelling—traditionally it was not taught, only tested and corrected. Much of the actual teaching of reading has always been handed over to children and parents through the practice of sending the 'reader' home to be prepared, and in spelling this was *always* done. For several generations children continued to perform the ritual of saying off the letter names repeatedly in the hope that they would learn and remember how to write words correctly.

At least the fact that children were clearly required to *learn* to spell, and no-one was very clear about how such a 'subject' could be *taught*, finally drew attention to methods of *learning* as distinct from methods of *teaching*. This, together with the excusable difficulty of mastering the irregularities of English spelling, generated the first attempts to understand how children learn one of the language skills.

Some insights arose outside the educational establishment in 'memory training' hints and courses offered to the adult population as secrets to success in life. As modern psychology developed, one of its first popular uses was the provision of systems and strategies for improving memory, and as a notoriously difficult memory task, spelling received considerable attention. Perhaps in consequence of this general public interest, teachers began *teaching* children how to learn spelling and the problem became one for academic interest and research.

In the past fifty years considerable progress has been made in understanding the learning of spelling, leading to insights about individual differences of sensory modalities[8] and learning styles (Schonell 1932; Arvidson 1963; Peters 1967). Stimulus was also provided by the work of remedial specialists such as Grace Fernald (1943) who pioneered the use of kinaesthetic techniques in both reading and spelling. The strategies recommended to children have become increasingly less mechanical and more functional, providing help to children in meeting the individual spelling needs of their written expression, and concentrating on words in the order of frequency of usage rather than phonetic or other traditional groupings.

Although these healthy developments have taken place (and helped to redirect the emphasis onto learning strategies and functional use in other language tasks) spelling remains a problem area. Recent research in the natural development of spelling generalizations (Elkonen 1971; C. Chomsky 1976; Clay 1977) provides increasing support to the idea that progressive approximation should be encouraged in the mastery of spelling. This notion, clearly pointed to in the i.t.a. research, is so foreign to traditional ideas of correctness that it is difficult to see how opposition to it could be broken down. Paradoxically, spelling—which began the movement towards understanding the process of language *learning*—is likely to be the last aspect of language in which children are permitted to approximate as they learn.

Written expression

Why is writing such a bore? By the time most of us have left school a pen has become the heaviest implement we will ever lift. Those few of us who took any pleasure in the thrice yearly composition on 'What I Did in the Holidays' may gain some esoteric pleasure from writing, but for the majority of us, even if we have a book burning inside us, writing will remain the worst form of hard labour.

The difficulties of handwriting and spelling tend to impede and delay any genuine desire to produce written language for a purpose. Traditionally this difficulty is met by inserting a more manageable task—copying. Evaluation of progress and ongoing teaching are narrowed onto the ability of beginners to achieve an accurate, mechanical copy before true written expression is expected. However, the real drive to produce writing, and to wrestle with the many conventions involved, springs from the belief that some personal meaning is being permanently recorded—participating in the magic and ritual of print.

It was not until the advent of language-experience methods that any real attempt was made to satisfy children's aspirations to use the mysterious symbols of print to record personal meanings. The practice of writing from children's dictation, and then allowing them to experiment with reproducing a meaningful script, constituted a much more fruitful intervention than providing copy which had not been generated by the children themselves. Discussing an experience with a child or a group and then writing their comments as they watch and participate is another fruitful technique associated with the language-experience approach. This practice leads naturally to participation by the children as they begin to 'cotton-on' to the way print works, and provides ideal opportunities to demonstrate and discuss the undertaking at a level suited to the children's development. 'What do I write next?' 'What letter do we need?' etc.

Expressive language is a fundamentally *generative* process whether in speaking or in writing—a process that is centrally creative and inventive. Perhaps in the early stages children need to 'babble' with a pencil for some time before we should expect genuine print forms to be learned and explored. Certainly, the major written output of very young children in natural or developmental ways has tended to be regarded as of little value or significance in traditional schooling. If this behaviour were better understood, were compared from week to week for significant growth, and as strongly rewarded as the first attempts at spoken words are rewarded, then a quite new perspective on early production of written language would emerge. The progression may then appear as moving from inventive play and exploration to insight about the complex conventions—directional, alphabetic, verbal and syntactic—which characterize the world of print. The formation of letters and the mere ability to copy accurately constitute a deeply impoverished view of what is involved in mastering the production of written language.

Current practice

It is always difficult to identify major trends in the hurly-burly of here-and-now. Many hopeful signs are in the air that lessons are being learned from mistakes of the past. New directions, guided by more realistic research of a developmental kind, embody a deeper and more sensitive awareness of what language is, and how its acquisition may be nurtured and sustained. These exciting developments suggest that answers to the perennial problems which we have analysed in this rather depressing historical survey lie in the realm of the possible. Many of these developments will be studied in detail as we proceed.

Before returning to the problems of the classroom, however, it may be fruitful to study the natural behaviour of pre-school children in the context of books and literacy. What constitutes readiness for reading and writing? Can reading and writing be learned in a purely developmental framework? What characterizes the early learning and experience of those children who become our high progress readers? What does the most healthy, optimal progress towards literacy from infancy look like? These are some of the questions which we will consider in the following chapter.

3
Literacy Learning Before School

A large group of children enter school at five and with remarkable confidence take to the business of reading and writing almost immediately. During the 'readiness programme' they display considerable knowledge about the conventions of print, and often take advantage of the special environment to role-play themselves as writers—which they do in ways that imply some familiarity with the process. They make rapid progress in reading almost regardless of how they are taught, and they show up in the most diverse programmes.

The success of these children cannot be accounted for by any simple explanation—intelligence and language background account for only a part of the effect (Clay 1967). They are a quite disparate group on most measures, yet they show a remarkable consistency in the ways that they operate in the contexts of literacy—at least, they rapidly converge towards similar ways of operating. They display meaning-oriented strategies very early, and without being taught to do so self-correct a high proportion of their errors (Clay 1972). They read with considerable accuracy from the first books, often above the level of one error in twenty running words. By what processes do they recognize the majority of words so early, or in what context have they learned some of the words previously? On what basis do they know so sensitively when they have made a mistake?

In many cases these rapid beginners display a deep familiarity with a number of favourite books which they love to read repeatedly regardless of whether or not they have an audience. They spend much more of their time reading than other children, and display an equal fascination for, and facility with, writing (Robinson 1973). They come to print with high expectations, not only that they will succeed in unlocking its mysteries, but also that the mysteries are *worth* unlocking. Even though they are often quick in everything they do associated with print, they will persevere and puzzle and practise with remarkable attention to the task, and in the more relaxed setting of story-time, they usually listen with rapt attention for long periods despite distractions. How did they develop these facilitating behaviours?

A number of children enter school actually reading. The evidence suggests that they were not deliberately taught but learned in natural, developmental ways. (Clark 1976; Durkin 1966). This group, too, display few similar characteristics apart from their ability to read. A significantly common feature in their *background*, however, is the presence of a certain type of supportive and emulative adult or peer who answers questions directly and readily without interfering with what the child is trying to do. What other factors in the pre-school environment may account for these very early readers?

A study of literacy-orientation in the pre-school years may provide answers to some of these questions and create a picture of what the entry to literacy in a developmental environment may look like. It is surprising how little this situation has been studied, and how little was known ten years ago about the conditions which produce our literacy-primed five-year-olds. It is almost as if the notion that nothing could be learned about reading outside the school environment had been accepted axiomatically by everyone. A few cliches summed up about all that was generally known. Everyone agreed that it was a 'Good Thing' to read to young children, and the virtues of the bed-time story were praised for reasons which remained vague and sentimental. Even in professional circles people joked tolerantly about the tiresome demand of infants to have their favourite books read again and again, and seemed to put this down to the quaintness of early childhood. As Holt (1975, pp.85–92) and others have pointed out, as soon as we regard youngsters as being 'cute' we become incapable of perceiving their behaviour accurately or taking its significance with due seriousness.

There was, indeed, a great deal of speculation about 'reading readiness', and people began talking about teaching 'pre-reading' skills, and setting up 'readiness programmes', without reference to the learning situations which actually produce the most literacy-ready children at school entry. Recently, there have even appeared a number of 'pre-literacy' programmes beginning with text-less books! More responsibly, research has begun to indicate that many of these purported pre-reading skills and activities which have been speculated into our schools seem to have little relationship to actual progress in reading. (Clay 1976a, p.75; Clark 1976, p.100).

Literacy learning in early childhood

Many parents in our culture read to their pre-school children regularly and provide them liberally with books and with the materials for writing. There may be a tendency for this custom to be associated with the middle class, but for our purposes this is probably not an important consideration. There are many other ways in which young children come in contact with print and we will consider these later. Our present purpose is to study the environment, the practices, and the outcomes of story reading and book handling in homes where these play a significant part in child-rearing.

Looking at the situation generally in the first instance, we find some surprising features. Most obviously, for the parents who engage in it, reading books to their youngsters provides deep satisfaction and pleasure. It is not engaged in as a duty or to achieve specific educational advantages for the child: it is a simple giving and taking of pleasure in which the parent makes no demands on the child, but is deeply gratified by the lively responses and questions that normally arise. It provides a stimulus for satisfying interaction between parent and child, different, richer and more wide-ranging than the mundane interactions of running the home. *The major purpose from the parent's point of view is to give pleasure, and the parent is sustained in this behaviour by the ample bonuses provided.*

From the child's point of view the situation is among the happiest and most secure in his experience. The stories themselves are enriching and deeply satisfying—there is something emancipating in the experience which trans-cends normal time and space. It provides an expansion of mental room, and freedom within it. The nature of the relationship with the parent is very special to the situation: the parent is giving complete attention; there are none of the normal distractions most of the time; the parent is invariably positive and interesting, with an enhanced being from association with the richness of the literature; and there is a feeling of security and special worth arising from the quality of the attention being received. *Thus the child develops strongly positive associations with the flow of story language and with the physical characteristics of the books.*

For these children introduction to books and book language begins at a very early stage of infancy, long before the tasks of oracy are mastered. The infant begins to experiment with book language in its primary, oral form while still using baby grammar and struggling with the phonology of speech. Yet this time seems ideal for such exposure: the sooner book-orientated activities begin, the more likely it is that book-handling and experimental writing will become an important part of the infant's daily preoccupation. *Literacy orientation does not wait on accomplished oracy.*

The language of the books used by parents even with infants below the age of two years is remarkably rich in comparison with the caption books and early readers used in the first year at school. Although the adults are usually willing to explain meanings and answer questions, they are seldom very worried about making certain that their infants understand every last word or have direct sensory experience of every new concept. The stories are usually allowed to carry growing understanding from an initial grasp of their central meanings. Just as speech develops in an environment which is immensely richer than the immediate needs of the infant, so *the orientation to book language develops in an environment of rich exposure beyond immediate needs.* In both situations *the infant selects appropriate significant items to learn from an immensely rich range.*

From the very beginning the infant is involved in the selection of those books which will deeply preoccupy him: the request to 'read it again' arises from a natural and important developmental demand. Furthermore, in his own play at 'being a reader' the infant quickly avails himself of the opportunity to practise and experiment with a selection from the material made available through repeated readings. As in the mastery of other developmental tasks, *self-selection rather than adult direction characterizes the specific tasks which will be intensively practised by the infant.*

Reading-like behaviour—a neglected feature of early literacy

By far the most surprising and significant aspect of pre-school book-experience, however, is the independent activity of these very young children with their favourite books.[1] Almost as soon as the infant becomes familiarized with particular books through repetitive readings, he begins to play with them in reading-like ways. Attracted by the familiar object with which he has such positive associations, the infant picks it up, opens it, and begins attempting to retrieve for himself some of the language and its intonations. Almost unintelligible at first, this reading-like play rapidly becomes picture stimulated, page-matched, and story-complete.

The time spent each day in these spontaneous attempts to retrieve pleasurable book experiences is often greatly in excess of the time spent in listening to books being read by the adults being emulated. The infant attends for surprisingly long periods of time until each book experience has achieved a semantic completeness, and the process may be repeated immediately with the same or another book.

Before going any further we should sample some of the behaviour to determine what sort of processes are in operation. First of all we will look at the behaviour in a fairly mature form after three years of exposure to books.[2]

Leslie has just turned four and will obviously be a high progress reader when she begins school. She is enjoying Sendak's *Where the Wild Things Are'*—which has been read to her four times. Note the way in which she determines the precise relationship between the story and reality as she 'reads' the title:

> " 'Where the Wild Things Are'—see? (sighs) I'm scared of these things but they're only in books—not in real countries. Only in books."

We now sample her reconstruction of the text beginning about a quarter of the way through the book.

Text	Re-enactment
and an ocean tumbled by with a private boat for Max and he sailed off through night and day	Max stepped into his private boat and sailed off one day and one night
and in and out of weeks and almost over a year to where the wild things are.	then when he came to where the wi—— OO look at that thing—he's blowing smoke out of his nose
And when he came to the place where the wild things are they roared their terrible roars and gnashed their terrible teeth and rolled their terrible eyes and showed their terrible claws	and where the wild things are they lashed their terrible claws—*oh no!* they lashed their terrible teeth—Hrmm!— (Interviewer: 'What did they gnash?') They *lashed* their terrible claws!—showed their terrible claws and showed their terrible yellow eyes (but we've got blue eyes)
till Max said "BE STILL!" and tamed them with a magic trick of staring into all their yellow eyes without blinking once and they were frightened and called him the most wild thing of all	till Max said,"BE STILL!" that's what he said. One of these ones have toes (turns the page to find the toed monster) Toes! (Laughs) until Max said "BE STILL!" into all the yellow eyes without blinking once. And all the wild things said, "You wild thing!" (Note the elegant transformation into direct speech.)
and made him king of all the wild things. "And now," cried Max, "let the wild rumpus start!"	And then Max said, "Let the wild rumpus start!"
No text. (Picture of wild dance)	That's got no words, has it? He'd better pull his tail out of the way.

The outstanding feature of this behaviour, particularly if it can be heard, is the deep meaning that it has for the child—the process displays language in proper use. The fact that 'gnash' is related to and transmuted into 'lashed' is not a matter for concern—as the interviewer obviously felt in making her pleasant attempt at a correction. It will not be long before this peripheral item comes under control. What we have here is another instance of the sort of approximation that goes on freely in speech learning. Another obvious feature is that the conventions of print are being mastered: Leslie knows that the message comes from print and not from the picture, she knows where to begin the book, and turns pages with unfailing precision.

A superficial assumption about this reading-like behaviour would be that it is a form of rote learning, based on repetitive patterning without deep comprehension or emotional response—that it would produce attempts at mere surface verbal recall. Leslie's performance clearly refutes this: at the very least, some of the parts she doesn't remember are filled from her own verbal inventory in an encoding activity springing from deep understanding.

A clearer picture of the actual linguistic and cognitive processes going on may be obtained from studying the re-enactment behaviour of very young children and observing its characteristic development in older children.[3]

A book that proves very popular and intelligible even for infants under two years of age is *Are You My Mother* by P.D. Eastman. This is a favourite book of David, aged two years no months. His control of syntax is still at a very primitive level yet he handles many aspects of book response with a remarkable range of skills which point to several months or prior learning.

Page	Text	Re-enactment
3	A mother bird sat on her egg.	The mummy bird sat at an egg.
4	The egg jumped. "Oh oh!" said the mother bird. "My baby will be here! He will want to eat."	Ow ow! A bumble bird baby here. ('Bumble' is a regressive form of 'Mummy' in David's speech.) Someping a eat. ('a' always used for 'to' and 'for').
6	"I must get something for my baby bird to eat!" she said. "I will be back." So away she went.	Must baby bird a (i.e. 'to') eated. Dat way went. Fly a gye (Fly to the sky).
8	The egg jumped. It jumped, and jumped, and jumped! Out came the baby bird.	Ig jumped and jumped. Out baby bird!
10	"Where is my mother?" he said. He looked for her.	Whis my mother? She look a her and look her.
12	He looked up. He did not see her. He looked down. He did not see her.	Her look up, look down, see her—[plus shake of head.] (Perhaps meaning, 'She can't see her'. Throughout, David shows no surface language for negation, yet operates meaningfully on what must be a comprehended deep structure.)
14	"I will go and look for her," he said. So away he went.	Look down. *Look* her! Way went. Way went. (The second 'look' is signalled by intonation to mean, 'I will look for her'—a typical syntactic elision by babies—cf. 'kiss' meaning 'give me a kiss'.)
16	Down, out of the tree he went. Down, down, down! It was a long way down.	Down, down, down, down, went. Down, down, down the bay went.
18	The baby bird could not fly. He could not fly, but he could walk. "Now I will go and find my mother," he said.	Could fly. Could walk. ('Could fly' turned into a syntactic negative by a violent shake of the head!) Now fin find mother (a self-correction).

This is as far as we will follow David. The point has been made that even at the stage where David is using baby grammar, what the linguists call 'pivot structures', he is still entering into book experience with considerable sophistication, especially in terms of identifying the action, page-by-page, carrying the whole story forward in terms of plot, and getting tremendous gratification from his own performance.

Now we will study a version by Robyn, aged two and a half, and youngest of a large book-oriented family. She enters with great gusto on the second sentence of page 8, beating out the rhythms of the language with a stick on each page.

Page	Text	Re-enactment
8	The egg jumped. It jumped, and jumped! Out came the baby bird.	It jumped and jumped. Out the baby bird. (We still have the remains of pivot structure, but Robyn adds the definite article. She then turns two pages impulsively as she is in the habit of doing.)
12	He looked up. He did not see her. He looked down. He did not see her.	He looked up and down. (Now another two pages.)
16	Down, out of the tree he went. Down, down, down! It was a long way down.	Looked down, down, down, down. (Another two pages.)
20	He did not know what his mother looked like. He went right by her. He did not see her.	Go wound the big wock.
22	He came to a kitten. "Are you my mother?" He said to the kitten. The kitten just looked and looked. It did not say a thing.	"Are you my mother?" "No said the cat."
24	The kitten was not his mother, so he went on. Then he came to a hen. "Are you my mother?" he said to the hen. "No," said the hen.	Den e came a hen. "Are you my mudder?" "No," said the hen. ('Den he came a hen' is a slight advance on David's grammar.)

Robyn becomes confused by the syntactically complex recapitulation sections in the following pages. We will take up her performance at page 44:

Page	Text	Re-enactment
44	Just then, the baby bird saw a big thing. This must be his mother! "There she is!" he said. "There is my mother!"	Den e came a big thing. "Are you my brudder—mudder big thing?" (Notice the early incidence of self-corrective behaviour.)
46	He ran right up to it. "Mother, Mother! Here I am, Mother!" he said to the big thing.	"No," said mudder big thing.
48	But the big thing just said, "Snort." "Oh, you are not my mother," said the baby bird. "You are a Snort. I have to get out of here!"	Itsa Snort!

50	But the baby bird could not get away. The Snort went up. It went way, way up. And up, up, up went the baby bird.	Went up, up, up, up. "Werya going put may—baby bird?" In the back the tree. (Self-correction of an earlier b/m phonemic confusion as she targets the first syllable of 'baby', cf. 'Brudder—mudder' above. Also David's 'bumble' equals 'mummy'.)

The first thing we notice in these two performances is the distance of the rendering from the text, especially syntactically. Yet there is no question here but that *deep* processing is going on. It is being expressed in syntactical operations at the level of spoken language mastery—both infants use their own primitive grammatical operations. They have encoded the *meanings* of the story into a unique structural form. They have remembered very little at the surface verbal level: what they have remembered most firmly is meanings.

Both infants self-correct what *they* perceive to be their errors—as we would find them doing also in their normal spoken language. They are mastering different aspects of the language at what might be called a 'working face' where they are making progress. This 'face' is quite narrow and no outsider would be able to determine exactly where it was placed. Any interference by an outsider is likely to be obstructive or harmful because it is not likely to be understood by the infant—as we saw in the 'gnash' case above. Yet both infants are working very conscientiously at their own current language 'face'. Both are monitoring their own output correctively *and* in confirmation of appropriate performance: their intonation patterns—not available, of course, in print—and the meaningful connectedness of the narrative, indicate that where self-correction does not occur, they are justifiably satisfied with their performance.

Even more complex syntactical operations can be seen in the performance of Emelia at three and a half years tackling the recapitulation section that was too much for Robyn. She displays most of the forms of normal, mature syntax, but this does not mean that she will pattern the text perfectly. She too encodes from meanings into an appropriate syntax which often stands in transformational relationship to the original text (like a translation into a different grammatical form).

Page	Text	Re-enactment
28	Then he came to a dog. "Are you my mother?" he said to the dog.	Now he came to a dog. "Are you my mother?" he said.
29	"I am not your mother. I am a dog," said the dog.	"No!" said the dog. "I'm a dog!"
30	The kitten was not his mother. The hen was not his mother. The dog was not his mother.	Den . . . so . . . The kitten wasn't his mother. The hen wasn't his mother. The dog wasn't his mother. (The 'Den . . . so' indicates awareness of a special structure coming up, and gives time for the thinking ahead required to get it rolling.)
31	So the baby bird went on. Now he came to a cow.	So the . . . so the . . . so the baby bird went on. Then he went to a cow. (The textual 'Now' or 'Then' beginnings are interchanged as at p.28,

		i.e. no word-by-word processing of print is going on.)
32	"Are you my mother?" he said to the cow.	"Are you my mother?" he said.
33	"How could I be your mother?" said the cow? "I am a cow."	"How could I be your mother? I'm a COW!"
34	The kitten and the hen were not his mother. The dog and the cow were not his mother.	Um . . . um . . . ummmm. The cow wasn't his mother, the dog wasn't his mother. The he . . . The kitten and the hen weren't his mother. (Starting at the bottom indicates that Emelia is not secure about the directional principle involved. The re-run at 'hen' indicates her awareness that this difficult structure changes from a single recapitulation to a double-barrelled one.)
35	Did he have a mother?	"Do I have a mother?" (Transformed from indirect to direct speech, and from past to present tense.)
36/7	"I did have a mother," said the baby bird. "I know I did. I have to find her. I will. I WILL!"	"Did I have a mother? Yes I'm did I had a mother. I know I did have a mudder. (Regression) I have to look for her, I do, I do, I do and I DO!" ('find' becomes 'look for'. The intensive construction of the text in 'I WILL' is perfectly echoed in the "I do" sequence with the intensive use of "and".)

Characteristic of her age, Emelia has difficulty in articulating the 'th' and 'r' phonemes in the next example. This is about the only thing which reminds us that she is still an infant making transition into the early childhood stage displayed by Leslie, who is six months older. We continue with Emelia's performance.

44/5	Just then, the baby bird saw a thing. This must be his mother! "There she is!" he said. "There is my mother!"	Then he saw a big Snort. (From p.48) "Dere, dere's my mother. Dere she is!" (To herself) Is that his mother? Naahohoho! (Big laugh.)
46/7	He ran right up to it. "Mother, Mother! Here I am, Mother!" he said to the big thing.	Then e went fwigh up to it. Said, "Mother, Mother! Here I am!" to the big HING.
48/9	But the big thing just said, "Snort." "Oh, you are not my mother," said the baby bird. "You are a Snort. I have to get out of here!"	But the big hing said, "Snor-or-ort!" And the . . . "Oh," said the baby. "You not my mother!" said the baby bird. "You are a Snort! I hafta get outa here!"

Emelia's false starts as in 'and the' and repetitions as in 'Dere' are automatic predictive devices which act as time fillers while she engages consciously in organizing the coming structure—a type of advance organizer. We often see this device in reading behaviour and fail to understand what is happening. Such a device is a useful strategy when confidence is low, or when the text becomes difficult. We should not interpret it as inaccuracy or error.

Very similar in many respects to Emelia, Leslie displays the great sophistication of mature reading-like behaviour. She has no difficulty in transforming to direct speech where the text uses reported speech and vice versa, making all the appropriate adjustments for grammatical agreement. The embroidery of the text indicates the semantic energy generated by the activity, and as a sub-vocal strategy will have powerful effects on the efficiency of Leslie's reading when she enters school.

4   The egg jumped and jumped. And the mother bird· said, "Oh, oh! I'd better go get some food for my baby bird to eat, 'cos he'll want to EAT."

6   And she said, "I will be back in a moment".

8   The egg jumped, and jumped, and JUMPED! Till the baby bird came out.

10   He said, "WHERE IS MY MUMMY? I'm going to go out and look for her."

12   He looked down, up down, up. He could not see her.

14   "I will go and look for her." He fought it was a path—see? Fought it was a path, doesn't he? But he'll fall—he really will—see?

Note the formality of the language, except when Leslie gets excited by the story: it approximates the tones and structures of the written dialect even when it departs from the text.

Page	Text	Re-enactment
26	The kitten was not his mother. The hen was not his mother. So the baby bird went on. "I have to find my mother!" he said. "But where?" "Where is she? Where could she be?"	And—so—the pussy went on, the hen went on, the baby bird went on. (Shades of 'Chicken Licken', another book Leslie is enjoying at the time.) I have to find my mother. "Where can she be?"
32	"Are you my mother?" he said to the cow? "How could I be your mother?" said the cow. "I am a cow."	He saw a cow. The baby bird said. "Are you my mother?" And the cow said, "HOW COULD I BE YOUR MOTHER?" said the cow. And the cow said, "I am a COWWW!" Hahmm!
34	The kitten and the hen were not his mother. The dog and the cow were not his mother. Did he have a mother?	So the pussy wasn't his mother, the hen wasn't his mother, the dog wasn't his mother, the cow wasn't his mother. And the baby bird said, "Did I have a mother?" An e DID! (Note the fluent transformation of the grammatical structure—similar in nature but more elaborated than Emelia's.)
36	"I did have a mother," said the baby bird. "I know I did. I have to find her I will. I WILL!"	What a sad face. That one says—"Did he have a mother? Did he have a mother? HE DID!"
38	Now the baby bird did not walk. He ran! Then he saw a car. Could that old thing be his mother? No, it could not. The baby bird did not stop. He ran on and on.	Now the baby bird did not run—he ran. (Leslie is going too fast to self-correct here—another sound strategy). He shoulda got in there—eh? It'd keep him warm. It would keep stopping the breath coming on him. He shoulda just sitted down in there—eh? Yes.

As Leslie completes the story it is fascinating to hear the lively and often subtle intonation patterns she uses in recreating the text, and to see the way in which she monitors and self-corrects her own performance. It is an experience of remarkable gaiety and verve.

During the leisurely period of three to four years of active literacy-learning before school entry most of these children become fascinated in print as a mystery that is well worth solving. They begin to play with writing in the same way as they play with reading, producing writing-like scribble, the central feature of which, for them, is that it *carries a message*. They learn to write their names, and explore creating letters and letter-like symbols with a variety of writing devices. They show intense interest in the print around them on signs, labels, advertisements, and TV, and often imitate these forms in inventive ways. By the time they enter school they are likely to know the alphabet and be able to recognize many of the letters in both lower and upper case forms, and name them. We will look more closely at this behaviour later.

Many of the same principles that we have been studying in reading-like behaviour of pre-schoolers are also clearly evidenced by very young children who have been exploring writing in a developmental environment in which approximation was tolerated. In a fascinating article entitled 'Invented Spelling in the Open Classroom', Carol Chomsky (1971) includes a lengthy excerpt from a 1970 thesis by Charles Read, who studied the spontaneous writing behaviour of pre-schoolers. He describes one of his cases as follows:

The beginning of spelling

The beginning of reading and spelling for Maria was typical of what parents reported, in that parental teaching was in response to the child's expressed interests and was of the most informal kind—there was no "training" in reading and writing . . . Maria, an Australian girl, recognized the letters BP on service station signs at 18 months. She then generalized this notion, calling all letters (not gas stations) "BP's". She quickly learned to recognize and name the letters that she saw in signs, licence plates, and books. After BP, Maria learned A and C (from books with ABC on the cover), then the M of her name. With three children quite close in age at home, her mother started using M to distinguish the toys and other objects that belonged to Maria. The mother emphasized that she told Maria the names of letters only when she asked, and used letters as a convenience only after Maria could recognize them. The informality of this process is illustrated in that although she could recognize all the letters before age two, she did not "learn the alphabet"—in the usual sequence—until age four. At twenty to twenty-two months, Maria had begun to learn the sounds that certain letters spell, beginning with the idea that "*b* says 'buh' ". On her third birthday Maria's parents gave her a blackboard; at that time she could write most of the letters according to their sounds . . .

At the age of three Maria began to go to an Australian nursery school two days a week. According to the mother, the school was comparable to an American kindergarten, but somewhat more formal. The teacher gave no specific training in reading and writing, but a great deal of what Maria's mother considered 'ear training', including listening to and telling stories. Sometime during this year, Maria began to write some words, beginning with DADE (Daddy).

The behaviour of the children was marked by an independent search for the significance of writing from an analysis of their own spoken language—the behaviour was essentially self-regulated and the spelling principles were largely intuited from their knowledge of the *names* of the letters. For instance:

One child of 4 produced this "get-well" message:
2 DADDY I EM SRY TAT U R SIC NED LUV DADDY

And a 5-year-old wrote:
DER MUMOY I HOP YOO OR FEELIG BEDR I AM MKIG THS PRESIM FOOR
YOO BI DIANE

It seems that the alphabetic method is alive and well among pre-schoolers!
It was something of a surprise in our study of reading-like behaviour that the
infants engaged in this activity for their own satisfaction and generally without
an audience. It seems that even in this early 'writing-like' behaviour, where we
would expect *communication* to be the driving motivation, the same principle
holds. Read says:

> Some children wrote messages to others who they knew could not read. Although
> they enjoyed having their parents read what they had written and sometimes used
> writing purposefully, their writings were usually messages intended for no one,
> stories apparently for their own amusement. Furthermore, the good readers often
> had more difficulty in reading their own writing (a few days later) than in reading
> standard orthography, and they would read their own writing only when asked to.
> The difficulty was increased by the distortions, such as ill-formed letters and
> sequences of words that wind in various directions around the page, that make a
> child's writing more difficult to read for extraneous reasons, but sometimes in
> reading their own writing, the children stumbled over just those features that
> distinguished it from standard spelling. It seems clear that they distinguished
> writing rather sharply from reading; the former was more fundamentally an
> expression than a communication.

We will consider the application of these principles as described by Carol
Chomsky to the classroom at a later point, but in terms of pre-school behaviour
it is clear that the incidence of writing-like behaviour complements reading-
like behaviour and displays the same characteristics of personal initiative and
approximation.

The relationship between reading and writing at the earliest stages is only
beginning to be worked out. Marie Clay (1975, p.74), in her comprehensive
treatment of early writing development, says:

> One frequently sees a statement which implies, 'How can the child write words
> until he can read them?' (This book's) analysis suggests the opposite point of view
> . . . If a writing program fosters the development of self-direction in locating,
> exploring and producing appropriate analysis of printed forms, then one is tempted
> to say, 'How can any child who is not exceptional learn to read until he can write
> some words?'

And Read reported:

> Among the original spellers, those who had begun to spell before they began to read
> predominated by approximately a three-to-one margin. Some children began to
> spell a few months or even a year before reading, some began reading and writing at
> about the same time, several parents were uncertain, and there is some vagueness
> in dating the beginning of either activity, but there were clear cases of both kinds.

Margaret Clark (1976) in her Glasgow study of thirty-two children who read
before five reports:

> Already before four years of age, ten of the children were also interested in writing.
> Some began by copying words, other letters, a few wrote their names or little
> messages—while one wrote the football scores. (pp.51-2)

In a short monograph, *"Write Now, Read Later": An Evaluation*, Marie Clay (1977) summarizes the scarce information available on this topic, and concludes with these words:

> Perhaps the challenge is this. How can we get young children to want to hear the sound segments in words and to search for these on their own initiative? That is worth thinking about. And *why is it easier to go from sound to print than vice versa?* That is a question worthy of an answer. (p.13 Italics mine—and we consider an answer in Chapter 5.)

At this stage we could summarize some of the major characteristics of these children as they enter school primed to become rapid literacy learners (unless they suffer radical setbacks of some form).

Literacy oriented pre-schoolers

Children with a background of book experience since infancy develop a complex range of attitudes, concepts, and skills predisposing them to literacy. They are likely to continue into literacy on entering school with a minimum of discontinuity.

They have developed high expectations of print, knowing that books bring them special pleasures which they can obtain in no other way.

They have built a set of oral models for the language of books and practised these models to the point where they have become almost as natural and familiar as the forms of conversation: they have developed native language control of the fundamental forms of written dialect.

They are familiar with written symbols as signs which are different in their interpretation from normal visual experience, and have become interested in them to the point of experimenting in writing them.

They have begun to understand the complex conventions of direction and position in print, knowing, for instance, that the message unfolds from the print itself, and from top to bottom of the page.

They have learned to listen for long periods to continuous language of story-length related in terms of plot, sequence, or central ideas.

They are able to attend to language without reference to the immediate situation around them, and respond to it in complex ways by creating images from their past experiences—they have learned to operate vicariously. This has opened a new dimension of fantasy and imagination, allowing them to create images of things never experienced or entitities which do not exist in the real world. By these means they are able to escape from the bonds of the present into the past and the future.

The concept of literacy set

Such children are all set up for reading and writing—they are *ready to go*. All their faculties have been trained to work in appropriate and harmonious ways whenever they are in contact with books or stories. Using the term 'set' in this psychological sense to mean an ability to tune in with appropriate action, we could say that the formidable range of early skills and attitudes which we have sampled constitutes a 'set towards literacy' or a 'literacy set'.

Children who have developed a strong literacy set begin to operate immediately and automatically in appropriate ways whenever they are faced with print. We should spend a little time exploring this concept, for the primary incentives to read and write at all levels, and the readiness to develop appropriate skills, are dependent on it.

A further example, Gregory, at the age of 4.0 displays many of the features of a sound literacy set. He is retrieving *Kittens* by Mollie Clarke. In his spoken language development, Gregory has not yet quite mastered such grammatical problems as irregular verbs, as in his 'drived' for 'drove'. This is another indication that the processing is at a deep syntactical level rather than a simple recall of the surface language which was modelled repetitively through listening to the story being read.

Text	Re-enactment
Here go the kittens with a fishing rod, and a red basket, and a bucket. This kitten goes to the pond to catch a fish.	This kitten goes to the pond to get a—fish.
But here come two ducks. The ducks say, "Quack, quack, quack! This pond belongs to us. Run away kitten! Poor kitten runs so fast that he falls into the pond. The little fish laughs.	But here comes some two little ducks. And the ducks said, "This is *my* pond. Run away little kitten." He runs so fast he fell into the pond. The little fish laughed. (Syntax adjusted from present to past and back again. The familiar concept 'my' over-rides the literary syntax of 'belong to'. Emotional reaction and indentification with the characters is at a high level.)
But along comes a kind girl. The kind girl drives away the ducks. She picks up poor kitten. She says, "Never mind, kitten! I know a kind boy. I will ask him to catch a big fish for you."	The little girl came and drived away the ducks. She picked up poor kitten. "Never mind, kitten. I wi——I know a kind boy. I will tell him to get a fish for you." (Note the rapid self-correction. Inflected verb forms are changed to retain grammatical agreement within the remembered structure.)
This kitten goes to the farm to find an egg. She has her little red basket. Brown Hen says, "Cluck, cluck, cluck! Here is a beautiful brown egg to put in your red basket."	This kitten goes to the farm to get a egg. "Cluck——" What now? (Request for aid—he was actually worrying ahead to the complexities of the next sentence.) "Cluck, cluck", said the hen. "Here's a beautiful egg," said the brown egg—hen. (The child is worrying about the complex structure one sentence ahead of his utterance—even the linguistic operation of a young child is immensely complicated and beyond our ability to analyse fully. Note the self-correction on semantic grounds.)
But here comes a barking dog. Barking Dog says, "Bow-wow, bow-wow. This is my farm-yard. Run away kitten!" Poor kitten runs so fast that she drops her red basket. The beautiful brown egg is broken!	But here comes the barking dog. The dog said "Bow-wow, bow-wow! This is *my* farmyard. Run away kitten!" (Very animated.) He runs so fast the beautiful brown egg is broken. He ran so fast he dropped his—he dropped his—basket (Knows there's something wrong but proceeds to next page. Intonation patterns are recreated as a major part of response. Syntax is the guiding road map.)

But along comes a kind boy. The kind boy drives away the dog. He picks up poor kitten.
He says, "Never mind, kitten! I know a kind girl. I will ask her to find an egg for you."

Here comes a kind boy. "Never mind little kitten." He drived away the dog. (This is said with a self-correcting inflection as he tries to achieve a logical sequence.) "Never mind little kitten. I know a kind girl. I'll get—I will tell her to ca——get a egg for you."
(The elaborated vocabulary of written dialect—as in 'ask'—has not yet been strongly enough modelled for utterance. But compare the confident use of 'fetch' on the next page. Highly appropriate substitutions are made.)

This kitten goes to the bridge to fetch some water in his bucket.
But here comes an angry goat.
Angry goat says, "Maa, maa, maa! This is my bridge. Run away kitten!"

This kitten goes to the bridge to fetch some water. (This time he gets the literary word 'fetch' even though he had replaced 'ask' by 'get' on the previous page.) But here comes a angry goat. The angry goat say, "Go a——Run away little kitten!"
(This experience of recreating a text can proceed at a pace which is both natural and satisfying. The laboured pace of later early-reading can be tolerated if it has been preceded by this type of processing.)

Poor kitten runs so fast that he falls over. He spilt all his water.
But see who comes to help him!
The kind girl, and the kind boy and the two kittens, come to help him.

He runs so fast he falls over and spilt *aaall* his water. See who comes. The kind boy, the kind girl, the two kittens (pause) come to help him.
(Self-monitoring is sufficiently careful to trigger completion of the structure.)

The kind girl puts an egg in the basket. The kind boy fills the bucket and catches a big fish. The kittens say, "Thank you!" and run home to Mother Cat.
Mother Cat takes the water, the egg, and the fish, and makes a big pie!

The kind boy catched the fish and the kind boy got a egg. The kind girl fetched some water. And that's the end. (Prompt, "What did the kittens do then?")
They said, "Thank you!" And then brought it home to Mother Cat.
Mother Cat made a big pie!
(The notions of plot, climax, and story-resolution are fully comprehended. This child displays a strong 'literacy set'. He is ready to begin processing print itself, and will persist through considerable frustration.)

In actual fact Gregory had a further year of consolidating experience before he entered school and began to be taught to read. His taste for stories during that year became much more sophisticated. He loved highly structured stories that had a special bounce to the language, like *The Magic Fish* by Freya Littledale, and books in the Ainsworth and Ridout Series, 'A Book for Me to Read' such as *A Name of My Own*. In these books his recall of the exact language became very precise, because that is required for the full savouring of the special effects. His self-corrections were directed to getting the language dead right from memory, intonation and all, and the subtle processing we see in the example above became sub-vocal and seldom appeared on the surface. In those instances where it did, he tended to use a re-run technique, returning to the beginning of the sentence to get a semantically complete utterance, and to savour it in its perfect form. For instance in the Ainsworth and Ridout story, *Huff the Hedgehog*, he says:

> I'm Huff the Hedgehog, and I want my dinner.
> If I don't get it soon, I'll g——
> If I don't have it soon, I'll get thinner and thinner.

The potential jangle of the two 'gets' offends his ear. This re-running is an important and effective strategy in the early reading stage ahead (Clay 1972a, p.19)—it provides insurance against becoming syntactically or semantically tangled, and re-illuminates the context before a problem of word-recognition is faced or corrected.

The marks of emergent literacy

From the examples we have been studying we can summarize some of the learning that has been achieved in the interactive and productive situation of the bed-time story. The examples of very early behaviour are particularly useful to us, because there the children are vocalizing most of their problem-solving.

Motivational factors

Predominant is the personal joy and motivational strength displayed in the behaviour. These children are impelled by the deeply rewarding structure of the listening situation into independent practice similar in its cyclic pattern of reinforcement to the practising of spoken language. They are sustained in approximation, self-correction, repetitive practice and modification by very powerful reinforcement contingencies of an intrinsic kind. Almost all book experiences have been highly satisfying so that the children gradually develop unshakably positive expectations of print, and powerful motives to learn how to interpret it for themselves. The quality of the enjoyment is global, evidenced in the facial expressions and toe-curling excitement that were going on throughout Gregory's retrieval, or in the page-beating displayed by Robyn.

Linguistic factors

Linguistically, the children are operating at a level of deep semantic processing, they are manipulating their own syntax in relationship to the deep syntactical structure of the text, and they are sorting out possibilities, striving to maintain grammatical agreement while experimenting with complex transformations. They are learning how to throw a syntactic rope across the abyss of meaning before they shuttle vocabulary over to the other side—a sort of flying-fox strategy of encoding. This process requires thinking ahead of where the voice has got to, in its realization of the surface level of language. It is a multi-level cognitive process going on simultaneously with the articulation. Another image for this would be that the child is engaged in a preparatory syntactic and semantic mapping of the tangled verbal path ahead.

The vocabulary chosen to fill the unfolding sentence-slots displays highly appropriate substitutions. New content words tend to be remembered and learned first, as in 'private boat' or 'Snort' or 'drived', while structure words (syntactical markers such as auxiliary verbs) tend to be drawn more frequently from the children's spoken language, as in 'look for' instead of 'find', or 'go get' for 'go and get'. Only slowly are the elaborated structure words of written dialect brought under control, as in 'said the cow' or 'I will ask'. Approximating is crucial and healthy: 'lashed' this week will become 'gnashed' next week.

Could fly. Could walk' this month becomes 'He couldn't fly, but he could walk' six months later.

The language of the children is remarkably alive intonationally—vigorous and full-blooded. The power of the intonational system to carry and refine meaning has become deeply associated with the written dialect for these children—the tunes of language ring in their ears and sing in their voices. When their pace is slowed temporarily during the early-reading stage at school, these children will continue to recreate the intonations crucial to meaning—it has become second nature to them. They will not be trapped into mindlessness by the slow, word-by-word visual checking of early reading.

Closely allied to this because of intonational involvement is the grasp of literary idioms—those special ways of saying things that are unique to particular utterances and sometimes depart from rule, such as, 'Never mind why!' or, 'That very night' or 'He made mischief'. These special literary forms are among the first things learned whole, perhaps because of their strong intonation, their freshness, and their emotionally complete semantic sting.

Operational factors

Self-regulating operations The most complex aspect of the children's behaviour involves *process*: they are learning much more than simple linguistic items, they are mastering ways of operating, strategies for generating language from meaning. They monitor their own output, yea-ing and nay-ing as they go: one part of their attention tastes their success or otherwise in encoding the deeply understood meanings. On the surface, this throws up self-corrections of an increasingly refined kind, entailing the strategy of semantic and syntactic re-running of confused sentences. All of the delicate operations of the task involving the organism at several levels, are under personal control. A product of this self-regulating behaviour is the steady flow of intrinsic reinforcement, confirming, sustaining, relaxing and restoring. Where in many typical reading programmes after five we find children unable to sustain attention through a tiny caption reader, and where the teacher sometimes 'sets' two or three pages of a reader to prepare at home, here we see children just turning two years old able to sustain attention for the full sixty-four pages of *Are You My Mother?*

Predictive operations We have already drawn attention to evidence of Gregory's concern foraging ahead into the difficulties of the sentence following the one he is uttering—he is operating predictively. By their ability to make appropriate substitutions, *all* of the children display a powerful predictive strategy. Placed in the interactive situation of the bed-time story as it is developed by the most sensitive parents, these children make appropriate predictions during the *first* reading of a story. This is particularly so when the story has a reliable structure of a repetitive or cyclic kind, as so many fine stories for the age group do. 'Father bear's bed was too hard. Mother bear's bed was too —— . Baby bear's bed was j —— r ——'. In such ways as this, these children learn how to use every clue available to find the precise word to fill a slot—even those of plot and story structure which lie beyond sentence limits. There is no more powerful strategy for decoding than this predictive search of the available verbal inventory—in reading, it is at the heart of word-solving skill.

Using the structures of written dialect   Infants are not born with the ability to understand and use cognitive structures and logical processes—these must be learned. Written language is distinctive in using a wider range of such structures, more rigorously developed, more crucial to understanding, and more sophisticated in their refinements, than occurs anywhere in conversational language. Lack of experience with these encompassing structures of logical arrangement, temporal sequence, cause and effect, plot, and so on, can present tremendous impediments in learning to read.

For three to four years of unpressured learning, these children work assiduously at understanding complex cognitive structures, and the stories they love abound in examples of the most central structures involved in early cognitive development—opposites, hierarchies (small, middle-sized, big), structures of logical relationship or consequence (because, if . . ., then . . ., however . . .). Often these structures are manipulated in their reversible functions at a quite early age, as in 'Little Red Hen', or 'The Five Little Chickens'. By the time they start school these children are very familiar with all the important cognitive structures which give stories their shape and meaning.

Context-free operations   Conversational language takes much of its meaning from the real situation in which it occurs. The sensory situation constantly provides confirmation and clarification of what is being said, and a glance at the speaker's face and his gestures, and an ear to his intonations, provide further clues to meaning. Normal spoken language is therefore a kind of composite message coming from language in association with sensory context. In consequence, spoken language structures may be incomplete or ambiguous in themselves without being confusing, because the situation adds its own components to the meaning. Written language cannot afford to be incomplete in these ways—it must carry the *total* load of meaning without ambiguity. This is the main reason why the written dialect is so different from conversational language. It is more formal, more complete, and more textured than spoken language, and to avoid ambiguity it has distinctive structures which do not appear in spoken dialects. For instance, people hardly ever use words like 'nevertheless' in speech.

We can call most speech 'situational language' and most writing 'non-situational language'. Learning to operate linguistically without reference to the immediate situation constitutes a much bigger task than is generally recognized. Many children enter school quite unable to interpret language which is not supported by the sensory situation around them. They are so used to gaining sensory confirmation or clarification from their eyes and ears that they become insecure and disoriented when they are denied such support. This is the major function of illustrations in early reading: they are special mediating symbols which replace the real environments of conversation until they can be fully replaced by mental images in mature reading.

The bed-time story situation is neutral in relationship to outside sensory stimuli except those of the human voice. The children we have been studying rapidly learn to transfer their outward-looking attention to pictures and to mental images induced by the language. They gradually learn how to operate in non-situational modes—to obtain total messages from language without external sensory aid. They learn to operate vicariously in the way that written language demands.[5]

This non-situational way of operating has its own semantic and syntactic conventions triggering responses of a quite different kind from those triggered by speech. For instance, when we hear a demonstrative such as 'this' or 'those' in speech, we look around us to find what is being referred to. The same demonstratives in written language require a quite different response—we must think back in the story or the discourse to locate what the 'this' or the 'those' refers to. Pronouns such as 'they' or 'hers' must be interpreted with the same backward-looking search. Non-situational operations of written discourse are time-oriented and energize memory for the previous part of the discourse—the language or the meanings must be held in mind in order to interpret some of the structures. Situational operations in speech, using the same syntactic signals, are here-and-now oriented and energize sensory exploration of the environment in which the communication is occurring. (When conversation is about something which happened in a different place or at a different time, these same signals ask for the 'as-if' explorations of that mental image, and the situational mode is thus maintained. Hence the way conversation about a film or even a story gets peppered with such structures as, 'Well this man points the gun at this other fellow, see, and he just grins and nods his head over to the corner of the room behind the other chap, and he turns—and there's this girl with the automatic pointed at his head.')

This is a complex and confusing matter—as the last four paragraphs have indicated! Perhaps we can simply say at this point that children exposed to book-language at an early age learn in this arena to take more of their meanings from the language and from their own *images* of reality than they would do in conversational speech. They are freed from the necessity or desire to clarify, complete or confirm meanings by looking around them. This is what we mean by 'non-situational operations' or 'situation-free modes of understanding'.

Imaginative operations   Finally in this operational field, the sort of children we have been studying have learned to use imagination in powerful ways. Stories are usually about the inner world of emotion, intention, behaviour or human purpose—things for which there are no clear verbal equivalents. We all know how vague and empty 'I love you' can be if not backed up by action and given body in metaphor. The images we use to represent and to explore the inner world operate in complex metaphorical ways which turn sensory experience into symbolic language. The images are often untrue to sensory experience itself and thereby signal their metaphorical purpose. The wild things of Sendak's powerful story about love and fear and power exist nowhere except in the mind, yet they are amalgams of sensory images. Lesley says they don't live in real countries, only in books, and so places herself in a proper imaginative relationship to the symbols. She enters the story with a zestful enjoyment knowing that the images are truly about real emotions (otherwise they would be trivial) and that she can experience her own fear and explore it in *total security*. If it's in the imagination, it's for real!

Knowing how to operate imaginatively is *learned* behaviour, and highly complex learning at that. The children we are studying have been introduced to these operations since infancy and spent several years learning how to make meanings from metaphors, symbols, and analogies. Because this behaviour is so difficult to study, its significance has been almost overlooked in traditional teaching of literacy. Sentimental things are said about the magical world of literature and the imagination, but few think of applying this driving force to the basic learning of literacy tasks. Nor do they think of remedying the situation for those children who have not learned to operate imaginatively. For such children, half their motivation for becoming literate is paralysed, and so learning to read must be like learning to walk with one leg.

This is such an important and little-understood part of the literacy under-taking that we must return to it in greater depth later. At this point we should acknowledge that the functioning imagination is crucial to literacy, and that early book-experience can be seen to develop a wide range of imaginative operations often associated with the deepest satisfactions that are to be experienced with print.

Orthographic factors   As traditional approaches to the teaching of reading and writing remind us, print is a system of visual symbols organized by complex conventions of directionality, punctuation, and letter-sound association. It is the mastery of this system, and the relating of its cues into the wider systems of language cues, which constitute the task of early reading and characterizes what we would call 'real reading'.

Children who are exposed to print as carrying fascinating messages become curious at an early age and usually attempt to create print in writing-like behaviour. There are many insights about the way in which print operates to encode language meanings, and these insights must be made before words or letters can have any real significance. Children must understand that the message comes from the print itself, and that it is preserved there in a verbally invariable way—that the story as read today will be verbally identical with the story as read yesterday. They need to know at which end a book begins, that the message starts at the top of a page and goes down the page before returning to the top of the next page, and finally, that the message is linear and moves from left to right, line-by-line, back-and-down. The directional conventions of print are intrinsically confusing and confusible and we should expect that mastery of them will be a lengthy process which is progressive in nature.

In the developmental setting, understanding of the conventions of print tends to be slow and late in developing. The features of print in the form of letters and words tend to be explored in a fairly unco-ordinated way before there is any understanding of their functional significance. Children may learn to make a few letters which are repeated in linear forms to approximate writing. They may learn to recognize their own names as signs similar to those which distinguish products on labels or advertisements, and yet have no clear concept of a printed 'word'. They may learn the alphabet as a cultural sequence introduced in books and songs, and even recognize some of the letters by name, yet still have no clear concept of a 'letter'. Finally, all of these unrelated insights and items of knowledge may begin to come together in systematic ways, but this is a very late development normally associated with the first months of schooling (Clay 1972a, p.137).

The emergent stage of literacy

These learnings add up to a formidable range of behaviours indeed. They enrich our notion of reading readiness, and present an ideal picture of what entry into literacy can be at its best. When we apply a term like 'pre-reading skills' to such behaviours we demean their real status as early literacy skills, for they actually display all the features of mature strategies already achieving sound and satisfying outcomes well beyond what could be called embryonic—or pre-anything. These strategies, if they are permitted to develop naturally, will lead into mature reading and writing without any discontinuity brought about by a regression into the print starvation of traditional readiness activities such as 'reading' picture books without print. From the point of view of reading, we should call this stage of development 'emergent reading', in contrast to the 'early reading stage', in which close attention to the visual detail of print in the final relating of cues brings about what we would recognize as 'true reading'.[7]

The vital learnings of this emergent stage of literacy development centre around the tasks of creating a healthy 'literacy set' in the terms discussed above. Most children enter school with a poorly developed literacy set—they have not mastered the tasks of the emergent reading stage. To pass them through a pre-reading programme which is not oriented towards literacy, and then move them on into early reading before they have developed a strong literacy set, seems very unwise in light of the sort of evidence we have been studying. Without adequately developed strategies for exploring written language, we would expect such children to experience great difficulty and confusion in facing the highly complex and refined processes of relating cues in early reading. The characteristics of a well-developed literacy set are summarized at the end of the chapter, and, at the beginning of the practical aspects of our enquiry, in chapter 4, we will use these characteristics as the objectives of a 'readiness programme'. However, to avoid traditional misunderstandings, we will refer to this programme as an 'emergent literacy programme'.

Language, ritual, and culture—the oral tradition

Closely associated with the experience of an enriching literature in early childhood and continuous with it in content, we find what might be called 'the oral culture'. Nursery rhymes and songs make up a large part of this tradition in our culture, but there is much more to it than this. Special forms of language have always been important in the enculturing process and often take the form of chant, song, dance, and ritual. The language of enculturing is usually highly wrought, firstly because it is, in fact, memorable, and secondly because it is designed to have a powerful and lasting effect on development.

In our society much of this special language is no longer transmitted from memory but has become embodied in print—it is therefore not possible to make a clear distinction between the oral enjoyment of books and participation in a purely oral tradition. In most societies much of this special language use is centred around religious belief and social custom, but since church-going has become a minority activity in our own culture, a great part of the tradition has been lost. Indeed, our modern secular culture must be distinctive in the small use that is made of linguistic patterning to implant important cultural meanings. Apart from some aspects of courtesy—'How do you do', 'Excuse me', etc.—little is left of that great wealth of common cultural experience which used to be so important in early education, and used to contribute so much to general language development.[8] Few mothers can sing a lullaby, and even the nursery rhymes may be disappearing. We can no longer expect that the rhythms of the Authorized Version of the Bible ring in every ear.

An important aspect of an oral tradition is that it is largely learned in unison situations—and gains in its social meaning from that togetherness. Much of the language is rhythmic and set to some form of chant or melody. Because of its purposes in forming attitudes, focussing emotions, and controlling personal interaction, it tends to be symbolic or metaphorical in form, using all the devices of a literature to make it penetrating, pleasurable and meaningful. Chant, song, dance and linguistic rituals are among the most powerful forms of human learnings, primitively satisfying, deeply memorable, and globally meaningful. Much of its power comes from the sense of security generated by repetition, familiarity, and universality.

Many of the features we observed in the bed-time story situation are shared with the transmission of the oral tradition. The oral tradition is linguistically enriching for many of the same reasons, presenting special styles and conventions of language which both stimulate linguistic awareness and introduce forms common in the written dialect. We can observe similar types of learning going on as in infants learning to talk. The following example displays this learning going on before the child has successfully distinguished all of the major phoneme boundaries in her speech (i.e. she does not discriminate yet between some related sounds such as /b-p/, /f-v/, /k-g/, /d-j-t/). Carol is two and a half years old:

> Umdy Dudty sad on the woll
> Umdy dudty ad a great foll
> Aw the king's orses and aw the king's men
> Couldn but Umdy dogether agan
> Ay Diddle Diddle an the gat an the fiddle
> A gow dump over the moon
> A liddle dog laughed to see da bort
> And the dis ran away with a boon
> (loud burp) Sowwy (Definitely coping with her world.)
> a b c d e f d h i day k l m n o p/b u r s t u fee w ax y z
> Now i know mine abc
> Gome along and zing with me

(The alphabet, of course, is part of the oral tradition, as are such common cultural sequences as the days of the week, the months of the year, the seasons, etc.)

> Dom Dom the biber's son
> Dole a big and away woo wa

(Parent intervenes—"Who's naughty there?")

> Dom Dom

("Why was he naughty?")

> Begos dat dole a big.

Quaint—if that is what you are attending to. But here is a child mastering the linguistic forms of cause and effect before she can articulate properly. The parents of this child realize that she is quite normal and therefore they don't persistently correct her.

Important additional insights we can draw from observing the transmission of an oral culture in our own and in other societies include:

the power of chant and melody to assist in the implanting of important language;

the reinforcement provided by the physical pleasures of language in rhythm and rhyme;

the rewarding nature of aesthetically satisfying and polished language;

the support provided by other art forms such as dance and drama, and their power to activate the learner globally;

and finally the sustaining influence of unison participation in learning language and associating this participation with acceptance and security.

A study of cultural and linguistic learning in any pre-literate society will indicate the effectiveness of these principles in establishing life-lasting attitudes and skills.

Reading before five

There has been great interest in the last few years in children who learn to read and write at a very early age. Before considering reports on spontaneous literacy-learning prior to school entry, we should look briefly at earlier research related to the *teaching* of reading during infancy.

The teaching of reading before five

We will look briefly at two approaches to *teaching* very young children to read. We may have serious doubts about the value of such early instruction and would expect to discover problems in the undertaking, but our main concern here will be to determine to what extent principles derived from the developmental model were important in successful early literacy experiments.

The notoriously popularized approach of Glenn Doman (1964) will be familiar to most of us in the form of the little bright red book, *Teach Your Baby to Read*, if not in the form of the kitset of teaching materials. Although massive sales all over the English speaking world have not produced the generation of literate school-arrivers which may have been expected, the efficacy of Doman's procedures in teaching three-and-four-year-old children to recognize words cannot be doubted. If Doman had known something more about the reading process and not been trapped into the traditional fallacy of equating reading with word recognition, the approach may have had some lasting contribution to make—'Nose is not toes' would be a good mnemonic for linguistically mutilated reading materials.

Nevertheless, his method, which arose from success in teaching disabled children to walk and to talk and simultaneously to read, reminds us of the power of positive teaching. Essentially, Doman suggests a programme of intensive positive reinforcement and the absolute avoidance of criticism, correction, or punishment of any kind. Such principles should be the foundations of any teaching programme. The two big questions are: Is it possible for parents to maintain such a programme without communicating some negative judgement of the infant in unconscious and invidious ways? And would not the positive attention given to the baby be better used to teach more appropriate and useful behaviour? The behaviour of parents in the bed-time story situation is *naturally* positive, without any form of illicit expectation, and the learning they encourage is immensely more rich and appropriate to the needs of very young children. Furthermore, it produces in the infant a drive towards self-seeking and self-regulation in the enjoyment of books rather than a dependence on adult instruction.

Of far greater significance was the work of Omar Khayyam Moore in teaching very young children to read in what he called a 'responsive environment' with the aid of a computerized 'talking typewriter'. His work is sympathetically reported by Maya Pines (1967, pp.62–86) (who observed Moore's work personally and discussed it with him) in her *Revolution in Learning: The Years From Birth to Five*. It is impossible to give a brief account of this research without producing serious misconceptions, and we will not attempt to do so—it was technically sophisticated and highly successful, but deeply humane. The important principles from our point of view were:

the programme was voluntary for the children—they could choose to have their half-hour a day, leave whenever they wished, or simply not attend it was individualized—the child was alone in the learning booth and he could choose what he wished from the resources available—consequently children learned to read and write by remarkably different sequences of activity

the programme was largely self-regulated—the environment (particularly the talking typewriter) responded to all they did without giving any instructions or advice, and they worked out their own strategies from there

it operated without *extrinsic* reinforcement in the forms of praise, blame, correction, or rewards other than success in self-chosen tasks.

> At no time was the child actually 'taught' anything. For many children, this phase proved somewhat annoying; they would frequently ask, and get, a chance to go back to free-typing of letters. But after periods of varying lengths—days, weeks, or sometimes months—the child would suddenly realize that the letters he knew actually made up words that had a meaning, and that he himself could now write such words. This discovery is so elating that when it happens, children have been known to jump up and down in excitement, or run out of the booth to talk about it.

> In Moore's opinion, this is the way to introduce learning to children—to make it so exciting that they are hooked for life. 'It's an affront to your intelligence to be always told, always presented with everything,' he says. Most systems in school alienate children for this reason. The children who are very able will learn anyway, but they won't like the learning part because it is too didactic. (p.67)

Each child learned to read, write, and touchtype effortlessly—most of the children in under a year. In the first and second grades at school they were so advanced and intellectually lively that they enjoyed an extremely rich programme in comparison with other children. As Moore left the programme to take up other aspects of his research, the project foundered on the age-old rocks of jealousy, politics, and finance.

'Spontaneous' reading before five

There is a growing literature about children who begin to read before school without direct teaching from parents. In two major studies Dolores Durkin (1966) working among children in California and New York, and Margaret Clark (1976) working among Glasgow children, present very similar findings about very early readers. The studies include a range of children almost as varied as a random selection of the child population except that the I.Q. averages are somewhat above the norm. (Although there is some evidence to suggest than an I.Q. around 115 is normal in large urban centres).

In these studies few of the children had been subjected to direct teaching. Parents or siblings tended to answer the children's questions, such as the request for a word, and leave them to continue the task on their own (Durkin, p.135; Clark p.53). A majority of the children began to read (or write) without any prompting from parents, and some of the parents were surprised, or even a little disconcerted, that their children had begun to read (Durkin, p.135; Clark p.49). Most of the children engaged in active writing as they learned to read, or before they learned to read (Durkin p.137; Clark, pp.14–15, and 17). It was evident that the children showed a great interest in print in the environment—on TV, on labels, in the names of cars, etc. (Durkin, pp.137–8; Clark p.50). Margaret Clark also reported on the importance of the local library in the experience of the early readers she studied (1976, pp.102–3).

Refining the developmental model

The behaviour we have been studying in this chapter clearly fulfils all the criteria of developmental learning, but in this case the learnings are directed towards *literacy*, and intimately related to the skills of reading and writing. The most important discovery we made was that the much-lauded bed-time story situation is only half the picture: practice of reading-like behaviour and writing-like behaviour completes the picture. A noteworthy feature of this behaviour is that it arises naturally without direction from the parents—and perhaps that is one reason why its significance has been overlooked. It is independent behaviour which does not depend on an audience of any kind and is therefore self-regulated, self-corrected, and self-sustaining. It occurs at just those times when the adult whose behaviour is being emulated is *not available*. The infant is not overawed by the need to please an adult—although delighted if the adult responds joyfully to the behaviour and encourages it. It would seem that *independent experience with books and with writing is natural in the developmental setting from the earliest stages of book-handling in infancy.*

The bed-time story situation should not be separated from the independent productive behaviour which it generates. Such behaviour normally engages the infant in extensive, self-monitored, linguistic behaviour for longer periods of time, involving far more intensive language use than is the case with the input activity of listening. Both activities are complementary aspects of the same language-learning cycle. In both aspects there is close visual and tactile contact with books, becoming increasingly focussed on the conventions of print. All of the most powerful strategies of mature reading are being established and the complexity of the behaviour makes the normal description of pre-reading skills look quite ridiculous. Going hand in hand with the practice of reading-like behaviour is an equally spontaneous involvement in writing-like behaviour. Both activities are message or meaning-oriented and support each other, especially at the stage when precise attention to print detail becomes appropriate.

In this developmental setting we have a further model for literacy-learning consistent in every way with the model derived from learning spoken language. It is based on the learning behaviours and strategies actually demonstrated in the learning of many high progress school beginners and in the majority of cases where children learn to read and write before school entry. A simplified version of this model is presented in Figure 1, page 63.

The crucial thing now is whether or not this developmental model can be applied to classroom settings in the school environment, and whether or not it is applicable to literacy learning of children above the age of five in that setting. Is there any way in which the school environment may be adapted to accept this model? How will the model operate in association with more traditional procedures? In what ways is the model changed by being applied to groups of children rather than to an individual learner within a non-competitive environment? We will consider answers to these questions in the following chapter.

Literacy Set

A. MOTIVATIONAL FACTORS (High expectations of print)
Enjoys books and stories—appreciates the special rewards of print.
Has had extensive, repetitive experience of a wide range of favourite books.
Seeks book experiences—asks for stories, goes to books independently.
Is curious about all aspects of print, e.g. signs, labels, advertisements.
Experiments with producing written language.

B. LINGUISTIC FACTORS (Familiarity with written dialect in oral form)
Has built extensive models for the special features of written dialect.
Syntax—grammatical structures learned through meaningful use. e.g. full
forms of contractions such as 'I'm' or 'What's', structures which imply con-
sequence 'If . . . then . . .'
Vocabulary—words not normally used in conversation e.g. 'however', 'dine',
'ogre'
*Intonation Patterns—appropriate intonations for literary or non-conversational
English* e.g. 'Fat, indeed! The very idea of it!'
Idioms—special usage contrary to normal grammatical or semantic rules e.g.
same example as for intonation—illustrates that idiom often works with special intonation.

C. OPERATIONAL FACTORS (Essential strategies for handling written language)
Self-monitoring operations: Self-correction and confirmation.
Predictive operations: Ability to 'use the context' to fill particular language
slots
Structural operations: Ability to follow plot, temporal and causal sequences,
logical arrangements, etc.
Non-situational operations: Ability to understand language without the help of
immediate sensory context.
Imaginative operations: Ability to create images which have not been experi-
enced or represented in sensory reality, and apply metaphorical meanings.

D. ORTHOGRAPHIC FACTORS (Knowledge of the conventions of print)
Note: Few pre-schoolers would have grasped more than a few of the ortho-
graphic principles.
Story comes from print, not from pictures.
Directional conventions—a complex progression:
    Front of book has spine on left
    Story begins where print begins
    Left hand page comes before right hand
    Move from top to bottom of page
    Begin left along line to right
    Return to next line on left margin
Print components—clear concept of 'words', 'spaces', 'letters'
Letter-form generalizations—same letter may be written in upper and lower
    case, and in different print styles
Punctuation conventions
Phonetic principle—letters have some relationship to speech sounds
Consistency principle—same word always has same spelling

Figure 1

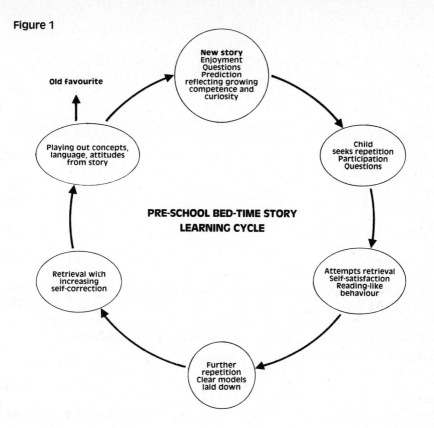

New story
Enjoyment
Questions
Prediction
reflecting growing
competence and
curiosity

Old favourite

Playing out concepts,
language, attitudes
from story

Child
seeks repetition
Participation
Questions

**PRE-SCHOOL BED-TIME STORY
LEARNING CYCLE**

Retrieval with
increasing
self-correction

Attempts retrieval
Self-satisfaction
Reading-like
behaviour

Further
repetition
Clear models
laid down

4
A Fresh Start: Shared-Book-Experience

We have reached a very critical stage in our enquiry. So far everything has been so theoretical, at least as far as schooling is concerned. The realities of pre-school learning are curious and fascinating, but are they *useful*? How are we to apply the model of developmental language-learning to the classroom? Is it possible? Will it work? Fortunately, yes—and there are many years of devoted practice to substantiate it.[1]

The major problem we have to face in applying a model of individual learning to the classroom is one of numbers. In what way does this affect the operation of the model? The individual infant in a home setting of delight and encouragement role-plays as a user of literacy in reading-like and writing-like behaviour. What adjustments will we have to make to compensate for the loss of this quiet intense concentration, and for the loss of the warm personal exclusiveness of the bed-time story? If we turn to our study of language transmission through the oral tradition in human societies less self-conscious than our own, and apply these insights to the classroom, the problem does not look so hopeless. We find that corporate experiences of culturally significant language have *always* been powerful modes of learning. In initiation ceremonies, in church services and festivals, and in playground games and rhymes passed down from generation to generation, we find models for intensely meaningful and satisfying corporate learning. If we are to avail ourselves of such vital learning energy, the most important insight we must carry over into the school from these models is that cultural learnings are non-competitive—they are entered into to be *like* other people—to be significantly human—and they have nothing at all to do with excelling for the purposes of personal power. Truly corporate activities are concerned with ego-sharing and not with ego-uppance. If we can achieve this corporate spirit, there is no reason why a large class cannot learn together.

Another aspect of the problem of numbers concerns the visual intimacy with print which characterizes pre-school book experience. Teachers have always used the special power of reading to a group of children as an important but separate aspect of their language teaching, but they have seldom brought that power over into the centre of the instructional programmes in reading and written expression.[2] Reading to a group of children in school has little instructional value simply because the print cannot be seen, shared, and discussed. The parent is able to 'display the skill in purposeful use' and at the same

time keep before the infant's attention the fact that the process is print-stimulated. Teachers can do the same by using enlarged print for the experience of listening to stories and participating in all aspects of reading.

Suppose we begin by taking half an hour from each day in a new-entrant or kindergarten classroom—it could be half an hour from the developmental period or just a slight extension of storytime. In preparation, we make a selection of books which we know are often favourites for young children or that we judge from our experience of children's books will be enjoyed and may become favourites. We look for fairly simple stories that the children will readily understand, but we don't worry too much about vocabulary—we are going to follow the model as closely as possible using good sound common-sense just as a reasonable parent would do. Some of the stories will be old nursery favourites. We need lots of books—at least twenty for the first fortnight—and we hope that ten or twelve of them will become real favourites.

Three or four of the books—the ones we feel most certain will be popular with all the children—we enlarge so that the bold print can be seen clearly from fifteen feet or so. We don't need to illustrate all of them because the children will enjoy contributing their own illustrations to some of the books. Nor do our illustrations need to be polished pieces of art—the children will return to the normal-sized book in their independent reading and be able to savour the original illustrations at that time. If we have ready access to an overhead projector, we may put one or two of the books on transparencies to obtain the enlarged print. This may seem a lot of trouble for a questionable return, but when we think that in the model situation each book may be enjoyed with the parent five or ten times and independently many more times, we realize that our work will be put to good use in the next few months.

On the first day we gather the children round as we usually do for a story. They don't settle easily so we sing a favourite song and a nursery rhyme or two. We have several books with us, one of them enlarged. We want to be sure that the first book we present is fresh to all of the children, and will be large and attractive enough to interest them visually. We choose *The Very Hungry Caterpillar* by Eric Carle which captures the magic of nature in the magic of print. There is a little discussion and comment during the reading and a satisfied glow at the end. We can see that real experience with a caterpillar pupating in the classroom would keep interest at a high level and help to make the book a favourite in the next few weeks.

Now we bring out our first enlarged book—a version of 'The Three Billy Goats Gruff'. We choose this partly because of the strongly emotional language of the repetitive section which may draw the children into prediction and participation even on the first reading. The children are delighted with the enormous book and many keep their eyes glued on it as we use a pointer to follow the story as we read. Sure enough, on the second occasion of the 'Trip, trap!' and the 'Who's that tripping over my bridge?' some of the children chime in, encouraged by the invitational cues we give off. They are delighted in the closing couplet, 'Snip, snap, snout, This tale's told out', and want to say it for themselves. We compare the idiom with 'This story's run out', and return to the original. We didn't expect this interest—youngsters are full of surprises. However, the children are obviously ready to dramatize the story and we have a first run at this to give them a little 'global involvement'—and it is very easy to improvize a bridge. We can see there is a lot more running time in this story in many kinds of activities.

Since the participation goes so well, we choose the Ezra Keats's version of *Over in the Meadow* as a closing experience. We have great fun with this, stopping to talk once or twice about how we know what to expect next. By the time we reach the 'little froggies nine' all but one or two of the class are chiming in, and at the end they ask for it again immediately—and we just have time.

As the session breaks up, we make a mental note or two. The children liked the song at the beginning—they're not shy about singing. Why not teach them some new songs using enlarged print on big sheets? Some of their instructional reading material can be their new songs—*and* poems. We wonder if we've been wasting our time—and our scarce supply of books. Three new stories in half an hour! And all the work in making that giant book! The youngsters were certainly delighted and it did seem to make a difference to their attention. But will they get interested in print that way? In any case, we don't feel exhausted—rather guilty in fact about enjoying ourselves so much. At least we can stand an exploratory week or two of this just so long as no-one complains.

On the second day we have our new song ready on a big sheet of heavy paper—a very simple old song, 'Love Somebody? Yes I Do', that didn't take long to print in gaily coloured letters. There was no picture—we couldn't think of anything but hearts—and that seemed a little corny. We wondered whether the children would be interested in the text just by itself. They certainly watched, and seemed to have some idea that they were acting at real reading.

Our second big book was 'The Gingerbread Man', and they did enjoy the 'Run, run, as fast as you can. You can't catch me, I'm the Gingerbread Man'. To tell the truth, we quite enjoyed it ourselves—a nice, secure, regressive feeling—it always was one of our favourites. The children asked for 'The Three Billy Goats Gruff', again, and we repeated dramatization. They also wanted another experience with *Over in the Meadow*. We said we would finish with that after our last story, *Nobody Listens to Andrew* by Elizabeth Guilfoile. Well, the talk that went on with that story! We had a long discussion about who had the most sensible suggestion for dealing with the bear. The boys finally came round to the view that Sister Ruthy made the most sensible suggestion of calling the zoo. It was good to see the children's satisfaction in dismissing the suggestions of the adults—fancy calling the police or the fire station! What would *they* know about bears! This self-satisfied feeling helped them to identify with Andrew on the last page looking Very-Pleased-with-Himself!

We ran over the half hour by a bit, but the sense of guilt was not so pricking as yesterday. We move around the room as the children engage in developmental activities. There are at least three bridges in the block corner and the fierce cries of trolls resonate through the room. Mr and Mrs Neighbour from 'Andrew' have turned up as new characters in the playhouse. The four children painting

gingerbread men are singing 'Love Somebody', and a quiet little fellow has a big copy of the 'Three Billy Goats' on the floor pointing at the story with his *foot*. What do you do about that? The model doesn't indicate what to do except to leave well alone.

The next enlarged text we use is the Rose Bonne and Abner Graboff version of *I Know an Old Lady* because that can be enjoyed first as a hilarious story, and then as a song—Alan Mills' score is in the back of the book. We present *Bears in the Night* by S. and J. Berenstain in an enlarged version and this brings an unexpectedly strong response—after all it's a very unassuming little story but it fascinates the children with its scary crisis and logical reversal back into the security of bed. When the two copies of the original are put out in the library corner, they are seldom out of use, and two children ask to take the book home. When we probe a bit to find out why, one of the children says she wants to read it to Mummy and proceeds to perform there and then. She doesn't point or follow the print, but she seems to have the words off almost perfectly. So off she goes home with it.

During the first fortnight we try to introduce at least one new poem or song and one or two new stories every day, but the children enjoy the re-readings so much that the half hour has become three-quarters of an hour and the normal developmental period each day expands the book-centred activities into the normal programme. Of the ten books introduced in the normal edition only two have not been requested again, and two have been so popular, *Drummer Hoff* by Emberley, and Paul Galdone's version of 'The Three Bears', that we decide to make large-page versions of them for further study.

Most of the children spend some time with the familiar books during the day. Some seem to prefer using the enlarged edition, and a group often forms spontaneously to enjoy a big book together. The idea of taking the books home in the original edition to share with parents has caught on, and one parent has popped in to comment on the enjoyment her child experienced in sharing *I Know an Old Lady*—much to the delight of the whole family. We decide to send a letter home to parents explaining in simple terms what we are doing, and helping them to accept the reading-like behaviour without getting anxious and trying to correct the children when their version is different from the text.

Thinking about the model, we decide to induce the children into predicting vocabulary more actively during the following week. For this purpose we read over some of the stories we plan to introduce and mark those places where prediction could readily occur. In the beautiful Emberley version of *One Wide River to Cross* we see the possibility of a good balance between structural expectation on the one hand, and on the other, prediction of vocabulary on the grounds of meaning or picture clues:

> Old Noah built himself an ark,
> He built it out of hick'ry bark.
>
> The animals came in one by one,
> and Japheth played the big bass ----.
>
> The animals came in two -- ---,
> The alligator lost his ---- (Picture clue if necessary.)
>
> The animals came in ----- -- -----,
> The ostrich and the chickadee.
>
> The animals came in ---- -- ----,
> The hippopotamus ----- -- ---- (Let the children try both 'got stuck in' and 'blocked'.)
> --- ------- ---- -- ---- -- ----,
>
> The yak in slippers did arrive.
> --- ------- ---- -- --- -- ---,

The elephants were doing -----.
--- ------- ---- -- ----- -- -----,
A drop of rain dropped out of -----. (Is the rhyme sufficient?)
--- ------- ---- -- ----- -- -----,
Some came in by roller -----. (Children may prefer '*on* roller skates'.)
--- ------- ---- -- ---- - ----,
The cats and kittens kept in ----.
--- ------- ---- -- --- -- ---,
Let's go back and ----- -----. (And so we will.)

The story goes on for four pages completing the biblical tale. There will be discussion and perhaps a fuller telling of the story. While the story is fresh in the children's experience we could explore Gerald Rose's *Trouble in the Ark*. There are some more opportunities for prediction, but, even more inviting, the opportunity to talk about written words, some of which are enlarged and decorated appropriately in the text. The idea may catch on with decorated name cards or personally 'special' words in the style of Sylvia Ashton-Warner's work.

It is beginning to look like a good month ahead with the chance to talk naturally about printed words and spaces, and finding words by pointing in a text we know. 'How can we find the word *two* or the word *hippopotamus*?' 'Why are they so different in length?' A secondary interest may be stimulated in the printed words that are our names. There is a delightful story in the Ainsworth and Ridout series 'A Book for Me to Read' called, *A Name of My Own*. This could be enlarged and read with the particular purpose of 'displaying the activity of reading in purposeful use', as we put it earlier. As reader, we will discuss how we go about working with print, inducing the children to participate in the problem-solving process. This works so well that we repeat it with another book in the series, *Come and Play*:

One day she met a frog.
She said -- -- ----:   'Who is she talking to?'
                                       'How many words?'

"Frog, frog,
please play with me   A repetitive section suitable for
I'm all by myself   chiming in.
As you can see."

"Yes," said the frog,
"I will ---- ---- ---.   'What does she want him to do?'
We will play at j------."   Perhaps discuss names beginning
                                       with j.

So the frog j-----   'Can this be *jumping* again? Why
                                       not?'
into the middle of a pond.
"Oh dear," said the little girl.
"I can't j--- like that."   We can play a little prediction game.
                                       'I can jump'. 'I like j------'.
                                       'I j----- over the fence.'

The second month actually turns out to be as interesting as we predicted. Several of the children display a quick grasp of the phonetic principle in problem-solving exactly as we had modelled it. They are fascinated and want to know more. We keep them working with the class group because their questions are so interesting to other children who have not quite caught on, and a few of these begin to see the light. This signals a readiness for alphabet knowledge—if we want to talk about letters, we have to know what to call them. So we pick up *Dr Seuss's A.B.C.* and one or two others, and incorporate a short time each day when we study the alphabet and a special letter.

BIG F   little f   F f F
Four fluffy feathers on a fiffer-feffer-feff.

We learn that alphabet song too—'Now I know my ABC. Come along and sing with me.'

We think we are going too fast, so we go back to the model to see what we ought to be doing. The independent, reading-like behaviour seems the important thing. Are the children actually exploring favourite books independently, as the model suggests that they should? Certainly they are, but often in groups with one of the children acting as teacher, pointing more and more accurately and being corrected when she goes wrong by the 'pupil children'. This isn't quite what we predicted—we didn't expect to have our function so rapidly eroded. But it is nice to see how meticulously the 'teacher children' follow the pattern we have laid down. It is quite an experience to see oneself so faithfully modelled—and be proud of it.

Two months! We are now spending an hour a day within the model—and this is not accounting for the way in which the children are extending the activities into other parts of the programme. Two of the children, including the little girl who went off home with *Bears in the Night*, seem to be really reading. They are pointing accurately, recognizing many words at sight, busily making their own books with strange collections of letters in linear file which they 'read' with bold assertion. Perhaps they were almost reading when they came to school. In any case we don't have to worry about them— we *use* them. They have been so attentive to our shy instruction that they not only ape us perfectly in playing teacher, but seem to have a genuine interest in sharing their new-found secrets with anyone who will sit down and listen.

After three months, sixty books, twenty poems, ten songs, and a chant or two, we give up the 'readiness programme' and are now busily answering questions and demonstrating literacy skill. We are enjoying the process—we hadn't realized that we were so literate ourselves. We are finding children's literature so personally fascinating and we are enjoying ourselves so much that we wonder how it was that we missed out before.

And then things outside the classroom start to go wrong. The principal is already considering re-organizing the department because some teachers, including ourselves, are carrying too big a load, and he wants to know whether there are half a dozen children ready to move on into the next class. One of the parents is proving difficult. Despite the explanatory letter, he thinks that what we are doing is unjust. He wants his child moved into a more organized class where he will be taught phonics and not encouraged to think he can read when he can't. And suddenly the lad who is already reading starts to throw his weight around. Somebody must have been telling him how brilliant he is! It never rains but it pours!

We start to worry. Where are we going and what are we achieving? Some form of monitoring would be helpful. We need some way of evaluating the literacy status of the children before they begin the programme and a checklist for observing progress. The headings in the analysis of the characteristics of 'Literacy Set' on page 62 could form a useful guide. It is fairly obvious to us that the children are making healthy development in the motivational, linguistic, and operational areas. Interest is developing in the orthographic area.

And so we decide to explore ways of evaluating our programme continuously. It will sustain our own security in a responsible manner even if it does nothing else. We could have predicted many types of opposition and criticism.

We will do our best to explain that what we are doing has a sound basis, and try to be in a position to justify the experiment by keeping personal records of children and being able to point to the progress of individuals. However, we won't allow outside pressures to influence what we are doing until we have assured ourselves that in some areas the programme is not working. This is clear in the model itself—*no pressures for results* either from inside or from outside the learning environment.

About this time we are fortunate in discovering the work of Bill Martin— he seems to be a fellow-thinker who has put together a wonderful range of literary material in the Sounds of Language series and in the Instant Readers, and backed this up with practical guidance of a rather special kind—he seems to convey the deep trust that an effective literature, well presented, will do its own job. In any case, we have a new store of useful material of high literary impact and an almost inexhaustible supply of teaching suggestions. The *Teacher's Guide to the Instant Readers* (Martin and Brogan 1972) is an inspiring presentation of developmental ideas about introducing print, and we feel comforted to have such support. Two quotations from his chapter headings will illustrate what we mean. 'Book experience should precede word experience in bringing a child to print', and 'An emerging reader needs a battery of books that he can zoom through with joyous familiarity'. That seems to describe what we are achieving in our programme at this early stage, and we feel more confident about what we are doing.

The developmental literacy environment

After three months of expanding activities in shared-book experience we have the courage to reorganize the language and the developmental sectors of our new entrant programme. Our aim is to incorporate these two sectors into a single developmental environment focussed on emergent literacy. Physically, the environment has all the features of areas for developmental activity except that the reading and writing areas have been highlighted and carefully furnished in a relaxed fashion. The total environment is alive with print, displaying all its functions, from things as simple as signs and labels right through to literature. A large area furnished with a carpet can seat the whole class of thirty-two children and has a large low easel for holding big books and charts.

At some time each morning we have our major sharing session, which corresponds to the bed-time story setting in the model—it is the major input or modelling part of the programme. This session may last for up to an hour on some occasions. On some days we have two shorter periods. We try to introduce at least one new literary experience every day—a poem, a song, or a story—and every day we complement this by exploration of the real world in language-experience ways. Thus, we have two sources of language to explore: the literary experience of books, and the language-saturated and personalized experience of the outside world, with all its real purposes for writing.

A new literary experience tends to go through three stages in the course of a few weeks:

A. Discovery.

Introduction of the new experience in the listening situation with maximum participation in predictable, repetitive structures, and in the problem solving strategies of decoding.

Objectives
To provide an enjoyable story experience to all of the children. *(This objective should not be sacrificed to any other purpose.)*
To induce a desire to return to the book on subsequent days.

To encourage participation by inducing children to chime in
    on repetitive sections,
    suggest an obvious word,
    predict possible outcomes,
    engage in suitable expressive activities.
To provide a clear and spoken model for the book language.
To induce sound strategies of word solving by encouraging and discussing suggestions, at an appropriate skills level and without unduly interrupting the story. Remember that the thrill of problem-solving is a natural and proper part of the enjoyment of a story.

B. Exploration.

Re-readings—usually on request—for familiarization and teaching where applicable. Increasing unison participation is natural to this re-experience.

Objectives
To establish firm oral models for the language of the book.
To deepen understanding and response.
To provide opportunities for all children to gain oral practice of the language of the story by unison, group and individual participation.
To help children become aware of the special structures of the story so that these may be used in reconstructing and decoding in later independent readings, or be used as patterns for personal expression.
To teach relevant reading skills in relation to the text, especially sight vocabulary, structural analysis and the use of letter-sound relationships in strategies of decoding.
To provide further expressive activities based on the language of the book both to personalize response and to provide purposeful practice of the language models.
To provide additional, enjoyable listening experience for slower children who require more repetition than others to develop strong memory models. Listening post activity is most useful for this purpose.

C. Independent Experience and Expression.

Independent retrieval of the experience in reading or reading-like ways by individuals or small groups. Creative exploration and expression of meanings from the experience, involving all the expressive arts.

Objectives
To provide opportunities for independent reading by individuals or very small groups (Sometimes one child will act as teacher in guiding others through the book).
To give a sense of individual achievement and competence.
To encourage the development of self-monitoring and self-correction, using the familiar language models.
To encourage expressive activities using the interests and the language arising from the book so that children will identify more fully with the story and internalize the language as a permanent part of their competence.

However, the total programme is concerned with a great wealth of literary experience happening together, and within this richness different children seek out their own preoccupations, determining for themselves where their own 'working face' in language learning will be from day to day. To give some order and security to this diversity of experience, the daily input session tends to have a predictable structure something like the following:

1. Tune-in Verse, song, and chant—favourite and new. Enlarged print and charts are always central

2. Favourite stories Re-reading of stories, usually by request but sometimes planned. Unison participation. Learning reading-skills in context. Dramatic and other relaxing counterparts. Exploring syntax—substitution, simplification, extension, transformation, innovating on verse and story structure.

3. Language activities Alphabet study and games. Learning other cultural

The bed-time story. David, just turned two (from Chap. 3, pp. 42-3) enjoying the input which he will later re-enact in reading-like behaviour.

At age four Leslie (Chap. 3, pp. 41, 45-6) engages in personal re-enactment of a loved story—the important converse of the bed-time story.

A talented teacher, Carol Blackburn, models the reading process with whole-hearted and emulative pleasure.

Attention is at a high level as the class become absorbed in the joys of a rich literature.
(Chaps. 4, 6 and 7.)

The children participate whole-heartedly in a corporate experience of familiar language—unison response in Shared-Book-Experience. (Chaps. 5, 6 and 7.)

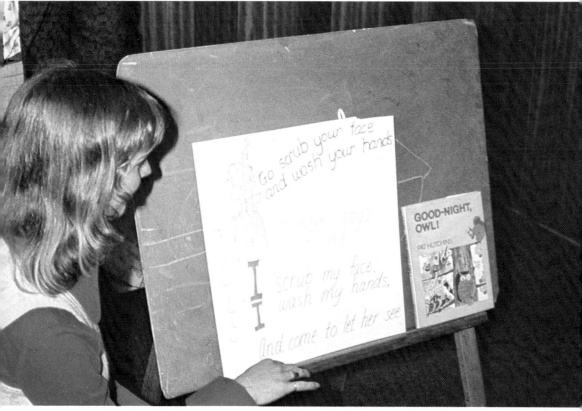

Verse, chant and song, using enlarged print become a vital part of the instructional programme in reading and a basis for innovating on literary structures in creative writing.

In a developmental literacy environment the children soon become engrossed in unsolicited, independent enjoyment of their favourite books.

The big books suit the immature level of muscular development and co-ordination of young children as, with deep involvement they role-play themselves as readers.

Role-playing as teacher, a vital developmental activity which mirrors all the precision of the teacher as model.

The children often illustrate their own big books, coming back later with fresh enjoyment to the original art in the published version.

Libby Handy introduces the *Tailypo* sequence described at the end of Chap. 10, pp. 195-6.
Lively mental images replace the need for illustrations on some occasions.

Reworking a personal creative response to the *Tailypo* story. (See Chap. 8, pp. 162-6.)

Permitted a wide range of materials and the time-scope to rework on successive days, the children move towards deeply satisfying experience.

A display of individual art mounted with proper respect for the children's highly individual exploration of meanings. (See Chap. 8.)

Group drama based on a favourite story, played out against the backdrop of a corporate mural of Jack and the Beanstalk. (See pp. 165-6.)

Children respond to the total environment of literary pleasure and aesthetic excitement—they mime symbolic meanings from the literature.

sequences. Exploring language—riddles, puzzles, vocabulary games; exploring writing—approximations towards spelling.

4. New story   Introducing new story for the day either in normal or enlarged form. Word-solving strategies induced within the unfolding context of a new language experience. Modelling how print is unlocked.

5. Independent reading   Enjoying old favourites—individual or group. Pointing encouraged—pointers available. Much playing at being teacher—children teach each other.

6. Expression   Related arts activity either individual or group. Painting, group murals, construction, mask-making for drama. Group drama, puppetry, mime. Writing—innovating on literary structure (teacher as scribe).
(Note: 5. and 6. interchangeable in order.)

After four months a few matters are becoming clear. As would be expected, the children have separated themselves out very quickly. Four are reading and we are giving them individual hint-sessions from time to time. The majority are enjoying themselves with print—exploring, puzzling, approximating. They are obviously in the middle of the emergent-reading stage, performing reading-like activities and writing-like activities with great abandon, and concentrating at their own individual 'working faces'. A large group at the tail—about eight children—seem confused. Some are only just beginning to enter fully into the unison experiences. They are interesting in that they follow the others in their own style, seeming to learn, or gain confirmation, from the surrounding full-blooded response of the rest. But they are miles away from reading.

Task control
We find that we actually have more control over the difficulty of tasks that children undertake than we ever had before. The difficulty a child experiences in 'reading' favourite books is in direct relationship to the number of repetitions he enjoys before attempting to read independently. We are using this factor to keep challenge at an appropriate level for different children. We can *all* enjoy the introduction of the same story, but some children will need less repetitions before they attempt independent reading. So we encourage the more advanced children to attempt the retrieval very much earlier than the slow-developing group. Sometimes the more advanced children opt out of repetitions into activities that preoccupy them more deeply. But what about the slower moving group?

The listening post
We gain much greater control over repetitions when we bring a listening-post into the room. The less ready children are then able to gain much more massive repetition before 'reading' than they otherwise would. The tape-recorder seems to be the second most important invention for literacy after the book.[3] We use mainly male voices because many of the slower children are boys and they must not get the idea that reading is a feminine occupation. In our chauvinistic society, if they once begin to think of reading as sissy, they're in real trouble.

Pace
We had never realized before how much young children can absorb in a few seconds. Attention problems only arise when there is not enough going on. We keep a very snappy pace. Then if some children get behind, they soon tune in. We've given up calling for attention and admonishing those who are distracted: they *are* so because nothing interesting is going on at that moment. And if we

break the spirit of the session to admonish one child, *all* of the children are likely to become distracted. So if attention flags, we crack on the pace. The result is amazing—if rather exhausting for us. Fortunately, we work only part of the day, and can relax among the children as *they* work for most of the time.

Positive teaching

The model suggests that there should be *positive* interaction and very little negative ticking off. That was hard at first, but *so* effective. In earlier teaching we were always telling children when they were going wrong—they did the performing, we did the correcting. Now that we are teaching reading skills in context there can be five or six suggestions for an unknown word—and to all of them we can say 'Fine, could be' or something similar. In introducing a story and throwing over to the children the prediction of some word, we can say 'Yes' ten times more often than we have to say 'No'. Let's imagine that we are enjoying the 'Discovery' session with Bill Martin's delightful ghost story *The Haunted House*, in which the reader is taken from room to room and 'NO-ONE IS THERE!' We came into the ------ ----! 'Lounge' says someone. 'Library' says another. 'Two words' says someone else. (There *is* a vague sort of picture, and it can't be 'bathroom'.) 'Living room' suggests someone else. 'No! We've *had* living room!' comes the response of the reflective reader. We write 'd--ing r---' on the blackboard. 'Yes, dining room!' says the phonetically forward Frances, 'It starts like dog.' The only thing we've said is, 'Yes,' or 'It could be!' Impatient correction *or* approval would have suffocated the development of skill and insight.

The phonetic principle

A few children have caught on to the idea of letter-sound relationships after three or four explanations, but the majority haven't seen it. We decide to take the matter very carefully and introduce two highly contrastive letter-sound associations: 'm' because the children can hum—and we have an extroverted Molly in the class—and 'f' because it has a primal slippery sound and feel. Then we go looking in the familiar books we know, and keep our eye out for 'm' and 'f' in the new stories.

Some of the little rascals scan the text way ahead of where we are up to and shout at inappropriate times, 'There's an EM!' We learn how valuable it is to know how to start saying a word that we're expecting. We get into that delightful *Fun on Wheels* by Joanna Cole and find quick confirmation in 'four' and 'five wheels' for our beginning 'f'. Then comes 'f------ on wheels' with a picture of a parading carnival animal on wheels—'Wow! FLOATS on wheels!' and then, later, 'Zip, Trip, F---, on wheels,' and sixty percent of them are there. Careful pairing of letter-sound relationships through 'b', 'g', 's' and 't'—all contrastive—brings insight for many of the children. The rest of the initial consonants and consonant blends are learned rapidly by those children in the following few weeks without specific instruction. For the remainder, a continuing programme of contrast and use brings insight at varying rates.

Alternative forms of large print

We have a friend who likes photography. He makes slides of Bill Martin's *When It Rains . . It Rains*. Well! We have a long strip of cardboard which we use to block out some of the words with a shadow. The word-solving excitement is fantastic. So we think about this for a bit. We make a large cardboard mask with a slot. Now, the word we want to highlight stands out with shadow all around.

What if we could progressively unmask a text as we read it? Wouldn't that be great? The obvious answer is the overhead projector, so we rush to Bill

Martin again in that beautiful version of Esphyr Slobodkina's 'Caps for Sale' in *The Sounds of a Pow Wow* and make a transparency. We cut little strips of cardboard to cover the text, and as we read, we slide the top one along exposing the words as we come to them. We have so much fun working out the words in that story, that we decide to repeat the operation many times.

The overhead projector is actually a lot of fun. You make a transparency with hinged words that can be flipped over into a slot at the right time—or even better, you make several hinges exposing letter detail progressively. In this way you can teach the strategy of prediction focussed on letter information, followed by confirmation with further letter information. And it's quite a lark!

Pointing

We have mentioned pointing many times as if everyone would agree that this was a Good Thing, but we haven't presented any evidence. Marie Clay's studies show very conclusively that pointing is a crucial strategy during the early reading stage (Clay 1972a, pp.71–3). Two vital insights are driven home by pointing: the insight that there is a one-to-one relationship between spoken and written words; and the insight that print moves from left to right along the line, back and down. Both insights are fundamental, but both can be confusing. So, in our teaching (and in the practice that children model from us) we are absolutely meticulous when we are pointing—not the sweeping movement that suggests a jet flight through the text, but that careful, word-relates-to-word pointing that suggests that reading is a strongly visual task.

Masking

If we were merely to talk about the print detail we would notice children's eyes wandering aimlessly across blurred details of letters and illustrations. It is vital that when we choose to talk about some detail of print, every eye is observing *that* detail at the same time as the accompanying sounds are uttered. Only then are we teaching that crucial eye-voice-ear link which makes print intelligible in the earliest stages of reading.

So, in our teaching we use masking devices. The best solution we have achieved is a sliding mask which allows us to highlight any word or letter or affix which we want to talk about.

Open versus graded material

We have already started off by choosing material that would fascinate children rather than material that was 'easy enough' for them. In our endless search for new engaging material, we often found delightful stories in graded texts—the old Beacon Readers with their wealth of simplified folk stories, or the brilliant simplifications of Seuss, or the early stories in Scott Foresman's Systems. (*The Bus Ride* is a classic).

But as children become conscious of their ability to decode print, it is important to make available to them caption readers and other simplified readers, which they can handle independently at a sitting—say, in five minutes. This seems to us the proper use of graded materials, rather than to attempt to use them as instructional material. We remember that we are committed to using a captivating literature in which prediction can operate at a deep level, and then we provide a wealth of more simple material upon which children can cut their teeth as independent readers. But, heaven forbid giving any child one of those linguistically mangled texts which have been designed to introduce words or phonetic elements in a so-called rational progression. 'Ratty on the Matty' is out.

Language experience and book experience

As the programme develops along as natural a line as possible, the distinction between language-experience procedures and book-experience procedures gradually diminishes. Book experience generates the thrust to use written language and to arouse new interests and curiosity, to explore the real world more deeply. Intellectual activity is stimulated by the impact of the developing meanings of literature and attention is turned outwards onto the world. *The Very Hungry Caterpillar* heightened interest in insect life cycles and led naturally to observation and discussion of live insects brought into the room and located outdoors. The keeping of a diary arose naturally and purposefully from this activity, and established a convention which was applied to a wide range of topics such as the weather, and personal records of what different children had accomplished. Often an interest aroused by observation of the real world stimulated a search back towards related books.

Dictated stories both in individual and group situations constantly display the enrichment of language arising from the deeply familiar literature—words, idioms, structures, intonations. From time to time a book idiom that has caught the fancy of the children becomes part of class-room language, carrying a special twist of humour and intimacy, and this helps to bind the class together as a group with very special common feelings for the world and for each other. For instance, the saying, 'No harm in that!' from *Just in Time for the King's Birthday*, had a popular run for two or three weeks as a humorously exclusive answer to any request to be allowed to do something. Sendak's distinctive locutions for the passage of time in *Where the Wild Things Are* keep cropping up in the stories that the children dictate—'In and out of weeks and through a day'. 'It's time for me to be on my wa-ay' from *The House of Hay* has become a favourite farewell, and 'I guess she'll die!' is a common comment when someone has been hurt or has done something shocking.

The more noteworthy and memorable happenings on an outing tend to be suggested for language-experience stories. 'Paul put his head in the culvert and yelled. His voice came out the other end. It sounded like a troll.' Instead of 'Our Visit to the Butcher', this adventure story received the title, 'The Day We Lost Anne'. In these ways the children carry over imaginative modes into their corporate living and expression—not only the *language* of books but also their *cognitive styles*.[4]

The procedures we use for encouraging and supporting written expression are fundamentally those of language-experience technique augmented by the acceptance of writing-like play. Examples of personal writing, both the tracing or copying of captions and the developmental attempts at independent writing are kept in individual files, and these display progress very clearly. Some children have attempted little writing and they tend to be those who have moved slowly in reading.

The children often attempt to copy words or phrases from their favourite books. We adopt Sylvia Ashton-Warner's approach, and each has a file of special, personal words both from books and from personal request. Following the procedure which worked so well for her, all the cards of a group are sometimes mixed together, and the children sort out their own, reading them to each other before placing them again in their own personal file. Those cards which are not recognized and are left on the floor are discarded—the words kept by each child are those that retain personal meaning and utility. Attempted copies of these personal words often appear as the only intelligible items in the exploratory expression of the children—but they are able to 'read' the complete message of their own scripts.

Innovating on literary structure

Following the ideas of Bill Martin (1972) we engage in analysis of the structure of stories and poems and create original versions of old favourites. This is usually a corporate activity in which we record the children's suggestions on large sheets of paper that can be made into books later. Often these personal versions of favourite poems and stories become popular reading material. An early example that proved so was based on the Instant Reader, *Brown Bear, Brown Bear, What Do You See?* After some fun changing the adjectives of colour to adjectives of size, the following structure was set up:

----- Bear, ----- Bear,	Which became	Huge Bear, Huge Bear,
What do you hear?		What do you hear?
I hear a ----- bird		I hear a tiny bird
----ing -- me.		Singing to me.

and so on with other verses. That big book now has the title, 'Huge Bear' and is illustrated by the children.

We visited a large sailing ship which happened to be open to the public at the time we were enjoying *The Haunted House*. Following Bill Martin's suggestion in the teacher's Manual, we rewrite the story something like this:

Once upon a time I came upon an old pirate ship.
I went along the wharf. No-one was there.
I went up the gangplank. No-one was there.
I went on the upper deck. No-one was there.
I went to the bow. (Stern. Down the hold.
Down into the bilges. Up to the wheelhouse.
Up into the crow's nest.)
I looked over the edge.
I was there. (Reflection in water.)

Not exactly a graded text with controlled vocabulary, but most of the children can read it. Many of the children are now experimenting with their own versions of favourite poems and songs.[5]

The early-reading stage

As children move from emergent reading into early reading, standard sequential or graded readers come into natural use in association with shared-book-experience and language-experience procedures. Many caption readers normally used in the preparatory stage are available in the room, and as individual children spontaneously display their ability to read these little books with appropriate pointing and matching, they are given the first little book of the 'Ready to Read' series. Their first reading is made with the teacher so that appropriate help can be given in response to direct questions. Many children are able to handle the first reading at a sitting and with a high level of accuracy and self-correction. In these cases the children are simply given the next reader in the series about a week later. All of the children are able to take these books home, and parents then feel secure in seeing their children use the same books as are used in other classes.

   None of the normal instruction associated with the vocabulary or themes of the basic series is undertaken, and there seems some advantage in the children coming to these books as completely fresh little stories. In the structure operating within our school, children are moved on to another class as they become capable of reading the 'Little Books' in the series. Two of the children, however, move rapidly through the twelve 'Little Books' and the first two of the big 'Readers' without the usual instruction and are then moved to a higher class.

Shared-book-experience—a tentative evaluation

During the year the shape of the programme became more settled. At the centre, based on the developmental model, were procedures which we first came to call 'co-operative reading', and later, more appropriately, 'shared-book-experience'. Figure 2 'The Cycle of Success in Shared-Book-Experience' displays the relationship of parts of the programme, highlighting the cyclic success-structure which seems evident in the children's behaviour.

   The relationship of shared-book-experience to other aspects of the programme as it developed is shown in Figure 3. Here we are to imagine that for many children the learnings of the emergent-reading stage would have begun through procedures of shared-book-experience in the home long before school entry. For a few children language-experience procedures may have begun through such activities as letter-writing and captioning introduced by parents and practised by children in writing-like behaviour.

   Our first attempt to apply the developmental model at the new-entrant stage of schooling seems more hopeful than we might at first have supposed. At least we are encouraged to go on and explore the matter more deeply and work out the implications for the traditional core of the literacy programme in the teaching of basic skills in reading and spelling. To what extent can developmental structures support the learning of central skills throughout the junior school? In what ways does the model need to be refined for it to apply more aptly to the processes of reading and written expression, or for it to apply more sensitively to the institutional nature of schooling? What clues can we gain from the study of related specialities and models in linguistics and psychology? What is the best of educational research in literacy saying about the matter? These are the sort of questions we should now proceed to study.

   Our classroom experiment has been stimulating, and if we must take a holiday, it will be with a load of books about all manner of related topics. We are becoming sufficiently fascinated by this business of literacy learning to spend some of our leisure hours teasing out the ramifications of it all. One of the unplanned results of the experiment has been the marked change in teacher role. Increasingly we have come to see ourselves as attendants and facilitators of natural processes rather than as instructors. Our major function in the active, input aspect of the programme has been to share pleasure with the children and to model literacy in operation. Although exhausting in pleasant ways, this activity has tended to make teaching a much more satisfying task. At first we felt somewhat guilty about having scripted ourselves out of our stereotyped occupation, and about the absence from the children of the typical first-year dependence on the teacher, but later, during the surge in growth of literacy, we recognize ourselves as observers and helpers. We reflect more deeply and with a kind of wonder on the intense preoccupation of the children and on their confident, self-regulated activity, which meets their individual needs more accurately than any sequential programme could do.

Figure 2   **The Cycle of Success in Shared Book Experience**

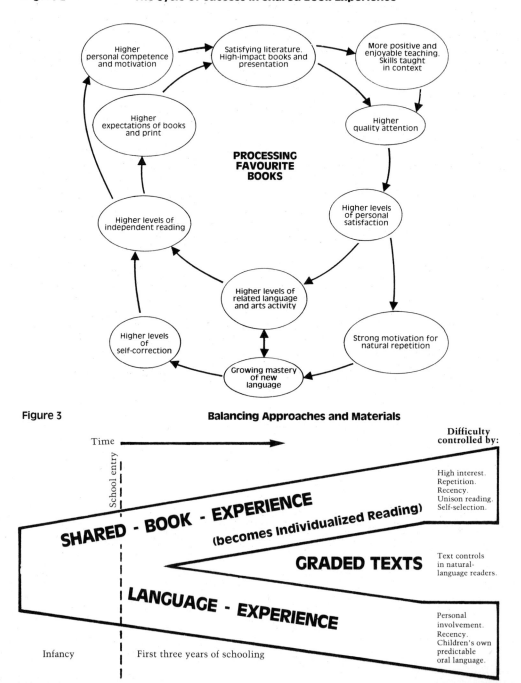

Figure 3   **Balancing Approaches and Materials**

5
Refining the Model

One of the advantages of the developmental model, especially as it occurs in the acquisition of spoken language, is that it accepts the efficiency of the learner's own system to govern the complexities of the process—it does not require a teacher to control the immensely complicated behaviour or provide a learning progression. The parents and others act as efficient teachers without having any deep understanding of the nature of the processes to be learned, except that they are of course efficient users of them. One of the pleasing results of applying this model to the classroom is that the teacher's role becomes more simple and natural and rewarding.

In shared-book-experience and related language-experience programmes teachers provide a favourable environment and an emulative model within it. They induce appropriate activity in literacy tasks rather than provide instruction. They give hints about how to solve problems in reading and writing and provide simple answers to direct questions. But the complex work of learning is carried out by the individual learners in a self-regulative manner and the teacher does not pretend to know what all children ought to be doing and how they ought to be functioning. The children learn by actually behaving in the skill, and by approximating towards mature function. They learn too, from the small proportion of self-corrected mistakes they make in this wider body of successful activity.[1]

But what is really going on in the experience of the learner? If we knew more about it, could we provide instructional short-cuts and make the learning process more rapid and efficient? Could we prevent failure occuring? Could we diagnose problems more accurately and provide effective guidance and remedial instruction? That is the unquestioned assumption of traditional teaching. To what extent can it be achieved? When *should* we intervene in the activity of a learner, and what distinguishes helpful from harmful intervention? If we want answers to these questions we must at least expect the questions to probe the tremendous complexity of the behaviour itself, and we will probably realize at crucial points that we cannot yet answer these questions fully.

The Meaning Systems of Language
Before seeking some insights from studying the actual behaviour of children learning to read and write, we should perhaps attempt a simple account of how language functions. But right at the outset we find many difficulties in

achieving such an account. It is impossible to say anything simple about language without being controversial and in some important sense plainly wrong. Any language is a system of sentences, (Chomsky 1957) yet it is not possible to define what a sentence is in any way that will meet general agreement or indeed account for the way sentences actually occur in the real world.[2]

To some extent the usefulness of a description of language is dependent on the purposes for which the description is made. Our present purposes are concerned with:

> how the operations of spoken language relate to those of written language
> how the learning of written language skills may best be supported in schooling
> and centrally, how language operates as a semantic system—how meanings function in language.

Our purposes do *not* include:

> the relationship of language to knowledge in a philosophical or epistemological sense
> creating a logically consistent description of English language which can account for its ability to generate the infinite number of meaningful sentences possible in it
> attempting to programme a computer to behave in language-like ways

It must be added that none of these purposes, including our own, can be achieved fully in terms of our current knowledge—or any system of knowledge that we can readily envisage for the future.

Modern linguistic science reverses the traditional tendency to study *written* language as the most perfect and correct form of language—it is concerned with speech. It underlines the primary nature of human language as a conventional system of speech sounds in which meaning is coded into sentences through inter-related sub-systems, none of which in itself can produce sentences. If we *hear* the storyteller saying the sentence

> And who's been sitting in *my* chair?

we can distinguish

> 1. the words
> 2. the sentence-relationships amongst the words
> 3. the 'marking' given to the words and to the syntax by the storyteller's intonation

Meaningful sentences of English are produced by a combination and interaction of the following sub-systems:

1. The lexical system

Words are the smallest semantic units in the language, yet they operate meaningfully only in sentences. (Words are seen as being formed from items in a wider class of semantic units known as 'morphemes'. In *smallest* there are two morphemes—*small* and *-est*. 'Free morphemes', *small*, for example—may occur alone in sentences. 'Bound morphemes', *-est*, for example—are affixes which always occur in association with a lexical item, or word. For our present purposes, this distinction is not crucial.) Words are constructed from a small set of speech sounds known as 'phonemes', and the set of phonemes in English is generally regarded as having approximately 44 items. Phonemes have no meaning in themselves—their role is to comprise words. The phonemic system, therefore, is *not* a semantic system. Words convey meanings in complex ways through their relationship in larger systems which transcend the lexical level.

2. The grammatical system

Words are put together in systematic, rule-abiding ways which give them relational or grammatical significance within sentences. Such syntactic patterns are established by—

a. Word order. 'The dog bit Bill' is different in meaning from 'Bill bit the dog'.
b. Function words. Words which have grammatical but not lexical meaning such as conjunctions, auxiliary verbs, and prepositions.

In addition to these syntactical operations words may be given grammatical significance by the addition of affixes—'Jim go*es* fast*er*'. This is known as the 'morphology' of the language. Hence 'grammar' equals 'syntax' plus 'morphology'.

3. The intonation system

Patterns of rising and falling pitch. ('Oh no? Oh no!')
Strong and weak stresses, or emphasis, or accent. (The lighthouse keeper and the light housekeeper)
Distinctive ways of breaking the flow of sounds, or *juncture*. ('I scream, you scream, we all scream for ice-cream'—in which 'I scream' and 'ice-cream' differ only in juncture.)
Variations in range of pitch ('flat', 'extreme')
Variations in tempo.

Non-verbal systems

Speech normally occurs in association with gesture, facial expression and other non-verbal messages such as grunts or sighs, or even significant silences. These interact as parts of the other systems. For instance, in the reading-like behaviour of David in Chapter 3 we noted that he used a shake of the head as a syntactic marker for the negation he was not able to make verbally.

Written language

Written language is a graphic system based on speech in that it uses the same semantic systems to convey meaning. Written English is therefore the same language in a fundamental sense as spoken English. No new semantic system must be learned in order to use written English. In our alphabetic system the graphemes relate very roughly to the phonemes of speech—but in the same way, they do not constitute a semantic system. (Graphemes largely record at a phonemic level how words were pronounced at some earlier time but do not necessarily correspond exactly to the way those words are pronounced today in our own dialect.)[3]

We think of the alphabetic principle as a wonderful invention BUTWEO-VERLOOKANINVENTIONALMOSTASBRILLIANTANDCERTAINLYMORES-IMPLE—namely the visual display of the lexical system as distinctive, perceptual units through the device of spaces. Indeed, written language is perceived as words, not as a series of individual letters. At the perceptual level, and operationally, the written language is largely lexical. It is only perceived as alphabetic for the mature user at rare moments of crisis.

If we compare the coded information in written as distinct from spoken English, we see that writing provides a deprived set of cues—quite adequate if compensated for by other factors—but essentially it is talking through the eye to those who already know the language and how to use it. It provides almost total lexical information but in an alphabetic/phonemic confusion. It provides almost total syntactic information, provided that the deficiencies in intonation and non-verbal cuing are compensated for by more precise syntactic markers. It does not provide clear intonational cuing in pitch and stress, but through punctuation and verbal spaces provides almost complete juncture cues. It is devoid of non-verbal cues—except through pictures and diagrams—which are however becoming more and more an integral part of print with the invention of off-set printing.

It has conventions of its own. The time series in which the sounds of language are heard are represented by a spatial series in which left comes before right in time. 'Beginning' and 'last' have quite different meanings in the two codes. 'Beginning' in speech means what I heard first; in print, what comes on the extreme left after the last space. Secondly, it has its own special conventions to avoid the ambiguities that arise from the loss of intonation and of non-verbal cues. These conventions include structural *completeness*, and the use of very precise structures with their own special syntactic markers such as 'however' or 'nevertheless'.

The actual individual sentences we construct stand in a wider context or situation either verbal or non-verbal or both. Many well-formed sentences would be seriously ambiguous if taken out of their context—in a certain sense every sentence takes some of its meanings from the discourse in which it occurs. In crucial cases it is impossible to determine the meaning of a sentence in isolation. For instance, in

John's shooting was terrible

there will be a fundamental difference in meaning depending on whether John was using a gun or a gun was used against John. In the first case we would have a subject feeling about John and a predicate feeling about the terrible shooting. In the second case we experience John as the object of the shooting. Given a context we have no difficulty in choosing the appropriate syntactic interpretation. The disconcerting thing, however, is that the surface features of the sentence itself do not display the syntactic relationships unambiguously—two quite different structures may underlie the same sentence. In other words, there is a deeper level of syntax beneath the surface and we cannot move directly from the surface syntax to the meaning.

Modern transformational grammar is concerned with this relationship between surface and deep structure and the ways in which surface structure in the form of spoken words or written words is generated from deep structure.[4] A vital implication of this characteristic of language is that we need meaning to interpret syntax—to determine what are the real grammatical relations of a sentence.

The lexical items in a sentence may also be ambiguous taken from their context. It is impossible to determine from the written surface features of 'reject' or 'tear' what word is represented. The meaning of the developing sentence, including the appropriate deep syntactic structure must be understood *before* the word can be perceived in its surface form. Here again we are faced with the apparent contradiction that we need to know something about the likely meaning of a sentence or a word *before* we can perceive it. And yet this is so obviously what happens in our ordinary experience. Nobody is likely to start refusing when faced with a 'REFUSE PLEASE' notice above a garbage can.

We noted the interplay between deep and surface structure in the reading-like behaviour of pre-schoolers described in Chapter 3. There we saw that the children were not recalling the surface structure of favourite stories but were re-creating *new* surface structures from deeply remembered *meanings*, and from deep syntactic relationships associated with those meanings. It would appear that from the earliest stages in healthy development towards literacy, meaning enters into the perception of surface features.

To what extent gaining meaning from written language entails awareness of speech sounds is a highly controversial matter. The massive domination of sound associations with language meaning, especially through intonation, and the cognitive structures they activate suggest there is. So does certain research (Edfeldt 1960) which invariably records some vocal-cord activity during mature silent reading. On the other hand, psycholinguistic research such as that of Kenneth Goodman (1973a) and Frank Smith (1973) would suggest that meanings are achieved *directly* from the visual cues in mature reading, without the mediation of sound in any form. We will not attempt to solve this problem: real experience does not fall into the neat logical compartments we would wish it to, and the truth probably lies somewhere in between. One thing is certain, during the process of *learning* to decode print, sound plays a major part, and the strategies for decoding new lexical items on the basis of sound remain important to the mature reader as something he can resort to when absolutely necessary. Even more clearly in learning to spell, resort is made to sound associations (Santa 1976).

'Knowing how to' versus 'knowing about'

Knowledge of human behaviour takes two forms: knowing how to do it, and knowing about it. We can know how to do something very complicated without knowing very much at all in analytical terms about how the skill operates or according to what specifiable rules. We can call the first kind of knowledge 'productive knowledge', and the second kind 'abstract knowledge'. Children master the syntax of their language *productively* almost completely by the time they are five years old, without knowing anything *about* nouns or verbs, tenses or agreement. Our major function as teachers is to help children to know *how to use language*, and this has very little to do with knowing anything academic about the way language operates. The traditional mistake was to imagine that in order to use language properly, it was necessary to know about it in abstract terms. In fact, sometimes such knowledge can deeply confuse our use of a skill—make us self-conscious, anxious and muddled. If we have to *think* about applying a rule before we utter a word, the first thing we are likely to do is stammer. When we speak, we have a feeling for meaning, open our mouths, and out it pours—every phoneme in the right order at the rate of ten or twelve phonemes per second!

A typical five-year-old in trouble can form his words into a complicated structure of tenses to get himself out of it without a single hesitation: 'If you hadn't've pushed me, it would'n've got broken.' Four seconds! But what has he done? He has manipulated the world of what actually happened in terms of a possible world that will never come to be, by syntactical processes of the most complex order. (In transformational terms at the deep level of meaning he has moved from, 'You pushed me. It got broken' to the beautifully conditional 'subjunctive' structure and a possible reprieve! 'If'—conditional; 'had have'—didn't but could've; 'not'—negation; 'would have'—prediction about a failed future; 'not'—negation. How do you put all that together in four seconds?)

We must be very clear about certain objectives which traditional teaching has overlooked, or worse, rucked over with sprigged boots—we want children to be able to read and write regardless of whether they know how it comes about—to be honest, we're pretty vague ourselves about how it comes about! Our job is to induce and sustain healthy behaviour, not to produce Professors of

Linguistics. Language use entails massive habituation, or the turning over to automatic functions what conscious deliberation would baulk at. What attention has this goal had in traditional methodology? How do you teach a child in such a way that he will rapidly achieve automatic control over his performance of language?[5] Reading and writing in their mature forms are as smooth and automatic in their performance as speech. By what path do children get there? Certainly not by the conscious application of unintelligible rules of syllabification!

Self-regulating systems

Each language skill entails a self-regulating system—not only automatic, and lightning-fast in operation, but also under sensitive, moment-by-moment control. Self-regulating systems are always complex: they comprise two systems locked together in special ways. Each system may be totally unlike the other, but they behave as one. A car being driven is an example.

The car alone is not a self-regulating system—it is a power unit that must have a driver. The driver is the regulating system. Self-regulating systems are like a car and a driver locked together into a single, co-ordinated function. The two systems are very different in kind, and the driver is by far the more complex. The 'driver' must be capable of sensing every change in the power unit and its environment and rapidly feed information back in the form of some instruction to change the behaviour of the power unit. This is why the 'driving' unit is called a 'feedback system'.

An essential part of any feedback system comprises the channels of communication bringing information from the unit and transmitting it back rapidly—before there's a crash—in a transformed message to the power unit. In the Apollo rocket, for instance, the power unit, massive and awe-inspiring, initially propels the enormous bulk, pencil-like upwards at a dangerously slow speed. It will topple for sure! But within the enormous machine a tiny system of great complexity monitors the perpendicular stance of the rocket through an electrical circuit energized by a small gyroscope. Within a split second, and a split degree off perpendicular, information is transmitted to small but crucial lateral rocket systems which correct any departure from the true line.

In a targeting missile such as a torpedo or a homing rocket, information is also received from outside the system causing alterations in course towards a moving target. Language depends on a feedback system of this second kind—sensitive to what is going on both inside and outside the system—and in far more complex ways than in simple targeting. How are such systems created in an organism? They are, of course, *learned behaviour*. So a child not only has to learn to utter language but to monitor and regulate it second-by-second simultaneously with the production. If something goes wrong or is about to go wrong in the productive system, such as choosing 'brudder' for 'mudder' as Robyn did in Chapter 3, this has to be corrected—or better still, avoided. If something goes wrong outside the system, such as mother's face beginning to show disapprobation, the language output must be modified immediately and appropriately. In speech a child is rewarded very powerfully for this movement towards control —for one thing, it is the difference between trouble and forgiveness. In reading and writing, some equivalently powerful system of rewards is required for the self-regulating strategies to be formed. That type of reward can only come from centrally satisfying meanings and purposes.

Traditional approaches to literacy teaching have neglected the fact that language is a self-regulating system of behaviour. By sacrificing satisfying meanings to the apparently mechanical nature of basic skills; by concentrating on the 'power' system alone, instead of on the more delicate and complex 'control' system; by usurping the corrective function which is the responsibility of the learner's own 'control' system; and by misleading children into the belief that problems are always solved by conscious application of abstract rules instead of by deeply automated processes—in all these ways ordinary teaching has misconstrued and therefore deformed the processes to be learned. This matter of the true nature of *literacy in performance* must be kept in constant focus as we proceed to observe more closely how literacy is learned.

The Psycholinguistic View

We can approach most closely an understanding of the complexities of literacy performance through the research and insights of the psycholinguists, of whom Kenneth Goodman and Frank Smith are leading spokesmen. Not surprisingly they insist that reading is a psycholinguistic process. Frank Smith (1973, p.6) says:

> Reading is not primarily a visual process. Two kinds of information are involved in reading, one that comes from in front of the eyeball, from the printed page, that I call *visual information*, and one that derives from behind the eyeball, from the brain, that I call *non-visual information*. Non-visual information is what we already know about reading, about language and about the world in general.

Essentially, the psycholinguists insist that reading is not a matter of perceiving or recognizing words first and then getting to the meaning but rather that meaning guides and facilitates perception. The influence of meaning in reducing uncertainty greatly limits the amount of visual detail which must be processed and in so doing makes perception more rapid and efficient, while at the same time allowing the greater part of attention to be directed towards comprehending. Kenneth Goodman (1976b, p.498) in discussing the prevailing notion that reading is a precise, visual process of word perceptions, states:

> In place of this misconception, I offer this: Reading is a selective process. It involves partial use of available minimal language cues selected from perceptual input on the basis of the reader's expectation. As this partial information is processed, tentative decisions are made to be confirmed, rejected, or refined as reading progresses

They take the developmental point of view that the most efficient way of learning to read and write is by actual reading and writing:

> A child can only learn to read by reading. Only by reading can a child test his hypothesis about the nature of the reading process, establish distinctive feature sets for words, learn to identify words and meanings with a minimum of visual information and discover how not to overload the brain's information-processing capacity and to avoid the bottlenecks of memory. Smith (1975, p.185)

And speaking of writing:

> Just as a reader comes to identify words as words, without reference to individual letters, so the practised writer commands a large repertoire of written word forms that he can put on paper, even by typewriter, without worrying about how they are spelled. The word is written as a unit, as an integrated sequence of movements. Such words are written much faster than if their letters were spelled out one at a time. Once again, however, this is a skill that comes only through experience. You learn to write by writing. (1975, p.190)

There is now such an extensive body of psycholinguistic research and speculation that it is impossible to give an adequate account of it in a few pages However, it will be a major resource as we proceed.

Goodman's findings about the nature of the reading process are based on research of the developmental kind entailing the close observation and analysis of actual reading behaviour. His major research technique, known as 'miscue analysis', is of particular interest and practical usefulness to teachers. He asks children to read orally a whole story which has been selected by the teacher as difficult enough to challenge the reader. The child is asked to read for understanding because he will be asked to retell the story after the reading. All discrepancies from the text are recorded, and these errors, or as Goodman more appropriately calls them, 'miscues', are analysed to determine the nature of the cues being attended to and the way these cues are related. This analysis is interpreted in relationship to a recording of the child's recall of the story which displays, among other things, his success or failure in comprehending the text.[6]

Discussing his findings Goodman (1973b, p.25-6) says:

> The readers of English I have studied utilize three cue systems simultaneously. The starting point is graphic in reading and we may call one cue system *graphophonic*. The reader responds to graphic sequences and may utilize the correspondences between the graphic and phonological systems of his English dialect . . .
>
> The second cue system the reader uses is *syntactic*. The reader using pattern markers such as function words and inflectional suffixes as cues recognizes and predicts structures. Since the underlying or deep structure of written and oral language are the same, the reader seeks to infer the deep structure as he reads so that he may arrive at meaning.
>
> The third cue system is *semantic*. In order to derive meaning from language, the language user must be able to provide semantic input. This is not simply a question of meaning for words but the much larger question of the reader having sufficient experience and conceptual background to feed into the reading process so that he can make sense out of what he's reading . . .
>
> Proficient readers make generally successful predictions, but they are also able to recover when they produce miscues which change the meaning *in unacceptable ways*.
>
> No readers read material they have not read before without errors. It must be understood that in the reading process accurate use of all cues available would not only be slow and inefficient but would actually lead the reader away from his primary goal which is comprehension. In fact in my research I have encountered many youngsters who are so busy matching letters to sounds and naming word shapes that they have no sense of the meaning of what they are reading. Reading requires not so much skills as strategies that make it possible to select the most productive cues.

However, Goodman is largely talking about the behaviour of mature readers and our major concern is how this mature behaviour develops. At least we can be clear about the sort of competence we wish children to develop, and without this clarity our progress towards understanding would be hazardous indeed. Some knowledge of how the proficient reader operates is necessary if we are to understand development towards proficiency.

Beginning Reading

We found confirmations of the psycholinguistic model at the earliest stages of emergent reading as described in Chapter 3. There we noted that infants in their reading-like retrieval of book language operated from deep meanings, using their own competence to carry out a predictive syntactic mapping of the performance before finally fixing upon the words and filling the language slots. To what extent do similar processes occur in early reading, and what strategies are used by successful *learners* in making sense of graphic signals in print?

Here again we can draw on an accomplished body of knowledge gained from conclusively descriptive and developmental research. From over a decade of research by Dr Marie Clay of the University of Auckland we have a clear picture of beginning-reading behaviour as evidenced by children between the ages of five and seven years. We will return repeatedly to this body of evidence and to Dr Clay's insights into the organization of early reading behaviours. These insights have important implications for the teacher's role in literacy instruction, especially in sensitive observation and monitoring of development. Her research techniques have many features in common with those of Goodman. She chose the 'current book' that a child was reading in the instructional programme and took weekly samples of reading. Again, all the child's discrepancies from the text were recorded together with other important behavioural information such as directional processing. These data were then analysed statistically in many different ways. Her studies are, therefore, both descriptive and longitudinal, providing a clear picture of individual behaviour regularly throughout development towards literacy (Clay 1972a).

Observing learning

The experience of observing the actual behaviour of children in the genuine learning and performance of a skill presents a picture of language learning very different in many ways from what we expect as a result of apparently logical speculation or even from common-sense assumptions.

The behaviour is more complex and variable than typical theories would suggest. There seem to be many different paths to success and failure.

Skills do not fall into the neat categories which we would expect, and it is often difficult to tell from what intuitions a learner's successful decisions spring.

Success is associated with purposeful, individual activity rather than with a particular method of teaching.

Developmental stages become more apparent, so that we become aware that behaviour useful at a later level may be an impediment when attempted at an earlier stage, and *vice versa*.

Children tend to work from their strengths—they use processes with which they are familiar before they master new ways of operating. They need the support of the familiar in order to learn the strange. For instance, they depend on spoken language competence in reading before they become capable of discriminating sound elements in the flow of language.

Another important insight for teachers from this developmental research arises from the descriptive investigative techniques. The investigator must take up a special passive stance in relationship to learner subjects. The investigator must avoid giving help, and allow a degree of deliberation—thoughtful silences—that would not be tolerated in ordinary classrooms. It then becomes plain to the investigator that these occasions of apparent blockage, of children puzzling with print, often entail valuable learning through the search-solve-and-check behaviour that is going on. Descriptive research emphasizes the need of children learning a complex task to have the mental room to engage in problem-solving activities in order to learn appropriate strategies or even quite specific responses. In normal teaching we tend not to wait for more than a second or two for a response before intervening in some way, and our interventions tend to disorganize fruitful processing. We need to respect the pauses and silences, interrupt less often, and encourage children to persist with those particular processes they have begun. Sometimes a simple question inviting a child to verbalize about his problem may give us the opportunity of more helpful intervention. A question like, 'What do you think has gone wrong?' or 'What is the problem?' asked in a warm, supportive manner, may be enough to elicit the information *we* need in order to offer real help. Most importantly, our demeanour during those awkward silences needs to express patience and optimism in the child's ability to use his own resources—it should not be a time when the child feels the tension rising and waits for the axe to fall.

There is probably no more enlightening experience than to be able to sit down and observe children's learning behaviour *without* for once feeling the responsibility to intervene. Some simple procedures for recording the behaviour we observe can be very useful both in organizing our observation and in providing material for later comparison and reflection. Children have many things to teach us that are very difficult to learn from text-books. But we will return to this later.

Early learning in reading

In her fine chapter on 'The Organization of Reading Behaviour' in *Reading: The Patterning of Complex Behaviour* (1972a, p.151), Dr Clay defines reading in the following way:

> Within the directional constraints of the printer's code, verbal and perceptual behaviour are purposefully directed in some integrated way to the problem of extracting a sequence of cues from a text to yield a meaningful and specific communication.

Our attention is directed in this definition to the importance of three types of cue which must be integrated in purposeful ways by the reader:

Directional cues
Language cues
Visual cues

It is significant that in studying the learning behaviour of beginning readers, Dr Clay sees the need to separate out the 'directional constraints' implied by what the psycholinguists call the 'grapho-phonic system'. The representation of sound in terms of direction and position—an intrinsically confusing system if ever there was one—underpins the conventions of written language more fundamentally than the grapho-phonic principle itself. Bound up as it is with very delicate control of muscles and a constant making and breaking of visual focus, it constitutes the most basic difficulty of early reading. Yet the whole great debate about phonic learning seldom adverts to this fundamental insight. Research such as that of Elkonen (1973) provides further clarification of the phonetic/directional learning which underpins success in early reading and writing.

As an introduction to processing at the beginning stages of reading we could take Dr Clay's summary of how her research indicated that beginning readers on natural language texts processed coded information (1972a, pp.161–2):

> Beginning reading is a communication system in a formative stage. At first the child is producing a message from his oral language experience and a context of past associations. He verifies it as probable or improbable in terms of these past experiences and changes the response if the check produces uncertainty.
>
> At some time during the first year at school visual perception begins to provide cues but for a long period these are piecemeal, unreliable and unstable. This is largely because the child must learn where and how to attend to print. Slowly the first sources of cues from experience and from spoken language are supplemented by learning along new dimensions, such as letter knowledge, word knowledge, letter-sound associations and pronounceable clusters of letters. As differences within each

of these dimensions gradually become differentiated the chances of detection and correction of error are increased.

The oral language habits of the linguistically average child provide a source of relatively stable responses which can give some success in predicting what a text will say and when an error has occurred. However, it is not inevitable that under the support of oral language habits visual perception will proceed to more refined knowledge of letters within words. Some children maximise the importance of oral language and fail to attend to the visual cues. Seen in perspective the child's oral language skills make an excellent starting point since they provide a set of well-established stable responses. Adequate learning must proceed in the direction of more and more receptiveness to visual cues which must eventually dominate the process. They do not do so in the first year of reading when the average 6-year-old can only discriminate half the letter symbols in his reading, and yet in the third year they are a dominant source of information.

The over-riding feeling of this summary is of human learners gaining increasing control of their own behaviour, bringing all their sense of probability to bear in recreating meanings and discovering how to make sense of arbitrary conventions—they are predicting, testing, and correcting as they go. We *don't* get the idea of learners accumulating a mini-pack of skills in a mindless dependence on outside instruction. We see them turning inwards with confidence to their own resources, knowing that they must find significance, if anywhere, from their own experience of the world and of language.

We see a psycholinguistic process at work—a determined exercise of thought in a two-way interaction with language—albeit language strangely coded. We see a self-regulating and self-improving process at work. We see a developmental process at work. We see learners teaching themselves to read.

The decoding process

An illuminating exercise is to place oneself in a similar position to the beginning reader by attempting to read a simple Welsh text, or by learning to use a new code such as Paul McKee presents in his 'Primer for Parents'. Taking a shortcut to such an experience, we can place ourselves in something of a comparable position by using our own alphabetic code with deprived cues. In the following exercise, 'x' is to be taken as representing any letter of the alphabet.[7] If we were to face something like the following, we would soon become discouraged and even feel that someone was trying to make a fool of us:

Xextexx xxx xox xxe oxxy xluxx xo uxxxowx xoxxs.

In that sentence we are given fifteen of the thirty-nine letters but have inadequate evidence to fix on any word with certainty. In the following version of the same sentence we are given only twelve of the letters, but feel immediately heartened by a degree of success, and are prepared to persevere:

Lxttxxx xxx xxt xxx xxly clxxx xo xxkxxxn xxxdx.

The fact that the first word leaps at us is very helpful because it provides the opportunity to get some sort of a run into the sentence.

Lxttxxx   Because the crucial letters beginning the word and those displaying its characteristic configuration are given, the mature reader makes an immediate lexical perception—what is called 'sight vocabulary' in the traditional corpus of skills. 'Xextexx' or 'lxxxexs' do not have the same effect. Furthermore, responding to the possible meanings of 'letters' we feel that the writer is, perhaps, still talking about reading and can be trusted to remain fairly in the familiar context of communication. The subject is not cabbages and kings (although some whole-earth readers may have got away to a horticultural start with 'Lettuce'). Meaning has already suggested limits which narrow the possibilities for other items, and it produces a sort of predictive tingle.

As we scan along the line, various possibilities present themselves, such as xxly/only and clxxx/class, but we retain an open feeling towards these proposals because there is nothing to confirm them with. But then—

xxkxxxn   That 'k'—silent as it may be—gives the show away, and the final 'n' which we didn't notice at first, clinches the matter in a surprising way. And as soon as the combined semantic pressures from 'letters' and 'unknown' begin to work on us, the appropriate noun being qualified pops into the slot:

xxxdx   It would have been comforting to see the initial 'w', but that 'd' was good to see, even though it was so useless at first.

clxxx   A possible next step might be an attempt at syntactic mapping—'the only class (yes, possible) of unknown words', but what we have done is somewhat dangerous—it would be more natural to normal reading to begin the syntactic run from the beginning of the sentence. Right, 'Letters . . .??'

xxx xxt   Probably 'are not'—we'd like to see the initial 'n' though. 'Letters are not the only class of unknown words'. A nice syntactic fit—which always makes us feel comfortable—but this will never do, even in educational writing! Letters do not belong to the class 'words'.

Then we see the misprint, 'xo' for 'ox'/of—or is it *our* miscue? Surprising how a little dissonance sharpens perception of detail. And then the penny drops: 'Letters are not the only clues to unknown words.' The semantic fit is now so perfect that, if we were in a classroom, we would fall over ourselves to be the first to let the teacher know that WE have the answer—fear of exposing our limited intelligence suddenly gives way to an assurance we are eager to display publicly.

Now let's study two more problem sentences tagged on to the one we have just successfully solved:

1. Lxttxxx xxx xxt xxx xxly clxxx xo xxkxxxn xxxdx.
2. Xxax xxxe xx xhxxe xn xxx pxxex xxxext xextexs?
3. Thxxx xxx pxncxxxxxxx mxxxx—xxx sxgxxxxxxxt spxcxx.

Sentence 2 is provided with thirteen letter cues against the twelve of Sentence 1, yet it is written in an almost undecodable selection of letter features. Why is it so much more difficult to read? Sentence 3 returns to the readable features of Sentence 1 and restores our confidence. The twelve letters selected provide immediate access to meaning—what is behind the eye can move out to throw light on what meets the eye and the minimum visual cues are adequate.[8]

Now let's return to Sentence 2 and see what sort of strategies may work in deciphering it. (If at this stage you were in a classroom and were instructed to write down your response under the teacher's eye, or were called on to read out what you had written, the possibility of operating properly would disappear. You would find yourself cut off from the ability you actually possess. Your failure then would be an unfair measure of your problem-solving ability—and you would probably feel deeply resentful. A problem-solving environment needs to be free from threats of any kind.) Collecting our wits after all that digressive teacher-talk, we finally get around to thinking through the problem of Sentence 2. We need more cues—grapho-phonic, syntactic or semantic—although a few determined readers may have reached a satisfactory solution. If we try a syntactic hint provided by the question mark and the high probability that the question will begin with an interrogative, we get 'What'. A semantic run on the text so far may give—'Letters not all there is? Well, what xxxe is on a page of print?' So we may now get something like, 'What else is there on the pages xxxext xextexs?' Without initial cues or configurational cues we may still have difficulty, but exxext lextexs?' and we are there. But suppose we were to look more closely to check our prediction of 'pages' and were to find 'pxpex'? Would it matter? There comes a point at which semantic closure is so adequate that correction of a miscue of this kind becomes merely pedantic.

The answer to the question posed in Sentence 2 presents no such difficulty because we have again returned in Sentence 3 to the device of providing the crucial letter cues—initial consonants, key configurational letters, and confirming letters. Note also how much more helpful the consonants are than the vowels. In the first syllable of 'punctuation' the 'pxnc-' is adequate to make a phonetic beginning with the indefinite vowel.

One of the artificial aspects of this puzzle-type exercise is that we have jumped around the words and made numerous fixations in a way that would be crippling to the highly selective process of fluent reading. (The exercise is not meant to do more than point to certain processes similar to those we may find in real reading.) However, it *was* necessary for us to keep in mind exactly where each word fell in the sentence, and what its precise relationship was to its neighbours—as for instance in moving directly from 'unknown' to 'unknown words'. These cues arising from directional conventions played an important part in solving the problem.

Cues used for prediction.   Firstly, we were able to read the spaces and perceive word items in which length was a strong feature. We noted the importance of certain letters in the perception of word configuration—letters which displayed the characteristic features of particular words (Smith 1973, pp.123–149). We also noted that there is no necessary phonic involvement in the use of these cues—the second 't' in 'letters' and the 'k' in 'unknown'. An important part of this feature analysis springs from familiarity with common affixes, which makes it possible to see the word form as made up of root plus affixes. In our puzzle we might have had the item 'ix/cxx/prx/hxxx/xblx.' These common letter clusters play an important part in early reading in the skill which is normally called 'structural analysis'. They display the morphological structure of words rather than the phonetic structure (Smith 1975, pp.180–182; Carol Chomsky 1971).

These quick recognitions of lexical items are important starting points in getting the semantic and syntactic probabilities activated in specific ways. At this point the phonic implications of initial letters, particularly consonants and consonant blends, become important. However, almost invariably two or more types of cue are cross-referenced in producing a proposal—like pinpointing a place on a map by using both co-ordinates of the reference. We could represent this diagramatically in the following way:

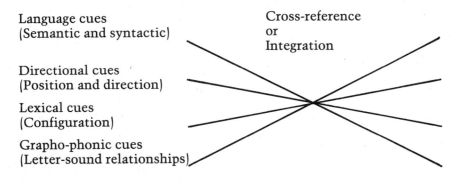

Language cues
(Semantic and syntactic)

Cross-reference
or
Integration

Directional cues
(Position and direction)

Lexical cues
(Configuration)

Grapho-phonic cues
(Letter-sound relationships)

Confirmation cues.   An important insight displayed by our puzzle was the peculiar psychological effect of certain letters which played no part in an initial guess or proposal: the 'n' at the end of 'xxkxxxn', the 'd' in 'wxxdx', the 't' in 'sxgxxxxxxt', and the 'c' in spxcxx'. These letters tended to clinch or confirm the specific proposal, providing an immediate feeling of assurance and self-satisfaction. This helped to keep the quest going until syntactic and semantic operations reached finality in the full sentence meaning which provided the *major* confirmation and reward.

Clearly, this letter-observation that confirms a lexical proposal—or self-corrects, as in the case of 'pages/paper'—is quite distinct from any simple form of phonics. It does not move from letters to sounds but in the reverse direction, from sounds to letters. As a proposal leaps to mind, it carries expectations for letter structure based upon the constituent sounds, especially those in terminal or stressed positions, or those giving a word a distinctive ring. In distinction from letter-sound association in traditional phonics, we could call this kind of perception 'sound-to-letter confirmation'. It uses letter details not needed to achieve the initial proposal—letters which become significant only as a proposal comes to mind. This type of grapho-phonic operation is important for at least five reasons:

> It is immediately rewarding, providing in-task reinforcement and relaxation, and it sustains attention to the on-going task.

> It is a feed-back operation sustaining the reader in self-regulating behaviour, and contributing to the development of the delicate and refined control system that is essential to reading.

> It is more natural and easy as an operation than letter-to-sound association and blending, in that it moves from something whole, meaningful, and easily retained in short-term memory, to the recognition of significant visual detail. It moves from the familiar and real, to the unfamiliar and partial.

> It has earlier utility to the beginning reader than letter-sound phonics, as will be discussed later.

> It is closely associated with the spelling operations required in the production of written language, providing a strong link between reading and writing.

In 'Call the ambxxxxxx!' the proposal raises the expectations of terminal letters for the sounds /n/ plus /s/ and throws the 'nce' into confirming positional prominence. The fact that we have here an alternate grapheme-phoneme convention causes no confusion as it may in letter-to-sound association—it perhaps induces the comparison with say 'dance'. Perhaps this rewarded observation may also take in the observation that in this case the indefinite vowel in '-ance' is spelt with an 'a'. Letter-to-sound phonics or 'sounding' often lays the reader open to confusion through alternate grapheme-phoneme correspondences. Sound-to-letter confirmation *teaches* the range of acceptable alternatives without confusion. It teaches because it provides immediate reinforcement.

Confirmation and self-correction use the same *sources* of cues as are used in recognizing or making an intelligent guess at a word in a display of print, but they use *additional* cues, some of which only become significant or useful *after* a proposal has been made. Some letters are *featured* by the proposal. At the visual level, it is as though the proposal has the effect of illuminating significant detail into rewarding prominence.

We have observed confirmation by expected letter detail and by syntactic and semantic coherence. A proposal may also be confirmed through a configurational insight—recalling the structure of a whole word as remembered from another context. A successful proposal for, 'Call the fire dexxxxxxxx!' may bring the confirming image of 'department' in another context or by such an image as 'Toy Department' seen in large stores. The essential component is the 'Aha!' response.[9]

Direction and position, vital at the lexical level, become meaningful at the sub-lexical or graphemic level as sound-to-letter confirmation begins to occur. The feeling for 'at the end' or 'near the end' produced by the expectation of certain letters to represent the sounds in the proposed word is rewarded by the observation of such letters *on the right* or *near the right* in the printed word.

We could now modify our earlier diagram by adding this dimension of relating or integrating cues to confirm:

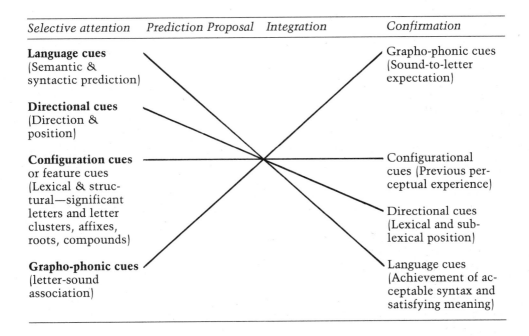

Selective attention	Prediction Proposal	Integration	Confirmation

Language cues (Semantic & syntactic prediction)

Directional cues (Direction & position)

Configuration cues or feature cues (Lexical & structural—significant letters and letter clusters, affixes, roots, compounds)

Grapho-phonic cues (letter-sound association)

Grapho-phonic cues (Sound-to-letter expectation)

Configurational cues (Previous perceptual experience)

Directional cues (Lexical and sublexical position)

Language cues (Achievement of acceptable syntax and satisfying meaning)

Problem solving in reading is structurally similar to other forms of problem solving as the diagram above begins to show—it is fundamentally a hypothesis-test situation. We can distinguish four phases in such an operation, each with its own psychological style and emotional overtones. Under the influence of syntactic and semantic expectations, the reader makes a rapid and largely automatic sampling of the visual detail. Uncertainty is reduced by this sampling to the point where a proposal or hypothesis presents itself—usually automatically and compulsively without deliberation. Confirming occurs in light of newly significant visual detail within a framework of increasing semantic coherence. Reassured and momentarily rested, the reader moves on with sustaining energy. In analysing what is almost always a very rapid, automatic process we inevitably make it *look* more ponderous than it usually is. (The term *sample* derives from Ken Goodman's work quoted earlier. The term *proposal* refers to genuinely predictive processes—not to mere guessing (Smith 1978, p.67). The term *test* refers to confirming processes, and the term *resolution* refers to the vital affective and organic outcomes.)

SAMPLE	PROPOSAL	TEST	RESOLUTION
Minimal observation of significant cues in relationship to ongoing meaning and sentence structure.	Possible slotfiller leaps to mind. One or more lexical items.	Checking newly significant cues. Weighing syntactic and semantic coherence.	Satisfaction Reinforcement Relaxation Restoration of faculties.
Emotional state: Pleasantly tense or anxious—tingling	Excited. Could it be . . .?	Calm and critical	Relaxed.
Example at 6 year level: 'Mother will *stay* at home.'			
'Mother will st--' —like 'stop' but different.	'stay'	Yes, 'stay at home'. Like 'day'. That's it!	Pleasure and relaxation. Readiness to proceed.
Example at 7 year level: 'The goat took a bite of *cactus.*'			
Texan goat—eats anything—but doesn't eat this— 'took a bite of cac---'	'cactus!'	Ends in '-us' Thought those things in the picture were potatoes.	Haha. That must've hurt. On we go.
Example at 8 year level: 'Wool makes fine hair and *whiskers.*'			
Making a mask? '. . . makes fine hair and w . . .' Like hair 'wisk---'	'wizzers' What's this? 'whiskers'	—No!—that 'k'! Right! There's the 'k' and the 'ers'	Of course—from animals like rabbits. I can do that.

Rhythms in complex behaviour

All organic behaviour is rhythmic. When energy is expended it must be restored. The heart beats and rests, we breathe in and out, we work and rest. Learning is no exception—it is very fatiguing. It requires tension and the right degree of anxiety to go out and meet the challenge, to adapt, and to accommodate. No muscle in the body, including those involved in perception, can function for more than a few seconds without rest. The secret of any continuous endeavour, any task requiring effort and perseverence, like learning, is the secret of rhythmic restoration of strength. We can further represent our analysis of problem-solving in reading, on the same four-phase structure that we examined, as a rhythm of challenge and relaxation, tension and reward. This rhythm, intrinsically controlled, sustains the organism in almost fatigueless activity.

The tension line

Challenge Proposal Confirmation Relaxation Challenge Error Self-correction Confirmation

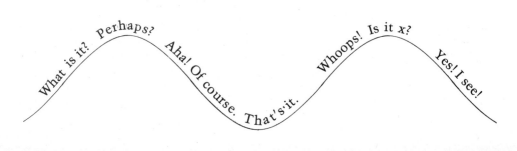

On the other hand, in a dependent, externally controlled system the tension line is quite different. It waits on outside relief, and if this comes not as help but as rebuff, as is too often the case when you are an inept reader, it may look like this:

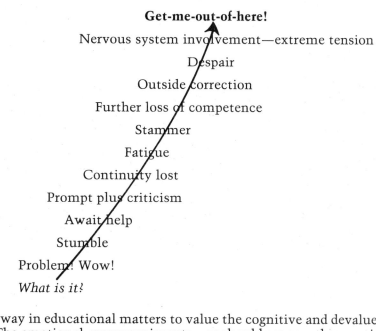

Get-me-out-of-here!

Nervous system involvement—extreme tension

Despair

Outside correction

Further loss of competence

Stammer

Fatigue

Continuity lost

Prompt plus criticism

Await help

Stumble

Problem! Wow!

What is it?

It is our way in educational matters to value the cognitive and devalue the emotional. The emotional accompaniments—or should we say, the emotional heart—of any human activity refuses to be ignored. No matter how meticulous we are about getting things intellectually right, unless things are *emotionally* right, human activity is tragically deformed. This is an indictment of the apparently safe and right intellectual analysis that leaves out of consideration so many of the available facts.[10]

The rhythm of challenge, effort, and reward is so fundamental to learning—indeed, to every few seconds of human endeavour—that to overlook it is to invite failure. Sadly, when we are concerned with literacy learning, we are frontally concerned with failure, ineptitude, defeat, inferiority, despair, and the terrifying injustice of finding yourself left behind. As teachers or academics most of us don't recognize this because we were the ones who weren't. Our competence rests in our ability to be sufficiently on top of the ball game to have gained pleasure from almost every stroke. Learning is always a question of emotional rewards, of awareness of success, of progressively achieving cognitively ratifiable advances.

The secret of learning a developmental task—one which is so complex that it will take many months or years to master—is the secret of momentary reward, the secret of an intrinsically satisfying way of being with a task or in a task. This is where the concept of basic skills most basically falls down. It does not build into the total learning structure a process of reward and restoration which allows the human organism the chance of remaining fully operative and autonomous, what you might call 'un-fatigued'. If we fail in this, it is as instructors who have made a gross cognitive mistake, and we impose our obstructions upon the learner. Attention, perseverance, moral rectitude in learning—these we impose upon children; responsibility, self-control, sheer competence—these we take away from them. It should be the other way around.

If there is anything we have a responsibility towards as adults and academics, it is the complex fabric of intellect and emotion which characterizes human learning, human endeavour, and human beingness. It is easy to sit in snug intellectual superiority from which we have taken a wealth of hidden satisfaction, and damn those who cannot learn without emotional support. In so doing we are, in the face of our own experience of success and pleasure, denying the deeply affective nature of learning. There is no such thing as human insight without human emotion.

The implications of what we have called the 'tension line' should be very clear as it affects the learner. Unless we can allow him a meaningful context of operation in which, moment-by-moment, he restores his own faculties, we drive him into despair, into autonomic-nervous-system shock, into learning neurosis.[11]

The implications for our own teaching are equally clear. Our task is to set up rhythms, both short and long, in which learners feel rewarded and restored in their faculties. Why it is that humour, for instance, with all its immense potentiality for relaxation and restoration has been almost banned from the serious engagements of schooling, only future anthropologists may be able to account for. The strategies of confirmation are crucial to these rhythms in the individual learner, as are the opportunities for experiencing satisfying meanings and insight through self-regulated behaviour.

Basic Skills

Traditionally we have divided the total decoding strategy into several parts which we call 'skills'. Each of the basic skills can be seen to have a vital place in the total strategy, but each working in isolation can be seen to be inefficient and misleading. The danger of analysing *separate* skills out from the total task is that they tend to be taught separately, and then *used* separately. Children gain the misapprehension that they should choose one of the skills and if that doesn't work, try another! It is the *integration* of skills working together which leads to efficient reading and writing. No single skill can be relied on to provide a solution which ought to be trusted.

Let's consider the traditional corpus of skills as refined in modern reading programmes:

A. Configurational or featural

Sight vocabulary.   The perception of whole words by immediate recognition. Of greatest importance is the 'basic sight vocabulary', which consists of the majority of grammatical 'function words' plus some others. Knowing some 200 of these words gives immediate access to 30–40% of running English.

Structural analysis.   The perception of structurally derived words through the immediate perception of affixes and roots, together with compound words ('un-fail-ing' and 'greenhouse').

B. Grapho-phonic

Phonics.   Letter-sound relationships or associations—involving the notions of 'blending' and 'sounding out'.

Syllabification. Letter cluster sound relationships which are 'sayable' because they include a vowel sound. The formal rules are difficult, conventional, and abstract—most teachers, even though they are good readers, cannot pass a simple test in syllabification—and so much the better for them! However, the skill as intuitively learned and productively applied is very powerful.

C. Semantic and syntactic

Using the context. A combination of semantic and syntactic considerations (quite properly grouped together) by which the reader predicts appropriate vocabulary. Too often this is taught only as the skill of 'reading on' when a powerful early strategy is the 're-run', or going back to the beginning of the meaningful structure, normally a sentence, to re-establish syntactic and intonational clarity.

What has been left out of the traditional corpus are all those skills we have noticed that are associated with confirmation and self-correction. If we add these, we have a reasonable *abstract analysis* of the constituents of decoding. But, as we observed in Chapter 1, the great fault of analysis is that it fails to put things back together again—the 'Humpty Dumpty syndrome'. The integrating notion we require is that of *strategies*: basic skills work together in complex ways controlled under the organization of an efficient strategy. And strategies are created and governed by a human mind. This is not to say that strategies cannot be taught: rather that our definition of teaching needs to move over towards inducing individual learners into mindful action rather than providing them with a pre-packed kit of rules.

The skills work together in two ways: they interact in the search and proposal stages to narrow possibilities into probabilities, and they interact differently in the confirmation stages to render probabilities into near certainties. Both types of operation are governed by the widely ranging propensities of a human mind seeking meaning and significance.

Furthermore, the combined skills, working in a strategy, rapidly become automatic or largely so. *A major reason why predictive and meaning-oriented drives must operate at the centre of any efficient strategy is that they provide the necessary conditions for fast automatic performance.* It may be possible with complex rules, consciously and meticulously applied, to decode most words of English—but at the rate of about one every three to four seconds. Efficient speech operates at three or four words per second, and efficient reading at more than twice that speed. The whole notion of conscious rule-application in relation to language skills is ridiculous and self-defeating. One only has to analyse the behaviour of children failing in literacy to realize the truth of this judgement. Most children experiencing difficulty know no other way of operating than consciously and conscientiously to struggle to apply rules for a single skill, and while they are locked in this activity they lose contact with central guiding purposes and overlook the implications of cues in different skill areas. The more difficulty the learner experiences, the more likely it is that he will be given explicit and narrow instruction in an effort to simplify the process for him. The child who does precisely what the instruction indicates and no-thing more, is likely to be in serious trouble linguistically. In consequence, it can be said with some truth that children failing in literacy tend to be those who are most conscientiously doing what they are told to do.

Developing basic skills

How do we teach basic skills and provide practice in them if they must always be used together in concert, and if their operation is to be as natural and automatic as possible? Surely it is irresponsibly confusing to teach many skills at the same time. And it would seem to make teaching itself impossibly complicated. These notions arise partly from thinking about language learning in terms of skills, instead of strategies, but the questions *do* represent an honest concern of committed teachers. Nor are we easily going to overcome the skills way of looking at things in the context of schooling—it is deeply embedded in our practices and in the materials we have to use. If the concept of separated language 'skills' is to remain with us, then we must endeavour to interpret that concept in more enlightened ways.

Clarity and simplicity are not achieved only by dividing things into smaller and smaller parts as has happened in the desperate attempt to make instruction intelligible to all children. The destruction of central meaning and purpose may make the task more difficult and less clear. A good instance of this has been the destruction of natural, intelligible language in 'readers' designed to introduce reading skills by a careful progression of simple steps. Because books then become instances of non-language, some children are deeply confused and paradoxically the task is made greatly more difficult. Clarity is heightened by seeing things whole and seeing parts functioning within a structure that gives them meaning. Clarity is also a matter of having clear purposes.

Three things seem to be fairly clear from our deliberations up to this point:

Firstly, language skills of any kind seem to develop most strongly and efficiently in a developmental framework. Before any teaching is attempted, a conducive learning environment should be set up in which the skills to be learned are modelled by the teacher and others and may be practised in purposeful ways. If these things have not been done, teaching of any kind is likely to be inefficient at best and deeply harmful to many children at worst. Children learning language in a naturally purposeful environment are just as concerned as the teacher about 'developing basic skills'. We should not allow the protagonists of 'teaching the fundamentals' to abscond with proprietary rights to the use of 'basic' and 'fundamental'. These are the words we are compelled to use when talking of the relationship of meaning and purpose to language learning, and of the powerful, skill-encompassing strategies which actually characterize the performance of successful learners.

Secondly, the teaching of 'basic language skills' should always occur in a wider language context which can make vital contributions to the efficiency and organization of the process. Whole stories are better than sentences, but sentences are certainly better than words. The larger the language context in which the skills are seen to be operating, the more the support they receive, and the more smoothly and rapidly—hence more nearly automatically—they operate.

Thirdly, it is better to set a real language process in motion and induce the learner to use and explore skills within it, than to give verbal instructions or rules about how the skill is to be carried out. Apart from making the fallacy of confusing productive use of language with abstract knowledge about language, such prescriptive teaching renders the whole operation cumbrously deliberative in a way which destroys true automatic function.

Having said these things, what teaching procedures remain open to use? How may we intervene in a developomental programme to provide helpful guidance and structure to the children's endeavours?

The Cloze Phenomena in Language

We all know how hard we work in listening to a slow or hesitant lecturer, ending up by delivering half his lecture for him in our heads—perhaps much to our own benefit. Filling linguistic gaps is a compulsive activity of the language user. We see this most clearly when any lack of clarity or pace, as for instance in a bad telephone connection, tends to be compensated for by the listener. The unit of significance in language is the sentence—a complete matrix of parts—and once begun, a sentence is driven on by the participants compulsively to an end which yields up the promised increment of meaning. Gaps are automatically filled in the sentence matrix and delays rushed to predictive completeness.

The easiest way of inducing meaningful language activity is to provide gaps in an otherwise complete flow of language. No-one can resist it. In reading, this impulse is almost as strong as it is in listening—and it has obvious implications also in talking and writing. Gap-filling requires the responder to be sensitive to all the linguistic constraints operating in the context, and it is therefore possible to control very delicately the nature of the induced language activity, or skill, by selecting the nature of the gap and the nature of any cues which may be allowed to stand within it. Gap-filling has been extensively used in research and in testing under the general name of 'Cloze-procedures'. Recently, the potential of gap-filling as a teaching procedure has been developed extensively in a move towards more effective ways of guiding language growth.

In Chapter 4 we explored how prediction could be induced in the shared-book-experience by inviting gap-filling responses in the flow of story language. In this way the teacher was able to 'teach' problem-solving strategies at the new-entrant level without at any time giving verbal 'instruction' or providing rules or procedures to be followed. The teacher may provide visual cues in an orally prepared gap by using the blackboard or a felt pen, and may select appropriate visual cues in a written text by progressive exposure using some form of mask. All of the basic skills may be taught within a strategy context, and with considerable precision, by Cloze procedures. And our ideal criterion of using material of story length may be retained.

Confirmation and self-correction—vital aspects of the problem-solving strategy—may also be 'taught' or induced in this way. By obtaining one or more proposals on the basis of minimum cues—for instance, developing meaning plus initial consonant—the teacher may induce the processes of confirmation or correction by asking what confirming details would be expected, and then exposing those details. When the whole word or sentence is always displayed, only the more advanced children, who are already using the strategy, are able to profit from the instructional setting.

In written language, especially spelling, a similar use of gap-filling in a text partially deprived of visual cues may be used to induce appropriate insights at a level suited to the children concerned. For instance, in writing dictated stories for either individuals or groups, *their* co-operation should be sought in suggesting how the next word will be written, or what letter will come next. Sometimes, the teacher may make a deliberate mistake at the 'working-face' level of a particular child or group, and invite their correction. The dictated story may be left with gaps at an appropriate language level for individuals or groups to complete. In written language we tend either to give *all* the cues for children to copy dependently—which may sometimes be appropriate—or we tend to throw them totally on their own resources to carry out, say, a piece of creative writing—which may also sometimes be appropriate. Between these two extremes, however, lies the most profitable and powerful teaching ground.

Observing and Teaching

Nothing can replace the sensitive observation of children's actual language behaviour as a guide to teaching intervention. Tests seldom provide information of equal sensitivity. They tend to be skills-and-item oriented rather than process-and-strategy oriented; they engage children in unreal language activities, and tend to distort behaviour in grossly misleading ways; and they attempt to replace the insight of the teacher by external expertise. Helpful intervention will always depend on the sensitivity and understanding of the teacher—even if a test *can* provide reliable information about language processes, the effectiveness of action based on it will depend on the insight of the teacher.

When a teacher takes responsibility for observing and understanding children's behaviour, she gains two bonuses: first she is likely to be presented with ideal opportunities for sensitive intervention then and there, when she and the child may best understand it; and second, she advances her own insight about the child's behaviour and about language behaviour generally. Familiarity with the literature about language learning and teaching may provide a framework for understanding and action, but there is nothing to replace first-hand experience. We will consider this crucial aspect of teaching in more detail later.

Models for Language Learning and for Language Teaching

We have made some progress towards understanding how language processes operate, especially the reading process. Although we have found nothing to contradict our basic, developmental model of language learning, we have added new dimensions, and we have opened up some hopeful avenues for teacher intervention in the literacy undertaking. It has been necessary from the beginning of our enquiry to emphasize the difference between learning and teaching in order to avoid traditional errors: now we are in a position to be more explicit about the model we have been implying for language teaching.

The induction model of language teaching

The developmental model of language learning appears to give the teacher a less dramatic role than any of the traditional models of teaching—it demythologizes teaching, and none of us likes to be cut down to human scale after enjoying a superhuman function. The model for teaching implied by our basic learning model is that of a skilled handmaiden or husbandman—attendants on natural processes beyond our full understanding or control. As we go on to refine the model we may find further functions arising properly from our professional responsibilities, but always, as we return to full engagement in our role, we return to this humility before individual human experience and functioning.

In language learning we face a range of problem-solving tasks integrating many skills in every moment of activity, and governed by complex self-regulative systems in the learner. The major task of teaching is not to break these processes up into simple parts and progressions to present to children in pre-cut packages; nor is it to instruct children verbally how these tasks should be undertaken and to lay down abstract rules for their proper execution; nor, further, is it to usurp the regulative and corrective role that lies with the learner. *The major task of teaching is to induce healthy activity in language, and to intervene in natural ways to sustain and to clarify that activity.*

An important responsibility in inducing healthy activity is to provide an emulative model of the activity in purposeful use—and to provide a congenial environment in which the activity may be practised purposefully. This practice may even be in the form of fumbling approximation similar to the clumsy targeting of early speech. And just as those around the baby need to *enjoy* the early clumsiness in constant awareness of progress, so we as teachers need to *enjoy* the early clumsiness of reading and writing in *constant and informed* awareness of progress. An important function generated by this need is the ability to observe individual behaviour sensitively and to monitor it longitudinally. We need to be experts in appreciating the significant signs of progress from ineptitude to mastery.

The hypothesis-test model of language learning

Many of the confusing and apparently contradictory aspects of language-function and language-learning were resolved as we considered the implications of predictive and confirming processes in the total structure. It became clear, for instance, why the language user from the earliest stages of learning must monitor and self-correct his own performance—that to see the pupil's function as lying in performance and the teacher's function as lying in correction was to grossly misperceive the process. We saw the way that traditional 'basic skills' fit into a wider concern for 'basic processes and strategies'. We share common goals with those who are impatient to see the fundamentals of literacy properly developed within schooling, but are building a far more real and accurate picture of what the fundamentals really are. The corpus of traditional skills includes much of what we would consider fundamental, but in a tragically dismembered way.

There is no escape from trusting children with the major responsibility for their own learning (Smith, 1975, pp.242-4). This in not just another soft appeal to human decency—it arises centrally from the actual nature of the tasks to be learned. When faced with the moment-by-moment necessity for self-regulation and self-correction in language function, it is soft and sentimental to believe that children are too immature to govern their own language behaviour. Unless they do, they are doomed. They are especially doomed if they follow instruction to the letter. To be tough and realistic in teaching is to put aside the temptation to control everything that children do, and to accept with the respect it deserves the stumbling efforts of early performance.

When we look at the 'childish' picture of learning to read and write which we present to children in a bits-and-pieces parody of language function, we can only stand in awe at the consummate skill so many of them display in cutting through it all to personal control of their own behaviour on a level of far greater complexity. But what about the children who lack the self-confidence to do so? They are likely to be met with further simplifications destructive of central functioning. The child who is forced to use a single skill when only an integration of skills will work is being cruelly manipulated and misinformed. The child who is led to believe that he cannot correct his own errors but must rely on some superior being to do it for him is being put down into false ineptitude and systematically denied the opportunity to succeed or to behave in a normal human manner. The child who is humiliated by his failure to carry out an analytic process which even his own teacher is incapable of performing unerringly, such as syllabification, ought to have a right to massive legal compensation.

When we are as honest as this about educational problems we are often met with the objection, 'What else can you do? Life's like that.' But is it? We refuse to believe that such a rational institution as the school cannot operate if it deals in good human sense and justice. By making learning unnecessarily difficult we mystify the processes of human development, and at the same time we attempt to justify the privilege and power we exercise by our claim to professional expertise. We don't need to understand all the complexities of language learning in order to teach supremely well. In accepting the inbuilt competence of the language learner, even the tasks of literacy become intelligible in the most practical terms. In the next chapter we will explore some of the classroom implications of this responsible conclusion.

6
Teaching Basic Strategies

Our first attempt to apply the developmental model to our class of new-entrants was described in Chapter 4. This foray into the new-entrant area proved so promising that the Principal encourages us to move forward into the early reading programme with a reasonably free hand to experiment. Instead of taking a new group of children, we simply move on with thirty-three children from the new-entrant or readiness stage—what we have called the stage of emergent literacy—into the serious undertakings of early reading and writing. We already have a repertoire of over twenty favourite stories in the enlarged format, ten or twelve songs on charts, and a large number of poems, chants and jingles with which we are familiar in varying degree.

All of the children engage in reading-like and writing-like behaviour at different stages of linguistic competence, and approximately one third have moved into the early visual matching and integration of early reading. Five or six of these children have a clear concept of the one-to-one relationship between spoken and written words. They can point effectively, guided by a relatively stable grasp of directional principles. They know a few words at sight, including personal words such as their names and those of a few friends. Most of them have learned the alphabet and can recognize and name many of the letters. Two or three seem to have caught on to the phonetic principle in relationship to some letters, but this is by no means an important part of their functioning in reading. The writing-like behaviour of this upper third of the class includes clear letter-like and word-like forms, and most of these children are interested in copying print, often asking how to write this or that.

Approximately one third of the children in the middle range are beginning to develop a concept for 'words' in a display of print. They can follow a text in enlarged type and locate words by moving through a familiar sentence from the beginning, modelling their pointing on that of the teacher, but it is not always clear that they know the significance of what they are doing. Their directional habits including the return sweep to a new line are secure only in very familiar texts, and not yet displayed consistently in their writing-like behaviour. They are interested in the alphabet and produce letter-like forms in their writing, but they are still a long way from understanding the notion of letters as distinct from words. All are easily excited by stories and spend a great deal of unstructured time both individually and in self-selected groups with their favourite books. Each has four or five very familiar personal favourites which they are able to process with great accuracy and enthusiasm in reading-like ways. They love to share this competence and regularly take books home to share with their parents.

The lower third of the class group are at various stages in the development of emergent literacy. All have developed a love of stories and other literary forms and have familiar favourites, but their reading-like behaviour does not yet closely pattern the words of a text unless they are extremely familiar with it. They are unable to follow directional conventions consistently except in familiar and simple enlarged text formats and are at various stages in grasping the idea that printed language represents spoken language in stable ways. Some can write their own names with reasonable assurance from day to day and recognize them in print, but this is more a matter of recognizing familiar signs—what might be called 'Coca Cola perception'.

Five or six of the children have obvious difficulties which may interfere with their literacy learning—there are problems in language background, intelligence, eyesight, hearing or motor co-ordination, together with problems of social adjustment or emotional immaturity. However, they are all reasonably settled in the school environment and are satisfied that they know what school has to offer and that they want to have a part in it.

The Groundplan

We begin our preparation by laying down a ground plan covering the basic structure of the programme, daily routines, and the sort of literacy strategies we will be looking to see develop among the children. We decide to spend large blocks of time for developmental activity, but there will also be certain fixed points every day for the corporate enjoyment of written language, establishing a secure routine which will give the day a predictable shape in every child's mental structure of the way time flows in the classroom.

There will be two regular times for coming together as a class, and group activities with the teacher will flow naturally from these situations. The first class session will occur about half an hour after school opens and will be structured in a shared-book-experience manner as described in Chapter 4, p.71–72. A second session, late in the morning, will allow discussion of outcomes and corporate enjoyment of creative work by the children. One of two shorter blocks for mathematics will occur mid-morning, and the other early in the afternoon. There will be considerable integration of literacy and numeracy activities, especially in the morning block.

Excursions out of the classroom will occur largely in the afternoons, these experiences providing the basis for language recall in a reflective mode on the following day. Visitors who are prepared to enter into the spirit of the programme will be welcome at all times, and will include some who can enrich the experiences of the children by formal or informal interaction. A close link will be formed with the local library, which is not too far distant for walking, and the librarian will continue to be a special friend of the class. The School Principal, who has a flair for poetry and drama and now has a special interest in the class, will be encouraged to participate as much as his duties will allow.

Some apparent difficulties

The use of a wide range of books from the trade literature for children presents a number of difficulties. Publishers do not all follow the same conventions, let alone use the same size or style of type. And few, even if they have studied the research, could agree on the most responsible way of setting out a page of print for children. The first thing we should notice from a developmental point of view is that children are exposed to print in real life from a very early age and in a confusing range of conventions. Advertising, labels, TV captions, signs, greeting cards, letters, shopping lists, and a dozen other print conventions bombard their visual experience, in addition to all the styles they see in books if they are lucky enough. Much of this material children want to read and do in fact learn to 'read', willy-nilly. The extreme regularization of conventions they find in their association with print at school will either be irrelevant to them in their demand to make sense of literacy in real life, or it will impede or delay their entry into true functional literacy. In some cases the delay may be beneficial, but it can be said with some confidence that the sooner a child generalizes about print conventions, the sooner he will be literate.

What do we mean here by 'generalizing conventions'? Let's take first the matter of print styles or fonts. The purists would say, 'For a child to be faced with many shapes, say for the letter "a", must be very confusing—upper and lower case differences are problem enough. We should be careful to use only one system in teaching.' Now this represents a misunderstanding of the *sort* of learning involved in perceiving print. Just as in the speech of different speakers there are many variations of the one phoneme which are all perceived as identical, so in written language there are many tolerable variations of letter form which the user must rapidly come to perceive as identical in significance. In psychological terms we are talking about the distinction between stimulus differentiation and stimulus generalization, between the recognition of two things as different and the ability to recognize two related things as fundamentally the same.

In print there is a range of forms that are instances of the same letter. An essential learning in dealing with written language is to develop a concept for each generalized *range* of forms which may be perceived as a particular letter. Because of the necessary variability in hand-formed letters, it would seem important that during the period when a child learns to form letters and to respond to the writing of others, he should develop these generalizations rapidly. Although variability of letter shape causes some confusion to all children, as does the variability of speech sounds in learning spoken language, the experience of our most successful learners seems to be one of wide exposure and rapid generalization.

Advertisers have discovered in how many ways print may be made interesting and appealing—colour, form, design, movement, and contrastive impact are all used extensively to grasp the attention of readers. It seems sensible that at an age when these factors are most dominant in perception their power should be utilized for learning. The print in children's books needs to be made more interesting and feelingful without losing its basic linear character. Bill Martin's version of 'The Teeny Tiny Woman' in *Sounds After Dark*, or Mike Rose's hand lettering in *Trouble in the Ark*, in our experience render the print memorable to children. With the widespread use of off-set printing, hand-lettering may be printed as cheaply as standard type-faces, and there is a tendency for it to be used increasingly in books. As a means of enlivening print and as a bridge between children's own printing and machine-type, hand-lettered books are a welcome aid to literacy learning.

We should be more imaginative and inventive in the ways we present print to children. Our own creation of print in the classroom using modern dye pens can be gay and sometimes humorous as we model the pleasures of writing for the children. In their own written expression children should be encouraged to experiment with interesting ways of forming written messages. Certainly there should be a ready supply of colourful pens and pencils as a stimulus to producing print and as an invitation to bring print to life in personal ways.

Inconsistencies in the conventions of print have often been blamed for the difficulties children experience in learning to read and write. Many careful experiments have been made using regularized spelling or phonetic systems in teaching, with disappointing results. Capital and lower case letters have received attention in such well-researched schemes as *i.t.a.* and *Breakthrough to Literacy*. Different styles or fonts of print have been criticized for unnecessary difficulty, and most education systems stipulate the use of a consistent style usually involving sanserif typefaces and perpendicular Roman printscript for use by children. Rather less attention has been given to what may be the most troublesome inconsistencies in early reading materials, namely directional and positional conventions (Clay 1972, pp.67–9). Research has failed to show that inconsistencies in the conventions of print are responsible for the *major* difficulties in learning to read and write. Attempts to simplify learning in these ways would not seem to warrant the sacrifices involved either on the side of narrowing children's experience of literacy in use, or on the side of instructional encumbrance and expense.

Of course, the sensitive teacher perceives confusions of any kind and acts to clarify them. But the way around these confusions does not lie with some artificial, non-real-life system. The sooner that children can be encouraged as problem-solvers to revel in the flexibility of print, the sooner are they likely to use it. Schooling has typically made the mistake of damning the variability of real life and imposing some simplified scheme which then makes it impossible for children to fulfil the very functions which schooling sets out to teach. This is not the way that most successful learning takes place. It takes place free from any deceit about reality, drawing on the richness of purposeful use within a community which actively displays the skills it values. The cause of literacy requires the school to be *this* sort of community, rather than one which sacrifices purposeful use for questionable gains through simplification.

This does not mean that variations in typography should be ignored. There are sound techniques for dealing with inconsistent conventions. Firstly, we need to watch children carefully and guide them when they become confused. Secondly, we can use devices which clarify early experience of sensory integration—we can point clearly, mask, enlarge, and highlight. Thirdly, we need to develop sound global strategies so that one skill or cue is supported by others and it does not have to bear too heavy a load. When a *single* skill is deployed, without any support, inconsistencies or irregularities can be disastrous, but when *combined* skills are used within a sound strategy, inconsistencies or irregularities cause little difficulty.

Stages of development in a first-year programme

An important objective of the programme will be to induce the development of basic literacy strategies in line with the general principles outlined in Chapter 5. Although children will develop in individual ways, we will be aiming to explore fruitful patterns of teaching intervention and to encourage development through a progression of stages something like the following:

Stage 1 Emergent Reading

Processes favourite stories in reading-like ways approximating to book language.

No sequential text attention. Self-corrects for sense.

'Reads' back short experience stories written by the teacher.

Engages in writing-like scribble.

Attempts to copy or write over the teacher's script.

Stage 2   Advanced Emergent Reading

Can follow a line of print in an enlarged text using word spaces.

Confirms and self-corrects by syntactic and semantic fit, and by word fit (i.e. knows when there are too many or too few words).

Realizes that texts have the same reading every day—that print is a stable, word-by-word record of language.

Can find any word in a very familiar text by checking off from the beginning of a sentence—what we call *matching*. Can locate the same word on a page of print.

Shows word spaces in writing-like behaviour.

Stage 3   Emergent to Early Reading

Knows some words from day to day in context.

Predicts actively in new material using syntax and meaning.

Has developed stable directional habits in processing familiar print.

Can identify and name most letters.

Can recognize words visually that begin with the same letter.

Forms some letters in an identifiable way in copying and in creative 'writing'.

Stage 4   Early Reading

Knows the meaning of 'beginning' and 'end' as applied to word limits.

Can use some initial letter-sound associations to predict and confirm.

Can recognize the most common affixes(-ed, -ing, -s) when used with familiar root words.

Copies with considerable accuracy. Can attempt a simple written message using personal words with a clear resemblance in structure to the correct forms and can read back these messages.

Can manipulate known word-cards or sentence-parts into a sentence-sequence.

Knows the meaning of capitalization at the beginning of sentences and of full stops at the end, and sometimes uses these conventions in creative writing.

Stage 5   Advanced Early Reading

In word-solving, uses many initial-consonant and some consonant-blend letter-sound relationships, together with context clues.

Can recognize letters associated with a sound heard in words, and can locate these for confirmation in the terminal and medial positions.

Probably displays 'voice-pointing', checking off each word in reading by some form of confirmatory process.

Shows signs of using letter-sound approximations in writing, attempting to spell words by principle as well as from memory.

Few of the children are likely to pass through these stages just as they have been analysed, and we won't be testing or checking the children rigorously to see that they have accomplished each step in the right order before being allowed to move on. The progression is meant to be only a general guide to give structure to the inducing or teaching side of the programme. However, we will watch children who seem to be going their own way and endeavour to identify faulty or confused processing before it becomes an inhibiting factor for them.

Materials

We have little difficulty in gathering together an exciting collection of books both from the open literature and from semi-instructional materials. We know more clearly now what sort of material we are looking for. Although we will use many books in straight prose, many of the stories we choose will use rhythmic or patterned language or will be repetitive or cyclic in structure. Many of the stories will be built on secure cultural sequences such as the number sequence, the months of the year, the alphabet, meals, and times of the day. Most of the stories and poems will reflect fundamental logical structures important to the age group, such as opposites, hierarchies, hypothetical thinking, and causal chains.

We have a number of useful series based on these literary structures such as the Beacon Readers of a generation ago (rich in old nursery stories and loved by those who learned from them forty years ago), Reading with Rhythm, and the Gay Colour Books, apart from collections such as those of Bill Martin mentioned in Chapter 4. We have books with records and books with tapes for the listening-post corner; many anthologies of verse and song; and a number of fine stories on filmstrip. We will have an increasing proportion of this material available in the enlarged text form as time goes by—giant books, charts, overhead transparencies, and 35 mm slides, with suitable pointing and masking devices to use with each.

We also have a standard range of caption readers and instructional graded texts of the natural language kind, which we will use to develop group and individualized reading as children break into competence with unseen material.

Some universal minor strategies

At all stages there are a small number of problem-solving strategies that are likely to be important within the major integration strategy outlined in Chapter 5. These are the simple techniques that can be demonstrated and discussed as stories are introduced and print is corporately demystified:

Re-run Used on being stopped by a mid-sentence problem. Before making a proposal or a correction the reader re-runs in order to gain a clear or refreshed feeling for the semantic and syntactic drive of the sentence. A highly effective and popular strategy in early reading (Clay 1972, pp.120–1). Also used as the last step after using one of the other strategies, if meaning has been threatened by the delay or by conscious deliberation. As competence grows and children become more able to hold meanings in short-term memory, the re-run becomes less and less necessary.

Read-on Especially useful when the structure of the sentence has not yet been adequately exposed. The strategy is greatly facilitated by using a gap-filler which may take common inflections—a good one is the word 'blank' (made famous in Australia by Graeme Kennedy's 'Blankety Blanks' game on TV). The blankety (adjective) blanks (noun) blanked (verb) their blankers (noun) blankily (adverb).

Picture A scrutiny of illustrations in light of the developing sentence may provide the elusive cue. Gradually the pictures on the page should be replaced by the 'picture in your head', i.e. personal imagery constructed as the story unfolds.

Identify The 'seen-it-somewhere-before' feeling ('Ah yes, it was in that poem about pigs near the bottom of the chart at the end of the line'. Young children usually have remarkably accurate concrete memories of where and under what circumstances they saw something before. Simply recalling the word in its context is often sufficient. However, actually going to the book or chart, or wherever the familiar word has been remembered, may provide a solution which warrants the time spent in searching. Once located and recognized, of course, a re-run is called for before proceeding with the reading.

Compare   Comparison with a more familiar word which may present a clue. These comparisons do not follow clear principles—different groups or clusters of letters with their sound associations have a different perceptual impact for different children. Natural word parts such as prefixes, suffixes, and known roots form the most helpful group. However, the comparison often clarifies into 'starts like', 'ends like', or just 'like'.[1]

Ask   A highly successful strategy is simply to ask someone, 'What's this word?' This is the favoured strategy of pre-schoolers who teach themselves to read (Clark 1976; Durkin 1966). The important thing here is for the helper to give the word directly without comment and let the reader proceed while sentence meanings are still alight in his mind. Any form of instruction about how the reader may have worked out the word for himself is likely to be counter-productive.

Sound   Probably the latest developing and least useful strategy, the sequential blending of sounds—'sounding out' as it is normally called—can be effective in association with a strong predictive drive from the context. All sounding techniques are humanly difficult, placing great strain on short-term memory and integrated function. Used often with quick success because of the involvement of meaning, sounding becomes a versatile, intuitive process—but this takes time. A natural feel for sounding in sayable mouthfuls—natural syllables—develops very late in the total array of strategies.

Characteristic strategy lessons

Using the basic pattern described in Chapter 4, pp. 71–72, we begin to extend the developmental literacy programme into the early reading stage. There is much more teacher involvement in the sense of structuring activity, and to that extent the programme may be less developmental and more instructional. However, we endeavour to preserve the essential principles of the developmental environment, especially in terms of modelling and inducing appropriate behaviour rather than telling children what to do. Of course, there is a verbal element to modelling—an opportunity to talk about how and why we do things in a particular way—which will become clear as we proceed.

Our objectives are now much more detailed and clear and we are aware that our own behaviour in displaying reading and writing must be more precise—both worthy of emulation and capable of emulation. Our major objective must be to help children find personally successful ways of getting sense out of print, and we expect to learn something from them also along the way. The following examples from the first term's teaching cover important aspects of the programme at the five progressive stages outlined above:

1.   A Sequence in Emergent Reading

Many of the children are still developing a 'literacy set' at various points in the emergent stage. Often the whole class profits from the sheer enjoyment of new stories. At other times the introduction of a new story or the repetition of a favourite is a very cosy and exclusive experience for the small group of slower children who enjoy the closer approximation to the bed-time story feeling. Some experiences of this kind will be with simply structured sequences such as 'What is Pink' as introduced in *Sounds of Numbers*, or with simple cyclic stories like *What Do You Hear* from the series A Book for Me to Read. Sometimes the children appreciate an emotionally cosy story like *Corduroy* by Don Freeman.

A sequence enjoyed by the whole class begins with the old story 'This is the House that Jack Built', which displays a cumulative causal sequence in a reversed logical form. It is enjoyed many times throughout the weeks, often as a dramatized experience ('I'm the' replacing 'This is the'). Later we discover the modernized version, *This is the House Where Jack Lived* by Joan Heilbroner. The renewed interest leads to the class developing their own version called, 'This is the Hut that We Built'. As the new story is created from the children's suggestions it's printed with a great deal of discussion about what should be written next and how to write this and that.

Observing our interest, our friend the Librarian produces *Apartment 3* by Ezra Jack Keats, which stimulates a study about buildings we live in. Many of the more advanced children build up a colourful word list and use it in creative writing for some weeks: 'Apartment, flat, house, town house, home unit, caravan, bach, hotel, motel, etc.' The four house books become popular among the slower children for personal 'reading', and their natural play is enlivened by the new language over which they gain confident control. The structure, 'This is the blank that blank blanked,' becomes a frequent sentence framework in the talk and 'writing' of the children in succeeding weeks. The visual display of these cumulative stories in the enlarged format seems to help less secure children arrive at the insight that sentences familiar to the ear have familiar visual patterns easily identified by pointing through the text with directional precision.

The emotional climax of this sequence comes from the experience of the old story, 'Titty Mouse and Tatty Mouse', from the Beacon Readers. This tragic tale of relentless woe has obviously been judged as too strong for modern tastes and has disappeared from collections of children's stories since the thirties. Essentially, as in all good tragedy, the emotional experience is one of cleansing compassion and special joy—what Aristotle called 'catharsis'

> Then the window said, "Door, why do you jar?"
> "Oh," said the door, "Titty is dead, and Tatty weeps,
> The stool hops and the broom sweeps, and so I jar."
> "Then," said the window, "I will creak."

For many of the children, the notion that books could echo with such beauty the most grievous realities of the human heart brings obvious and lasting satisfaction. Sorrow is a part of life and books are not dishonest about it. 'Titty Mouse and Tatty Mouse' receives tender attention for many weeks and one of the slower children seems to be teaching himself to read from it.

2. A Sequence in Relating Spoken to Written Words

Advanced Emergent Reading   This sequence begins with the selection of a book which displays how a simple kernel sentence grows by the addition of words. In *One Two Three Going to Sea* by Alain, a new phrase is added to the sentence at each page, and memory for the expanding complex structure is supported by the intensive repetition—almost like the re-run strategy writ large. The story is presented on the overhead projector to emphasize the additive principle and allow active prediction of new vocabulary.

> If nine fishermen meet one fisherman going to sea, that makes . . .
> Ten fishermen / going fishing / in much too small / a boat / on the rough / and windy sea.

We are tempted at this stage to use the delightful word-string story, *The Little Fish That Got Away* by Bernadine Cook, but decide that we'll wait until directional habits are more firmly implanted before exploring print which departs from the usual conventions. This is probably a good decision since later we find that the children enjoy the experience from a more secure directional base when they begin exploring some of Bill Martin's shaped stories which move in squares, circles, and spirals. Such a surge of creative writing comes from this discovery that it is as well the children are sufficiently competent by then to sustain the interest spontaneously.

Our choice of a story for more intensive study falls to *The Magic Fish* by Freya Littledale. This is a book we have in multiple copies with a good recording for the listening post, so it's possible for less advanced children to gain extra running time in the read-along situation following our introduction. It includes some familiar vocabulary and displays a secure cumulative structure. An enlarged text is prepared with very simple, stylized sketches, leaving the delights of the original art to be enjoyed in the original. We want the print itself to be the dominant thing in this case because our major purpose is to match a flow of familiar speech with a pattern of printed language, and within it to isolate a few familiar words and word groups such as 'Why?' 'Never mind why!' 'I don't want to go' and 'Go!' For this purpose we make three simple cardboard masks with slots of appropriate sizes to highlight these features.

We begin in the usual way using the oral Cloze technique with which the children are very familiar, and pointing carefully with a pointer which allows the text to be seen clearly without an intruding arm:

Once upon a time there was a poor fisherman.
He lived with his wife
In an old hut by the sea.
Every day he went -------.
One day the fisherman felt something
on the end of his ----.
He pulled and pulled.
And up came a big ----.

Here we repeat the last line, pointing off the words and using a mask at the end to highlight 'fish'. 'Have we seen this word before?' 'On the cover.' 'Yes, in the title,' and we locate and mask the word. One child jumps up to get the enlarged version of 'One Two Three, Going to Sea', and locates the 'fisherman' there. A mask is used to locate the 'fish' part of 'fisherman'.

We turn the page and one of the children volunteers to find 'fish' there, using the mask. 'Let's see how the story goes and decide whether "fish" will fit in there.'

"Put me back in the water," said the ----. (Of course.)
"I am a magic ----.
I am really a prince."

As the story develops its power after the first repetition in the cumulative extravaganza, the children become fascinated by the outbursts of the wife and the puzzlement of the fisherman. They chime in feelingly:

Then she said to the man,
"Go back to the fish.
Tell him I want more than a pretty house.
I want to live in a castle."
"Why?" asked the man.
"Never mind why," said the woman.
"Go back and tell the fish I want a castle."
"But I don't want to go," said the man.
"Go," said his wife.

The mask is used to highlight the visual form of the utterances, and they are then written boldly on a large card and dramatized:

Why?
Never mind why.
But I don't want to go.
Go.

Other utterances are picked out as we proceed through the story. Next day the whole class enjoy the story as mass drama, some children taking the part of the fisherman, others the wife, and others again the magic fish. The cardboard lists are cut into strips each containing a cue which is held up and used as a visual prompt. This set of cards is in constant use during developmental play in the next few days. The cards are also used in subsequent readings of the story to be matched back into the text.

3. A Sequence Identifying Sight Words

Emergent to Early Reading Once most of the children have developed a concept for words as visual entities located on the page by spaces, and can point along a line of print to isolate particular words, the focus is changed somewhat to encourage memory of words in the configurational sense from day to day. The idea is not to isolate these words from the context and teach them as sight words which could be recognized in a non-linguistic manner, but rather to have them immediately recognized in changing linguistic contexts. At the same time individual children are building what Sylvia Ashton-Warner (1965) calls an 'organic vocabulary' of highly significant personal words which carry sentence-like significance. We had better dwell on this concept a little before proceeding.

The first utterances of infants involve single words, and later two or three words, which carry sentence implications. Although it is clear that five-year-olds can never again use those one and two word sentences which they used as infants, they do as they attempt to become literate suffer similar difficulties of scale in attempting to read involved sentences, and especially in attempting to write them. Some powerful single printed words or phrases can capture and fascinate them, and may be used to form the kernel ideas of satisfying short sentences.

These words with power are likely to differ from child to child and therefore need to be provided on a purely individual basis. They tend to be words with deep symbolic meanings which are emotionally charged in personal ways. When they are provided to children on large cards at their request they are likely to become once-seen-never-forgotten words, and be used extensively in the creative writing of the children. There needs to be an accepting environment in which the children soon learn that they can obtain their own private words on request. To make sure that the words are in fact of this personally memorable kind, it is necessary to have a regular screening procedure. Once a week, the words of all the children are put together on the floor, and each child locates his own. Cards that are not claimed are simply destroyed, since they no longer fulfil any deep function.

Personal words of this kind are usually nouns or verbs. Apart from a few rare exceptions which might include 'No' or 'Don't', they are not likely to include the grammatical function words that have come to be called the 'basic sight vocabulary'. Certainly, recognition of these function words brings ease and fluency to reading and writing, but they are difficult to learn, often phonetically irregular or confusing in their likenesses, and above all, they carry no clear meanings or images. However, a powerful *personal* sight vocabulary establishing kernel meanings provides the semantic drive to *extend* sentences and so begin to elaborate structure and explore the function words. We will consider other ways of encompassing the 'basic vocabulary' later, but an excellent starting point for building an early written language repertoire is the use of highly meaningful personal words. Children's names, of course, come into this category.

Often some new or emotionally powerful word or phrase will make an impact in an exciting story or poem, and individual children will want to claim it for their own personal use. For instance, during the enjoyment of the dramatic language from *The Magic Fish*, we discussed similies for the wife's 'Never mind why,' and 'Go.' Among the phrases which came out were, 'Don't ask me why,' 'Mind your own business,' 'Don't be nosy,' and 'Never you mind!'; and 'Get going!', 'Scat!' and 'Be off with you!'. Several children claimed one or other of these idioms for their personal files and used them extensively in their creative writing. Together with some of the personal 'organic vocabulary' such as 'brute', 'love', 'yell', 'bomb', 'Bulldozer', 'Shut up', and 'I love you', they provided the energy for some very expressive creative writing.

Returning now to recognizing words in context, we first of all make a deeper study of *The Magic Fish*, using a sliding word mask and discussing differences between words such as 'fisherman', 'wife', 'magic', and 'Go'. It's easy to draw out the insight about size, and that large words like 'fisherman' and 'beautiful' *sound* long (the children are already familiar with clapping word rhythms and verse rhythms), and that short words like 'go' and 'Why' *sound* short. Some children are able to point out that the big words have more 'letters' and to count them. Other children point out that one of our favourite phrases, 'Never mind why', is made up of three short words. The words we discuss are printed on large cards and recognized by checking them off in the text. It's then agreed that we will put the cards away and see if we can remember which is which the next day.

After recognizing the words from *The Magic Fish* with gleeful ease next day, we discuss other words we know, especially children's names. Likenesses and differences are discussed and the way that the capital letter at the beginning helps to pick the word out. Then we choose three names that are rather similar, 'Penny', 'Peter', and 'Patsy'. The particular children are able to pick their own names, but many of the others are confused—much to the delight of the three concerned. It is agreed that they look alike because they start with the same capital letter and each has five letters. 'Penny' and 'Patsy' look especially alike because they both end the same. But Patsy herself can point to the tell-tale 't', and Penny is proud of the double 'n'.

As we introduce a new story on the following day, we explain that we will be finding words that look very similar and trying to see how we can remember them. The story 'David Was Mad' by Bill Martin in *Sounds of a Pow Wow* is chosen because it deals with strong emotions and introduces some simple emotional words in powerful use—'mad', 'hot', 'red' (also in the form 'RED') and later 'hit'. As the story proceeds the children locate these words and mask them with ease. When we come to 'They shouted and pushed and kicked and h-t', it is easy for the children to see that meaning helps to distinguish between 'hit' and 'hot' even though the words are so alike.

Next day the word cards for this vocabulary are looked at and identified in isolation before re-reading the story. A range of words for anger and aggression is located—'angry', 'argue', 'shout', 'kick'—and new words are suggested and listed—'wild', 'cross', 'fight', etc. The children enjoy miming these words. We then go on to write a class story discussing together what to write and how it will be written—even at times what letter will come next. The children's story is called 'Daddy is Angry' and it brings into focus some of the emotions from the miming. Of course, the children insist on the happy ending that stories normally have, and Dad, who has in any case been expertly provoked in the story, turns out to be a pretty jovial, laughing sort of character after all. The large book, illustrated by children working in a team, becomes very popular reading material. Most pleasing, however, is the impulse this theme gives to personal writing, and the increased request for personal vocabulary of a largely memorable kind.

Although we are not following a prescribed syllabus in Social Studies —hoping to develop sensitivity to social values in natural and active ways, and in response to the literature—there is a great deal of discussion about controlling emotion and a great deal of subsequent developmental activity. The spin-off in handling personal interactions in the classroom is interesting to observe as children use their growing ability to verbalize feeling and use language as a mediator in relationships. The idea from the original story that 'Anger is like wet paint—it rubs off on everybody who touches it,' catches the imagination of the children in an appropriately symbolic way with just the right touch of humour that the metaphor evokes.

While interest in words and distinguishing them runs high, we decide to move into the area of function words and see how far we can take the children. We prepare an enlarged version of Dr. Seuss's hilarious *Green Eggs and Ham*—with our eye on repetition of the auxiliaries 'do', 'would', and 'could'; the negative 'not'; the pronoun 'them'; the prepositions 'in' and 'on'; and the adverbs 'here' and 'there'. In our version we use colour in the text together with bold and very bold for emphasis. A number of original versions are produced in subsequent days by interested groups, including, 'Blue Cheese and Jam', 'Pink Fish and Pips', and 'Raw Bones and Beer'. There are the usual wild and silly suggestions, but working in a group of eight or ten the children are usually able to select suitable vocabulary and decline the purely inane. Since none of the children is yet able to make a really presentable text, we are kept very busy with the felt pens.

Interest among the slower group leads to the revival of *Bears in the Night* with its repetitive prepositions, and to the introduction of *Out and In* by Elizabeth Hulbert. It is about this time that themes and songs from 'Sesame Street' begin to be popular, especially among this group. As the muppet craze begins, it's satisfying to see that the children have such a wealth of new vocabulary with which to enjoy this very verbal art form. A favourite occupation is practising muppet songs for use on special occasions.

4.   A Sequence on Using Initial Letter Cues

Early Reading   One day we discover Bill Martin's version of the old song 'K-K-K Katy' in *Sounds of a Pow Wow*. We soon locate other children in the clas' with 'K-K-K' names—Karen, Ken—Carol! and Christine! What a confusing way to start an interest in using initial letters—or is it? In any case the interest is compulsive and irreversible, so we end up with many versions including 'T-T-T Teacher' and 'M-M-M Mummy'. The final verse we write up is called 'K-C-Ch Christine'. They might as well know from the beginning what to expect from letter-sound relationships.

In establishing letter-sound associations we decide to stay with three or four letters that are highly contrastive in sound, in feel in the mouth, and look—in the mirror. We choose M, S, F, and of course are stuck with K, but we encourage each child to develop an interest in the letter-sound association of his or her own initial. (Often we make these apparent compromises between systematic method and personal method, and it seems to work.)

Before moving into this area we have done a lot of thinking about how we would explain and talk to children about letters and the sounds they represent. We decide we need to be very clear about some things if we are to avoid confusion. We won't, for instance, talk to children about 'the sound of a letter' or even 'the sound a letter makes', since neither locution is accurate—letters are among the most silent things in the world—they are what at one time children were supposed to be, 'seen and not heard'. When we want children to think of a letter—a visual.shape—we need a name for that association. We will, therefore, use the alphabet names whenever we want to draw attention to the visual symbol. The children have already learned the alphabet as a cultural sequence from books and songs, so this presents no problem.

The relationship between letters and sounds we will refer to as letters *standing for* sounds. When we want the children to attend to *sounds* in words, we will ask them to *listen*; when we want them to attend to *letters*, we will ask them to *look*, or to think of the letter recalled by its name, that is *visualize*.[2]

We will be particularly careful in using the ambiguous terms 'beginning', 'starts', 'last' or 'at the end', making certain that the children are always clear whether we are talking about sounds or about letters on the page. We will say, for instance, 'Listen to the word "blank". What sound to you hear at the beginning? Listen! 'Blank'. Or we will say, 'Look at this word,' pointing or masking or writing it, 'What letter do you see at the end?'. In this way it would be possible for us to talk about multiple sound associations for letters like 'c' (cat, city, chop), or about multiple letter representation for sounds like /k/ (kick, cap, chemist), without contradicting ourselves and without confusing the children more than the orthography itself does.

In the language-activities time each morning we play 'Cloze games' as we talk about each letter-sound association that we introduce. There is the old 'I spy with my little eye' game (which is really a situational Cloze game), and also true gap-filling games in which we tell a story in sentences, leave oral gaps indicated by intonation and a raised eyebrow, as we point to or hold up the shape of a letter.

> 'Yesterday m------ we went for a walk to see the ducks on the ----. We could hear some f---- croaking in the reeds. Patsy hurt her f--- and cried. She couldn't keep up so she just s-- on the side of the road and c----.'

We introduce the minor strategies and talk about them.

> 'We heard a loud ----. (Language prediction—no letter)
> It was like a c----- (Read-on) *blank* going off. (Then re-run.)
> We all s------. (Re-run—What did we do?)
> We all s------. (Compare—Do we recognize any part of 'stop-ped?')
> Was it a g--? (Compare—Starts like 'go'.)
> No, it was too ---- for a gun. (Read-on, compare—starts like 'look'.)

It was a very b-- b---. (Context plus initial letter.)
(We stop to draw a brightly coloured BANG! with explosive symbols.)
It was *an* ---------! (Language prediction. Big word.)
The ducks were f---------. (Context plus initial letter.)
They took off into the s--. (Context plus initial letter.)
We watched them ------ *around* over our heads. (Read-on.)
Then Patsy said, "It's only a b---" (Identify—oral recall) and we all -------. (Re-run)
and we all blanked.
She was thinking about her f---.
"There aren't any bombs around here," someone said.
"Yes, it was a bomb", said P----.
"Don't be s----," said K--
"It was an old car b---------."
We all ran over to have a ----
And who do you think got there f----? P----!
In the end we saw the ducks and f-- them on -----------.
But we didn't see any f----.
They were too s-----.
And who was the first back to s-----?
P----, of c-----.

In the introduction of the next few books and poems we discover ways of using initial letters to assist in working out new words. Although we concentrate on the letter-sound associations we have practised, we allow those children who have made a wider range of associations to use them. A story we had been keeping for the slower children, *Fun on Wheels* by Joanna Cole, proved a real invitation for initial letter prediction, especially in association with picture cues:

One wheel, Two wheels, Three wheels, F---.
F--- wheels, S-- wheels, S---- wheels, M---.
M---- on wheels (Mobile takeaway) Squeals on wheels,
Coats, Boats, F----- on wheels (Street parade) etc.

The fact that the slower children will come back to this lively little book with its bold print in the listening post, means that they can observe these letter-sound associations even though they may not have caught on fully in the introduction session. They will not be pressed to learn the associations, or do exercises on them, but the idea will be in the air.

A more carefully planned session next day is centred on the Instant Reader, *Old Mother Middle Muddle* by Bill Martin. In this cumulative story a sequence of animals each dreams about what it would do to the previous one:

"Oh joy!" said the cat, (Picture of cat leaping on mouse)
"When the m---- comes out to eat the crumbs,
I'll p----- on him."
"Oh joy!" said the dog,
"When the cat comes out to pounce on the mouse
I'll b--- him on the tail."
"Oh joy!" said the p--, (Picture withheld)
"When the dog comes out to bite the cat
I'll p--- in the s--- (Read-on and re-run)
I'll blank him in the blank." (Picture suggests 'side' or 'stomach'.
                    Length suggests 'side'.
                    Picture plus p--- suggests 'poke'.
                    One child notices the 'k' as evidence.)
"Oh joy!" said the cow,
"When the pig comes out to poke the dog.
I'll *hook* him with my h----. (Not 'hit'—compared card from 'David Was

Mad'. Read-on gives 'horns' very readily)
I'll blank him with my horns.'' (Compare —like 'look'—'hook')
"Oh joy!'' said the donkey,
"When the cow comes out to hook the dog (*sic;* misprint in book)
I'll k--- him over the f----.''

Protest here by one alert child who insists that 'dog' should be 'pig'. (Rerun) Yes, the text says 'dog', but we all agree it *should* be 'pig'. And so we are able to demonstrate that our strategy is so strong that we can find the printer's mistakes. The children are fascinated by the new concept—'misprint'. We point out that these can be found most readily in newspapers.

An interlude

'Poetry', said Wordsworth, 'takes its origin from emotion recollected in tranquillity.' The tranquillity we enjoy in the classroom is largely in a quiet session near the end of the day. We come together and ruminate, bringing our inchoate feelings into the language. We have been active outdoors and sit or lie on the rugs and bean-bags with some relief. 'It's good to relax sometimes,' we venture in the mood of meditation. 'Oh joy! We can have a rest,' says someone with all the right intonations. 'That old lady was sure stupid,' says Mark, who is just catching on to the joke of the story – 'She didn't have any tea a-tall!' Patsy says, with meditative resignation probably cued by the mention of stupidity (and after a careful physical examination) that her foot no longer hurts. Jill comments that she got a real fright when that bang went off. Fiona expresses disdain for the whole matter. 'Why!' she says in a Magic-Fish-Wife voice. 'That was just an old car.' 'Old cars are beautiful,' says our veteran-car-fanatic-fathered Peter, 'You can't expect old cars to go like a Mercedes Benz!' We are all put in our place, and quietness settles momentarily on the group. We catch a second's reflection ourselves. 'It's working.' The calmness of these children in their slow mastering shows that literacy already means more to them than getting words right. 'Titty is dead, and Tatty weeps' and so we sleep. And when these children sleep they will not only hear a bang, they will see the way we wrote it:

5. A Sequence Emphasizing Letter Position and Confirmation

Advanced Early Reading Developing the confirmation part of the major strategy has proved relatively easy up to this point—it has been fundamentally a resort to sense and meaning, including syntactic appropriateness. Questions such as 'Does that make sense?' 'Does it sound right to you?', 'Do people talk like that?', and so on, are all that were required to set the process going. A few of the children have shown signs of using sound-to-letter confirmation—an instance was in confirming the proposal 'poke' above, with the 'k'—but we have not yet drawn attention to the process. We're thinking carefully about how to introduce the idea and talk about it when the matter is forced on us unexpectedly—in a far from ideal setting as so often happens.

We are enjoying the introduction to Sendak's delightfully whimsical poem 'Chicken Soup and Rice' in *Sounds in the Wind* using typical Cloze prediction techniques. The children are tuned in and prepared to take on anything. Then we come to this beautiful big new word that the children have never heard before. So we tell them it's 'concocting'. But someone has got there before us, and she won't have it—she has her own proposal which makes more sense than our gobbledegook word. The stanza goes like this:

In May (Picture of a bird stirring   Mix it once
soup in a nest!)   mix it twice
I truly think it best   mix that chicken soup
to be a robin   with rice.
lightly dressed
con------- soup
inside my nest.

Fiona insists that the word must be 'constipating', and we are somewhat perplexed. She has a viable personal meaning for 'constipating' which we cannot deny, 'That which causes stomach ache'. Perhaps the nest has suggested something indigestible. Now according to the psycholinguistic view of reading, such a meaningful miscue should be allowed to stand, but for some reason we feel particularly pedantic on this occasion. We begin to remonstrate. We know she sees the 'con' and has made an appropriate prediction on that basis, and she has probably noted the '-ing' in a confirming perception—a good use of the major decoding strategy. She has some right to her assurance, and the matter has now become very personal—Fiona against us.

Only the precision of print can get us out of this, so we ask, adult-powerfully-omniscient, 'If it's "constipating", what letters do you expect to see after the "con"?' And she says, bless her, 'st'. So we look. Fiona's brow begins to furrow, and we press the advantage. We write up the middle syllable 'coct', and unfairly trading on our advanced knowledge of calligraphy, ask, 'Can that be "stip"?' 'No,' she says, 'But it *should*—it's a *disprint!*' So we are in trouble again. Nothing for it now but an appeal to authority. The dictionary? But no child's dictionary would include 'concoct'. Serves us right for trying to teach reading with ungraded material.

In the end good-will wins the day and our explanation is accepted even by Fiona. This is a lovely *new* word for mixing, for trying things out in the kitchen—for taking the *contents* and *cooking* them together. We try it on the tongue, experiment with it in various forms—'concoct', 'concocted', 'concocts'. This is reward enough for the interruption. But as we move on we wonder what we have concocted for ourselves. At least we have hit on a way of talking about letter confirmation which seems to be intelligible to the children.

Let's try to tease this matter out a little before getting into the teaching. When a reader is engaged in a confirming or self-corrective activity he has a proposal in mind which he wishes to check off rapidly as he moves on. The proposal suggests that he should see certain details in word form or letter detail, and provided his expectation is fulfilled, he feels satisfied and hastens on. In this way the letter detail keeps up a moment-by-moment affirmation which sustains effort and pace at high levels. The letters themselves are saying, 'Yes, yes, yes!'—or sometimes in self-correction, 'No, of course *blank*, Yes!'—the process always ends in 'Yes!' If we can get this process going, we have turned phonics back-to-front to become a primary rewarder—a real ally rather than a fickle friend or a plain spoil-sport.

We give some thought to this before embarking on the introduction of our new story, a real favourite of ours, *Red Fox and His Canoe* by Nathaniel Benchley. We use the overhead projector and a progressive exposure mask as described in Chapter 4 p.75. We read into the story, uncovering the text as we go. Red Fox and his father are looking for a large tree from which to make a bigger canoe for Red Fox. On p.14 we have (and imagine this text sliding out word-by-word and letter-by-letter from beneath the mask):

Finally his father cut down a tree and made a f--- in it. "This is too big for you. But *never mind*. You'-- gr--," he said.	Except for the opening, *Finally*, the children read. Good picture clue.
	Seen that before—Magic Fish—the identify strategy.
	Read-on to *grow*. Then re-run—'You will grow . . . you'll grow!' We say, 'And there's the double *l* that we would expect.'
Red Fox who was helping scr---	We look at the *scr*. *Scratch? Scrape?* 'Yes, could be,' we say. 'If it's *scrape*, what letter should we expect to see? Yes, a *p* and (as we slide the mask) there it is.' Re-run.
burned w--- out of the tree,	Impulsively, *wood!* 'Then what

said,

"No canoe is too big for me.
The big--- --- ------
I say."

When all the burned wood was
scr---- out, his father said,

"All r----, here's your canoe.

Can you l--- it?

"*Sure*," said Red Fox.

"Eas---"
"Sure," said Red Fox.

letter would we expect to see at the
end? Yes *d*.' We expose the *ood* and
someone says, 'It's like *good*—the
contrast strategy.'

After a moment at *big-* someone says
excitedly, 'The bigger the better.'
'O.K. what letters will we expect to
see at the end of *bigger* and *better*?
Listen again.' And as we slide the
mask, 'we were right.' 'And *better*
starts with *b*,' says someone.

'What ending?' *ed*! We check.

Impulsively from several, 'All right!'
'What letter will we see at the end?'
'O.K.—but hullo! (as we slide the
mask) what's that *gh* doing there?'
Someone volunteers, 'It's like night,'
and we write this on the board. (A
positive learning from letter-
confirmation.)

Picture clue—Red Fox struggling.
'*Lift*, and it'll end in *f*.' 'No,' says
someone, 'in *t*!' We look. 'Well, in a
way both of you are right. Let's
listen, *lift*. Which sound do we hear
first, the /t/ or the /f/. That's right,
we hear the sound of the *f* before the
sound of the *t*.' (At this stage we can
abbreviate from 'the sound that *f*
stands for' without causing
confusion.) We compare *left*.

'What's this?' (at *Sure*). An argument
breaks out. 'He can't lift it.' 'Yes he
can.' 'No he can't—it's too heavy.
Look at him.' We discuss the
problem. Does he think he can lift
it? What sort of thing is he *likely* to
say, whether he can lift it or not?
Someone says, 'He'll say, *A course I
can lift it!*'
'Yeah,' says someone else, 'He'll
say, "F'shor I can!" 'That's it!'
shouts someone else, '*sure*! It's got a
s! 'Alright, let's go on and see if
we're right!'

'Easily!' comes the chorus.

We re-run for clarity and to savour
the special effect. 'There's *ly*,' says
some bright spark.

So they put it in the -----	Before any letter of the word is unmasked, 'River.' 'Water.' 'Could it be anything else?' 'Stream.' 'Pond.' 'Let's peek.' (showing just the *w*)
w----.	'Water!' they all shout. Re-run from *So*.
and Red Fox p------ off.	Read-on to *off* keeping *-addled* covered. 'Pushed off.' 'Paddled off.' Picture favours *paddled*. What letter would we expect to see in the middle? We check. 'Two of them,' says someone.
"Oh b---! he said	'Boy!'
"Now watch me catch a m------fish!"	Read-on to *fish*, covering the *-illion*. 'A million fish!' 'What letter should we see in the middle of *million*? Let's listen?' 'That's like my name,' says William. 'It's got two els.' And we note this double letter phenomenon in *little*, *Middle Muddle*, and recall *paddled*.

This lesson had a faster pace than the analysis suggests, but even so, the reaction of many teachers and others would be, 'What a terrible thing to do to a good story.' Not so. We tend to overlook the immense pleasure children get out of the problem-solving aspects of decoding. We assume that learning the mechanical aspects of a skill must necessarily be drudgery, but as long as children feel they are succeeding and gaining mastery, they enjoy the problems of decoding as part of the whole adventure.[3] Working at a word need not be threatening or boring, it can be exciting and satisfying, as crossword puzzles show. Of course, the sensitive teacher watches the attention and involvement of the children, and keeps the pace just right. One of the great advantages of Cloze teaching in story material is that at any time the teacher can drop the analysis and speed the story on its way until attention and curiosity are at a pitch again. Then too, the trouble taken to present the material in the exciting progressive-exposure mode helps to obtain the desired level of interest and participation.

Work on the strategy of sound-to-letter confirmation seems to have an immediate effect on the writing of the brighter children. They begin approximating in spelling and lose their insecurity over the difficulty of making some attempt at writing English words. Their approximations are, of course, received with delighted approval, and we soon have three or four children writing English in the quaint old style of Shakspere—who spelt his name, they say, in five different ways.

Refinement and self-correction towards conventional patterns of spelling will come slowly and surely in developmental ways as the children are exposed more and more to traditional spelling patterns. It is necessary to send another letter home to parents at this stage explaining what is going on in these intelligent attempts to spell English. (We will consider this whole matter of spelling later when we work with older children.)

Independent reading of unseen texts

We use our large supply of graded, natural-language texts to move children from that emergent reading in which they rely to some degree on memory for the text into reading of a quite 'unseen' nature. It's surprising to see the way children approach these simplified readers without any preparation, except that we do make a comment or two to produce interest and an appropriate 'set'. The strategies developed in shared-book-experience and language-experience procedures stand up well in the 'unseen' situation. Children in the main know how to tackle a page of print and are supported by the clarity and simplicity of instructional presentation in the little readers. Print size, regularity of directional conventions, clear picture-cues, repetitive vocabulary, and familiar homely contexts all make these readers ideal 'read-at-first-sight' material. However, children are not invited to explore these readers until their searching and matching strategies are well developed.

An advantage of using this material is the opportunity it provides to monitor individual progress. We use a streamlined version of Marie Clay's techniques for keeping 'running records' (Clay 1972b). We make heat copies of a carefully constructed sequential set of readers, and annotate these as individual children read to us. This is the sort of code we use for annotating monitored reading:

Substitution:	Word written above word in text.
Self-correction:	Substitution struck out.
Attempt:	Exact sounds made recorded above word in text.
Insertion:	Caret sign plus insertion. ∧
Direction:	Lines showing any deviation from conventional direction.
Repetition:	Underline. Double or treble for further repetitions.
Pauses:	Bar through the text.
Request for aid:	Question mark.
Aid given:	T (told)
Omission:	Word circled.
Intervention:	Brief account.

The following script indicates how these conventions are applied.

"I will hose the car/today,"
said Father.
"Please will you hose me?"
said Helen.

"Please will you hose me?"

Michael (T)

said/Mark.
hoses
Father hosed Helen and/Mark.

"Please will you hose me?"
~~said~~
~~b~~arked Boxer.

Father hosed Boxer (too.)

These records are dated and filed individually as a criterion for later comparison. Even after several months it is possible to reconstruct fairly accurately how each child had been functioning at an earlier stage.

Dated examples of creative writing and copying behaviour are also filed in this way. It becomes evident from time to time from these records that children are experiencing difficulties or confusions, and some attempt is made on an individual basis to clarify the behaviour.

Individual progress

The developmental approach we have taken does not solve the problem (if it is one) of individual differences: rather, it seems to accentuate it. After a term the spread of competence is very marked. Three or four children are already capable readers and writers, forging ahead into independent reading and writing as if they were bred for it. The large middle group display a wide range of abilities, but are confidently 'strategy-oriented' and assured in their own success. The slower group of seven or eight children do not seem unhappy or frustrated with their achievements—they relate well to literature and are happy in the environment. In the main, they are simply making slower progress, but in a few cases it's apparent that confusions are arising from special difficulties in the physical, sensory, emotional or social status of the children. Those from what might be called 'deprived backgrounds', however, show few signs of anything other than a slow start.

The experiments in developing basic strategies are difficult to evaluate in any objective way. None of the current instruments for testing reading is capable of evaluating *process*, and in any case few are suitable for the early reading stage. The evidence we have about these children is encouraging but we need to go a great deal further. To what extent has the success of these children been dependent on our own knowledge and enthusiasm? To what extent will their positive attitudes and developing competence be sustained in future years of schooling? Is it possible for the accomplishments of early literacy to be destroyed as children continue their schooling? If so, how rapidly may this occur?

In the next phase of our exploration we will attempt a modest extension of developmental learning to other classes in the junior school. What aspects of traditional sequential teaching will integrate naturally with the type of progamme we have been operating? What difficulties may be faced by teachers as they begin to adopt the developmental model? To what extent may current materials be adapted to more healthy ways of living literacy? We will work with other teachers towards answers to these and similar problems.

7
Integrating Approaches

As the months go by we find that our fellow teachers become more and more interested in what we are doing. The Principal, who has played an active part in the drama and poetry aspects of the programme, suggests that we get together as a junior staff and explore ways of integrating shared-book-experience with other programmes operating in the department. This seems an ideal opportunity to explore ways of providing central coherence to an eclectic approach. To what extent can methods and materials already in operation be adapted to a developmental framework and used as aids in achieving learning strategies?

Our learning environment has increasingly been open to interested observes and it is not difficult for all the junior staff to become familiar with the things we are doing. There is a great deal of discussion about different aspects of the programme and we spend a few weeks clarifying some of the issues which emerge. We all have a lot to gain from open discussion, positive criticism and the sharing of ideas. Some members of the staff have very genuine anxieties about some of the things we are doing. Initial misgivings centre around the most obvious ways in which shared-book-experience procedures depart from normal teaching. The following matters cause most concern and arouse the most detailed discussion:

Memory for text

When children process favourite books it is difficult to tell whether they are really reading or not. To what extent can 'reading' based to some extent on the recall of familiar material be regarded as real reading? Clearly, the extent to which memory for the text contributes to a 'reading' varies widely from individual to individual, from stage to stage, and from time to time. To some extent it is dependent on the number of repetitions, the recency of those repetitions, and the place of that particular 'story' in the total range of material for which some recall through familiarity is available. The narrower the range, the more recent the experience, and the greater the number of repetitions, the more involvement of memory that can be expected.

For efforts to memorize to be focussed on a *single* reader, or worse, a few pages of a reader as has so often happened in the past, would be disastrous in the development of problem-solving strategies. Yet it must be noted that many children have actually learned to read in the past hundred years in just this way. The real teacher has so often been the anxious parent attempting each evening or morning to 'prepare' those few pages set as 'tonight's reading'. One of the sad facts about traditional methods has been the tendency for teachers to 'set' what must be learned, and for the pupil to have to find some way of 'learning' that material willy-nilly with or without the help of an untrained adult.

There is in fact good reason to believe that memory for text *always* plays a significant part in competent reading at the beginning stages. Even when moving through a series of carefully graded readers as normally happens today, children need to process each reader several times before they can handle it competently. (Clay 1973a, p.104) In other words, memory for text still plays a hidden role in reading progress in the carefully structured sequential programmes of our time. That degree of fluency and connectedness required for 'real reading' is dependent on the ready recognition of most words in the text and on a high enough level of predictability for the beginning reader to assure himself or confirm that his responses are appropriate.

There is much to be gained from a situation in which we cannot always determine to what extent memory for text is contributing to a reading. If we have a *fixed* idea of what real reading is—remembering words, being able to work out new words, being invariably accurate at the verbal level, or some such criterion—we find it very difficult to allow children the opportunities for approximation which we found to be a fundamental principle in our developmental model. Furthermore, the appeal of the familiar story helps to sustain children in active reading behaviour without supervision and maintains the central focus on meaning and enjoyment. It provides the most basic conditions for the operation of a healthy literacy set as described in Chapter 3.

Regardless of method or materials in early reading, some involvement of memory for text seems necessary in developing smoothly operating automatic functions. It allows predictions to be made rapidly and naturally most of the time, freeing conscious attention for deliberate search-and-match activity on a small proportion of verbal items. We will discuss the importance of this a little later when we consider techniques for controlling the difficulty of tasks. However, it is in the area of confirmation and self-correction that memory for text plays the most essential role in early reading. As soon as a child has made an appropriate proposal, his familiarity with the language assures him of his success—his endeavours are rewarded by satisfying meanings and affirming echoes of the language in his mind, or subtle dissonances redirect his search towards self-corrective effort. Ideally, he should not be able to recall the material accurately word-by-word as in rote recall, but should reconstruct the material at the verbal level by genuinely linguistic processes from central meanings and familiarity. *The most important aspect of memory for text in early reading is not the exact recall of word items learned by heart but the proper assurance of the reader through his own language system that he is operating successfully.*[1]

Bearing this in mind we can see that an important principle in using shared-book-experience procedures is to maintain such a flow of *new* material that none can be processed repetitively to the point of perfect rote memorization. As we saw in the reading-like behaviour of pre-schoolers, total story meanings and a familiarity with major semantic sequences provides the impulse for creating a personal rendering of the text. Similarly in shared-book experiences, children should have just sufficient support from memory to be induced into successful decoding-strategies at the verbal level. They should not be so familiar with all of the material that they can rattle it off word perfectly by rote. They should have a strong feeling for meanings and major sequences such that when they apply appropriate decoding strategies the language will flow meaningfully, and they should have sufficient familiarity with the language at the verbal level that they immediately feel 'right' when they make their reading. In other words, involvement of memory for text to the proper degree supports the early development of functioning within the total, complex strategy—it allows every part of the strategy to operate simply and often automatically.

The teacher can control this proper level of familiarity very delicately by the number and recency of repetitions to which different groups of children are exposed. In this way also the *same* material may be used effectively with children at different levels of early-reading competence—the teacher may control exposure differentially. We could display this in a tabular way as follows:

Level of Competence	Degree of Exposure	Nature of resultant reading behaviour
Emergent (Pre-reading)	Five or six repetitions No delay between last modelling and attempted 'reading'.	Reading-like reconstruction with no attention to print detail—or limited attention. Page-by-page directionality.
Transition emergent/early	Three or four repetitions. One or two days delay.	Full rendering of meanings in sentence form, becoming increasingly matched to print detail.
Early reading	One or two repetitions. Longer delay after exposure before reading.	True decoding using all cues supported by memory for text particularly in confirmation.
Fluency or later 'remedial'	Full introduction but no repetition. Delay variable as required. or Partial introduction— 'reading-in', tuning-in producing 'set'.	Reading facilitated by familiarity. Reading at sight assisted by 'set' and after oral familiarity with the exclusive vocabulary of the text.

Although this should not be taken as a prescriptive system (many children in a proper developmental structure will operate either regressively or aggressively within the structure) it is clear that a teacher in control of input has very great powers to match competence with desired performance. *By allowing memory for text to play an important role in learning to read, the teacher gains rather than loses control over what is happening.*

Unison activity

In the repetitive enjoyment of stories, the read-it-again side of the programme, children participate increasingly in unison responses. Superficially this appears like another aspect of rote learning and offends the critical teacher who did away with meaningless drills long ago. However, there are a number of important differences here from the mindless repetitive droning of rote learning. Firstly, the children participate by choice. They feel drawn into the language and gain support and confidence from the togetherness. If we listen to them carefully, their responses are all somewhat different and personal. They fade in and out depending on confidence, they make gross 'mistakes' without drawing attention to themselves, they approximate, they precede or follow the major pace of responses by a split second, and they put in their own intonations. Each of these differences is important and guarantees the usefulness of the learning. Highly *individual* learning following the principle of approximation is taking place.

It was in the field of second language teaching outside the mainstream of normal schooling that the power of unison practice received its first experimental success. In that context pupils were usually paying for tuition and could complain and walk out if the teaching was not successful. There are two outstanding practical problems in language teaching with large groups. Firstly, each individual is unlikely to have sufficient opportunity for actual language use and practice. A good language lesson will involve active use of the language by each pupil most of the time. In a traditional classroom the teacher does most of the language using and individual pupils are likely to gain very limited opportunities to actually process language through their own learning system.[2] *The unison situation, properly controlled in a lively and meaningful spirit, allows for massive individual practice by every pupil in the teaching context.*

Secondly, early attempts to use new language forms are likely to be clumsy, underconfident, and abounding in 'error'. This leads to intense personal embarrassment and inhibition, especially if individual reponses are demanded under the attention of competitive and critical peers. *The great advantage of unison practice preceding individual performance lies in the provision for gradual approximation towards competence without personal embarrassment.* There is probably no more inhibiting factor in language learning than the fear of making a fool of oneself.

In the home setting, infants practise book language *without an audience*. Hence they are able to gain massive practice in actual use of the new language within a framework of approximation controlled by themselves and not by an outsider. The only way of achieving comparably massive individual language practice in a classroom is by the *proper* use of unison settings.

A healthy unison learning situation has the following characteristics:

It provides a very lively model for the language.

It must arise from free choice by each individual participating—the responsibility of the teacher is to provide an emulative model which will draw the participants into language action.

There should be no forcing of children to take part—if they wish to opt out or simply remain silent, this should be allowed.

It encourages natural intonation and maintains natural speech rhythms—it must never be permitted to become a boring drone.

It is confident and full-blooded in the first instance—refinement comes by degrees, you can't obtain a refined language response when what you have to start with is an underconfident and stilted mumble.

Using enlarged texts

The major concerns about using enlarged print are practical in nature. Most of the junior staff have borrowed one or more of our big books at some time and enjoyed using them. But the idea of providing enlarged print formats for daily teaching appeared irksome at first, to say the least. How necessary was it to teach from enlarged print, and how could a supply of enlarged texts be built up without undue strain on the staff?

Although it is not necessary to introduce every new book in an enlarged format, the objectives of shared-book experience cannot be achieved without daily use of enlarged print. The central task of the teacher in a developmental

programme is to display and model literate behaviour as something both rewarding to do and possible to learn. When large groups of children are involved
they must all be able to see the print being processed or discussed if the
situation is to be experienced as intelligibly literate. There seems to be no
logical escape from this simple requirement. As children pass through the early
reading stage there should be many occasions every day when, at the moment
they hear a flow of language, their eyes should see and their brains should
perceive the visual detail which conventionally embodies the language ringing
in their ears. Matching spoken to written language in the early stages demands
a meticulous linking of eye, voice, and ear. *Clear pointing and masking with
print that is clearly visible to all children characterizes the most efficient
teaching.*

In answer to the second part of the question concerned with *providing* enlarged texts, we decide to organize our resources in such a way that we can share
our stock of charts, big books and overhead transparencies, and we can call on
our panel of interested parents to lighten our labour. To be quite honest, the
staff are more apprehensive about this additional burden than about any other
aspect of using shared-book-experience procedures. The published programmes
at their disposal have the *appearance* of self-sufficiency: the prospect of having
to use teacher-prepared materials is dismaying. Publishers would soon meet
this need if a general demand were voiced, but in the interim teachers have to
back their convictions with ingenuity and hard labour.

Controlling task difficulty

We all agree that if children could work on literacy tasks most of the time
at a level of success, we would have solved the biggest problem in learning to
read and write. But how can this be achieved without the use of a controlled
vocabulary? How can children possibly cope with the uncontrolled vocabulary
of an open literature? For nearly two generations we have relied upon graded,
sequential programmes to match the difficulty of materials to children's abilities. Even then we have too often failed—we still see children struggling with
material that is far too difficult for them. Abandoning controlled vocabulary for
an ungraded literature would seem to be an act of sheer madness.

As we discuss this problem with the rest of the staff a number of interesting
considerations arise. One teacher who depends heavily on language-experience
methods points out that children are often able to handle quite difficult vocabulary if they have had recent personal experience of the topic or if they themselves have dictated the material in the first place. A teacher of third-year
children has used individualized reading procedures extensively and she makes
the point that given the opportunity to select their own material from a wide
range of books at different levels most children seem to choose books that they
can cope with. Our own submission is that if children are reading favourite
books that they have enjoyed several times, they can cope with a surprisingly
rich vocabulary. We all begin to see that we have been making too much of this
problem of vocabulary control—there are many ways of making an appropriate
match between difficulty and ability without reliance on graded materials.
Indeed, the match cannot be achieved by considering vocabulary alone—meaning, purpose, motivation, satisfaction, familiarity and many other factors enter
into the question.

We decide to take a fresh look at ways of controlling task difficulty. What
resources do we have in different methods of teaching for bringing reading tasks
within the control of children? What are the factors which make reading
material easy or hard for children? We come up with a list something like this:

Vocabulary and other linguistic features:
    Simplicity of vocabulary and syntax
    Controlled density of new vocabulary
    Progressive repetition of vocabulary
    Memorable language—special effects
    Patterned language—rhyme, rhythm, cyclic structure, etc.
    Naturalness of language

Prior experience:
    Familiarity of concepts
    Familiarity of plot or other story features
    Recency of exposure to material orally
    Recency and impact of related real experience
    Memory from previous experience of the text

Personal reaction:
    Intellectual satisfaction
    Aesthetic satisfaction
    Emotional satisfaction
    Desire to return to favourite or remembered material
    Social satisfactions—peer support and social solidarity

Self-determination:
    Personal choice of material
    Personal control of pace

Purposefulness of content:
    Practical objectives, e.g. construction or recipes
    Relatedness to desirable activities

Presentation of material:
    Stimulating illustration or textual layout
    Size and layout of print

Teacher introduction or discussion
    Read-in, i.e. teacher reads into story orally to arouse interest
    Discussion prior to reading—preparing 'set'
    Relating material to prior experience

Putting this list together we begin to wonder why we have remained so imprisoned by the controlled vocabulary concept for so long—with such a range of techniques for controlling difficulty there should never be an excuse for children struggling with material that is too difficult or being bored by material that is too easy. But how do we bring this range of techniques into action? It has already become clear in previous discussion that different approaches emphasize different techniques for controlling task difficulty. We analyse the methods and materials in use in the department and reach the conclusion that *a balanced use of different approaches will greatly extend our ability to match materials to the coping ability of different children.*

Graded, sequential programmes are particularly strong in controlling purely linguistic factors such as vocabulary. Language-experience techniques have the advantage of using children's own language, of recency and real experience. Shared-book-experience is strong on impact, memorableness of language, and memory for a previously introduced text. Individualized reading maximizes control by choice and personal pace and interest. Many practical activities pursued in the developmental environment require reading and writing and these display the purposiveness which induces children to accept the challenge of a task. *By using all the resources we have in different materials and approaches it should be possible to avoid entirely that debilitating situation in which children are working with a sense of failure and frustration.*

We agree that the ideal is to have children sufficiently self-motivated and free in their choice of activities to determine for themselves what task they will take up and attempt to accomplish, but there is considerable difference of opinion as to how practical that ideal actually is. We are now aware of the wide range of options open to us in adjusting tasks to the competencies of different children. If we observe a child failing or another child under-challenged and bored we need not feel trapped by the inflexibilities of a particular programme, or feel bound to it for the sake of continuity or sequnce or some other mesmerizing principle. Since working at the level of success is so fundamental to progress, it is more important to achieve this for all children than to stick with the superficial requirements of a particular programme.

Combining programmes

The basic programme in the junior department for some years has been the *Ready to Read* series consisting of twelve 'Little Books' used during early reading and five 'Readers' in normal format used in the second and third years as fluency develops. This series is written in lively natural language and the vocabulary is not so rigidly controlled as to destroy the spontaneity of the text (Clay 1972a, pp. 79–93). However, over the years several publishers produced 'supplementary' readers for this series, and many of these readers so slavishly reproduce the vocabulary and style of the original series that the intended naturalness becomes another type of artificiality. Trapped within the unimaginative sameness of this diet many children learned only that they were failing—the series and its innumerable supplementaries accurately informed some children of their comparative ineptitude in this new skill, as it informed others of their success.

The 'little books' were designed to be read at a sitting, but experience showed that many children remained 'on' a book for many weeks, gradually processing it bit by bit to the point of rote memorization (Clay 1967, p.14)[3]. This was not the way the series was intended to be used, and it would be quite unfair to denounce it because it was being wrongly applied for the needs of many children or because the supplementary materials provided a diet of unpalatable sameness. If by one means or another we could see to it that no child was 'placed' on one of these readers until he could process it successfully, the series would become a valuable part of the programme. It would form a standard basis for monitoring progress and at the same time retain freshness and appeal to the children.

Other programmes in use included *Breakthrough to Literacy* in one first-year class; individualized reading in the second and third years based on the *Scholastic Core Library, Level B*; and *S.R.A. Reading Laboratories* used to supplement third year programmes. All of the staff made confident use of language-experience procedures to some degree, and felt philosophically comfortable with the ideas involved. There were, however, extreme differences in the teaching of phonics, some teachers insisting on a separate 'phonics period' and strongly justifying this in terms of the written language programme, others teaching phonics 'incidentally' in relationship to any other programme in operation. Consistency in sequence of phonics-teaching or in the vocabulary used to talk about it was sadly lacking—for instance what some teachers called 'digraphs' other teachers called 'diphthongs' and others again called 'double vowels', and there was little agreement about when or how these vague concepts should be taught. We would have liked to introduce a little lighthearted humour about these matters but soon learned that we were dealing with very serious issues, and levity was quite inappropriate.

First Year Programmes

Applying the insights of shared-book-experience at the first year level presents us with few initial difficulties—the procedures are simple to understand and greatly enjoyed by teachers and children alike. There is some stress in providing an adequate supply of big books and charts, and because most of the children have not yet reached the stage of visual matching, there is some question as to the necessity of using a visible text as distinct from just enjoying the wealth of stories. The reading-like behaviour of most of the children departs so much from the text that the bogey arises as to whether the children's *thinking* that they are reading will establish ineradicable errors. However, as the children's approximations become more and more appropriate and their interest in print develops into aggressive curiosity, it becomes apparent that, just as in other forms of active play, the children are not confused about their own attempts being something less than the real thing. They become increasingly interested in finding out how to *do* the real thing, asking questions about words and copying more and more accurately in their own production of written language.

The developmental environment

The most deep-seated problems centre around misconceptions about the developmental environment. In certain respects the concepts that have grown around the idea of a 'developmental period' within the schooling system depart radically from the model of developmental learning displayed in the home environment. Free-choice and non-interference have become formalized to the point where teachers dare not even demonstrate desirable behaviour and they remain unnaturally passive towards the children. Developmental learning in real life is not like this. It is generated by emulation. The child sees a skill in active and effective use by adults and peers and attempts to model his behaviour on that purposeful use.

Another surprising thing about the developmental period as it has developed in the schools is the almost total absence of literacy-oriented activities available to the children. Perhaps it has been imagined that such activities belong to the area of instruction and could not be profitably explored by children in developmental ways, or that such activities are artificial and difficult and that therefore children would not choose to explore them. It is probably nearer the truth that as teachers we could not tolerate the bumbling approximation and error that would accompany such activities—we would be unable to resist the temptation to correct, to 'teach', and to insist on proper ways of doing things. However, as we saw in Chapter 3, the natural home environment which tends to produce children with a strong literacy set includes reading and writing both as modelled behaviour and as behaviour which the children *choose* to practise in developmental ways. *If we see our aim as producing a strong literacy set at this stage rather than accurate reading and writing, perhaps we can tolerate the necessary approximation.*

After some discussion and clarification, we decide to modify what we have come to think of as a developmental environment in line with the natural model as we have studied it outside the school. We would try to display active literacy as an enriching and enjoyable part of living and we would provide materials for developmental play in literacy modes. At first this is quite a challenge, but gradually the environments come alive with print.

There are many favourite books and charts of many shapes and sizes in enlarged print and in constant use.

The library corners are comfortably furnished for prone, semi-prone and seated reading and writing. They include many books which have been enjoyed together and reached some degree of familiarity.

There is a liberal supply of writing materials of many kinds and ready access to colourful dye pens which invite and reward experiment.

There are many activity areas decorated in a lively way with print that gives instructional or retell experiences. Among the most popular are the cooking areas, the construction areas, and the typing areas (we managed to locate and acquire a number of old typewriters from local supporters).

A Dymo strip printer is in constant use.

One room has a small 'printer' provided with a range of letters and word stamps much larger than those normally available in retail shops, and filed on labelled racks.

Teaching materials—big books, pointers, masks, chalk and a small easel—are part of the developmental equipment in each room. Without a doubt the favourite activity is role-playing teacher and this provides an opportunity for profitable emulation.

A sign-writing area has been set up in one room following a visit to the road-sign department of the local Automobile Association.

A photographic exhibition, constantly changing and captioned with written comment and story provides stimulus in another room where the teacher has photographic talent.

A plant-propogation annexe has also come alive with print in an area adjacent to the room of our resident naturalist.

We expect the ideas to keep developing rapidly enough to maintain freshness and change, and we enjoy the cross-fertilization of ideas from one environment to another. Plans are in the air for joint activities of the three classes, especially concerned with dramatic presentations of favourite stories, visits to such places as a newspaper office and a printery, and the sharing of experience stories. Two exciting developments deserve some description at this point.

Shared-book-experience and Breakthrough to Literacy

Lorraine, who has been using the *Breakthrough to Literacy* materials for two or three years, is welcoming new motivations into her classroom. After the first big books have been enjoyed several times a remarkable change takes place in the sentence-making activity of her children. The vocabulary and structures of the books begin to appear more and more in the children's production of written language. Quite suddenly the deadly little sentences about liking Mummy begin to be enriched by the personages and preoccupations of favourite stories. It seems that the intensive repetition of enjoyable stories involved in shared-book-experiences gives the children sufficient confidence for new vocabulary and structures to flow over into their desire to write. We often talked about children role-playing themselves as readers or role-playing themselves as teachers: our colleague now talks about her children 'role-playing themselves as authors'.

Language-experience gets off the ground

Our photographic enthusiast, Jill, sees the possibility of using the print displayed in public places. She takes her camera on a class visit to the airport and makes a point of getting clear shots on slides of the signs and instructions guiding passengers at the airport and aboard the aircraft—together of course, with the appropriate range of pictorial shots. This material is put together into a slide-tape programme following the de-briefing discussion with the children.

The actual text is printed up in large book form to be used in a read-along manner by the children as they view the slides. Most of the children are now able to write 'Fasten your seat belt' and 'Toilets aft occupied' with varying degrees of accuracy. (Discovery of toilets on an aircraft seemed to have much greater interest for some children than the dial-packed cockpit.)

Second Year Programmes—Towards Strategy

It is during the second year at school that children are expected to master reading and writing, and anxiety is consequently at a high level amongst teachers, administrators, parents—and children. We try to be calm without really fooling ourselves. If we abandon strict sequential progress through the basic series or tolerate mistakes in word recognition, will the sky fall on our heads? We decide to take our courage in hand and avoid playing the Chicken Licken script.

What are the important ideas standing beyond methods and materials which can be used to form the guiding principles in a combined programme? It is not good enough to be eclectic and simply take what we like or what we think will work—we need a few touchstones against which to test our teaching behaviour from time to time. At the practical level we find that the simple structures of the bedtime story and its outcomes in reading-like behaviour give us a reliable model to which we can return whenever things go wrong.

Our primary responsibility is to provide an enjoyable experience of written language and an emulative model of what successful literacy looks like. Within that framework we actively teach whatever we think appropriate, but if things go wrong—attention flags or children become confused—we get back to our primary role as quickly as possible, we move the story on, show enthusiasm, recapture attention. It doesn't matter whether we are reading to the children or writing for them, the fascinating power of written language is what it is all about. Unless we generate this awareness in the children all our instructions will be to little avail.

Skills and strategies in teaching

When we come to talk about what we are supposed to be teaching it is difficult to avoid the traditional mistakes of abstraction, and sheer wordiness or verbalism. In our discussions we seem to be committed to abstract terminology by the need to be professionally responsible and to avoid the confusions of ordinary language, but so much hinges on what we understand by this abstract terminology or jargon. Is it possible to talk about something as complex as literacy learning in ordinary language without ambiguity? Probably not, but we can try. What we are trying to do is to set up favourable conditions for the efficient learning of reading and writing. We can look on these human behaviours as 'skills', as has been done traditionally, provided we understand the characteristic distortions involved. Firstly, the idea of 'skills' devalues the human and cognitive aspects of the behaviour and emphasizes the mechanical, mindless, must-be-practised aspects of the behaviour. Secondly, the idea of 'skills' invites analysis into unrelated parts—'sight vocabulary', 'phonics', 'syllabification', etc.—parts which the learner may never be able to put together again into any sort of integrated behaviour. It also suggests that the different skills should be taught separately.

Our group of three second-year teachers decide not to abandon the notion of 'skills' altogether—familiarity with this way of looking at the matter simplifies communication—but we all opt for the notion of 'strategies' as a more suitable, *over-riding concept* with which to refer to major instructional objectives. In a certain sense, skills, as we have become used to talking about them, form identifiable aspects of those complex processes or 'strategies' which coordinate human behaviour in effective and purposeful action. We agree among ourselves that *our teaching objectives are concerned with developing sound central strategies for reading and writing, and that the traditional 'skills' are given meaning when they are seen to be abilities that may be called upon in applying strategies.* The major difference between a 'skill' and a 'strategy' is the co-ordinating control of a human mind operating in purposeful, predictive, and self-corrective ways. The major difference, then, between 'skills teaching' and 'strategy teaching' concerns the presence or absence of self-direction on the part of the learner. In skills teaching the teacher tells the learner what to do and then 'corrects' or 'marks' the response. In strategy teaching the teacher induces the learner to behave in an appropriate way and encourages the learner to confirm or correct his own responses—*the teacher does not usurp the control which is crucial to mastering a strategy.*

Oral Cloze procedures in shared-book-experience

The procedures of shared-book-experience lend themselves most naturally to this strategy-oriented style of teaching and we all concentrate on developing our abilities in this area before applying the insights to other parts of the programme. The style of teaching which we have to master is not prescriptive or instructional but what might be called *invitational*—an enthusiastic invitation to participate, contribute, take over the operation. The most important technique involves sensitive use of oral Cloze procedures—providing a flow of language which induces prediction or creative involvement. Another way of describing this type of teaching would be in terms of *gestalt* psychology. What induces activity of any kind is a felt incompleteness or need—an urge towards closure. An incomplete structure is highlighted (i.e. set in contrast as figure against a ground) so that the incompleteness is obvious, suggestive, compelling. A sentence is made to unfold against a story background and all the energies generated to complete the sentence or fill the gap are put to linguistic use. Unless there is the drive towards closure under the control of the learner's directing mind, 'skills' are meaningless impediments to action.[4]

We all practise this style of teaching, comparing notes and learning from each other. The most important part of our determination to develop as teachers is our willingness to have others observe and discuss our teaching or to tape-record segments of our teaching for later self-criticism and discussion with colleagues. In the end we all develop our own peculiar way of doing things, but become increasingly clear about the objectives which we share. Sheila is a naturally quiet, low-key sort of person, and she develops a bland, non-committal style of teaching which brings the children out into confident participation more efficiently than any of us can manage. Carol is lively and boisterous. She puts everything she has into her teaching. Her enthusiasm and expressive intonations are infectious. Her face is so expressive that the children can readily judge her approval or otherwise, and she has to work hard to learn not to give the show away when seeking a range of possible solutions from the children. Janet is unflappable, exuding a spirit of 'We can do it'. She accepts the children's predictions and approximations naturally with a 'Could be', or a 'Yes, it might be x', and then leads the children to home-in on confirming detail with something like, 'Well, if it is x, what would be the last letter be?' or 'What would come after the p?'

Carol and Janet both run fairly 'straight' *Ready-to-Read* programmes with four groups at different levels. This keeps them very busy, and sometimes harrassed. The instructional reading period is too often a hectic, joyless time for them and, one suspects, for the children. Furthermore, it generates few real purposes for writing. Shared-book-experience procedures help to relieve some of this strain almost immediately: there is the injection of lively language and the opportunity for corporate learning and enjoyment by the whole class in socially cohesive activities. The basic series begins to fulfil a properly supportive function in the total programme rather than a dominating one. Children come to them later, with greater competence, and process the books more rapidly and naturally.

An increasing amount of time is spent in the creation of written language stimulated and supported by the new vocabulary, structures and themes of a rich literary input. Drama based on favourite stories and involving the whole class becomes popular in Carol's room. The children use large, hand-held masks for the central characters and the familiar language of the parts is printed on the reverse side of the mask. The class as a whole or in appropriate groups form a chorus carrying the narrative line and using the relevant parts of the initial big book as their prompt. Carol used language-experience techniques to deepen understanding of favourite stories and provide new opportunities for reading and writing. A very popular sequence of activities combining real experience and drama involving the whole class rises through the children's enthusiasm for the story 'Dragon Stew' by Tom McGowan

A castle kitchen is set up in the classroom, and the children prepare a giant stew, creating a recipe with detailed instructions with the teacher as they go. The dramatized version of the story is played out using the recipe as a central part of the text—this is read by all the children as the dragon performs a complicated mime.

Janet on the other hand uses the manuals of Bill Martin's *Sounds of a Pow Wow* and the second series of the Instant Readers, and the idea of playing creatively with the language of books—what Bill Martin calls 'Innovating on Literary Structure'—catches on. A constant flow of written expression, motivated and sustained by the secure patterns of favourite verse, songs and stories, provides deep confirmation to the children that anyone can enjoy writing.

One favourite poem is 'Beans, Beans, Beans' by Lucia and James L. Hynes.

Baked beans,
Butter beans,
Big fat lima beans,
Long thin string beans—
those are just a few.
Green beans,
Black beans,
Big fat kidney beans,
Red hot chili beans,
Jumping beans too.

Pea beans,
Pinto beans
Don't forget shelly beans.
Last of all, best of all,
I like jelly beans.

Other possibilities are discussed and she presents a pattern on the overhead projector:

Hands, Hands, Hands.
_____ hands,
____/____ hands,
Big fat ____/____ hands
Long thin ____ hands—
Those are just a few.
____ hands,
____ hands,
____ ____ ____/____ hands

____/____ hands too.
____ hands,
____ hands,
____/____ hands,
Don't forget ____/____ hands
Last of all, best of all,
I like ____/____ hands.

Here are two of the forty to fifty versions produced in the next few days:

Hats. Hats. Hats.	*Bears! Bears! Bears!*
Black hats.	Black bears.
Funny hats.	Skinny bears.
Great big floppy hats.	Big fat growling bears.
Long thin witch hats.	Strong mad grey bears.
Those are just a few.	Those are just a few.
Ladies' hats.	Brown bears.
Men's hats.	Smooth bears.
Big fat itchy hats.	Big tall King bears.
Round soft warm hats.	Round soft nice bears.
Crazy hats too.	Dancing bears too.
Show hats.	Dumb bears.
Circus hats.	Singing bears.
Don't forget the crowny hats.	Don't forget the moaning bears.
Last of all, best of all,	Last of all, best of all,
I like sloppy hats.	I like father bears.

The children respond with a delighted feeling of authorship, enjoying the opportunity for a genuinely personal and creative experience yet supported by the familiar structure. The opportunity is taken to discuss and clap one and two-syllable words in a purposeful way and the children are encouraged to experiment with the spelling of unfamiliar words. When the children make 'errors', Janet discusses the peculiarities of English spelling and asks such questions as, 'How else could we spell that word?' or 'How do you think they spell it in books?'

In Sheila's class, stimulated by the literature, there is an upsurge of activity in the visual arts. She encourages the children to paint boldly on very large sheets of paper, and, if initial impulse is still strong, to return to the painting on successive days to rework and enrich it with a variety of materials from crayon to *collage*. The children become preocccupied with particular stories or topics and a search is made for related poems, songs and stories. Corporate art forms become popular and satisfying. The children enjoy illustrating their own 'big books', sometimes working in a large team to complete a book in a day or two. Some of the children's paintings expand into group undertakings which provide the experience for creating large murals expressing a thematic interest. A mural about 'Jack and the Beanstalk' begins with a ten-foot high giant created by several children working together. A simple sky and mountain background is prepared by other children. Eerie trees with faces in the bark and limb-like branches are created by some children working on the floor. These are cut out and attached to the mural. All manner of smaller details such as leaves, stars, strange insects, and birds are added as the days go by. Someone works on the castle to stand among clouds in the distance. Story captions are added last to become an integral part of the design and highlight the verbal delights of the story, such as 'Fee, Fie, Foe, Fum'. The end result is rich and evocative, providing an exiting backdrop for dramatic explorations.

Third Year Programmes—Active Literacy

By the third year individual differences have separated the children into very extreme groups—some are still at the stage of emergent reading, deeply marked by a sense of frustration and failure, but some have achieved almost mature literacy displaying rapid silent reading, flexibility of language styles, and some sophistication in spelling. Not only do teachers face great difficulty in handling these extremes, but at the lower end of the range they face rapidly cementing negative attitudes towards literate pursuits—many children have opted out of the contest as contest. A major challenge is to re-establish proper motivations for learning and to remove the falsely competitive forces which, no matter how humanely teachers handle the matter, maintain a punishing barrage on the failing children.

In our department each of the third year teachers is responsible for a mixed ability class. The alternative organization of ability grouping has been abandoned by general consent, but there is growing pressure to re-establish streamed classes. The use of the basic series in these mixed classes is very difficult, requiring at least four ability groups at very different stages of the sequential programme and still failing to meet the needs of many children who cannot be accurately placed in the structure. For this reason two of the teachers have favoured multi-level programmes such as individualized reading and the *S.R.A. Laboratories*. After experience with individualized reading in the previous year, Jan has developed an ingenious scheme for individualizing the basic *Ready-to-Read* programme. This is so effective that her plan deserves some description.

All of the books of the series and supplementaries are arranged in cardboard boxes on an open shelf. The names of the children at each stage are attached by a clothes peg to each of the boxes. Where four or more children are temporarily at the same level they constitute an instructional group and receive tuition of the guided silent-reading kind from the teacher. Where less than four children are at a particular level they operate on the individualized reading structure, and are permitted to gain help from anyone in the next group if the need arises. They enjoy a weekly conference with the teacher and from time to time have the opportunity of sharing their expressive work with other children. This scheme works reasonably well in that all of the children have some time in group instruction and some time in which they are responsible for their own programmes. However, the strict hierarchical nature of the scheme continues to deliver competitive feedback to some of the children, and this false motivation tends to be a distracting influence for a few children, who are removed from the scheme to a more open shared-book programme.

The feeling among this group of teachers is that shared-book-experience procedures will not be suitable in their classes because of the extremes of ability. We look at the ways in which these procedures can be used to meet differential needs. Firstly, a very rich literature can be introduced since controlled repetitions bring the material into the competence of less able children. The whole class can enjoy *some* sessions together on the same material either at the introduction stage or in subsequent repetitions. By organizing listening-post settings in each room those children who require greater exposure can obtain this in the read-along situation without interfering with what other children are doing. By organizing some of the class activities around themes, the more competent children can undertake challenging tasks and still contribute to matters of general concern.

Our first experiences reflect those at the lower levels. After all, what group of children would not become expansive on a diet of strong literature. Jan's class is the first to bubble over into the corridors. They already have a considerable literary background through individualized reading and they become fascinated with giants and witches. They take up the idea of innovating on literary structure from their enjoyment of Bill Martin's *Sounds After Dark* and from the Core Library theme of 'Monsters: Real and Imaginary'. Soon they are creating their own poems and spells and stories about modern monsters. The topic is obviously relevant since many of the giants and witches are barely disguised versions of real people—selectively viewed and aesthetically transformed.

Bronwyn's class take matters a step further. They obtain the co-operation of local shopkeepers and mount several displays with literary pretensions. The butcher's shop is strung up with mobile skeletons inviting the populace to a concert of bony songs and rhythms. (They intend to present their own local version of 'The Kneebone Connected to the Thigh Bone'.) The grocer has a display about 'Chicken Soup and Rice' inviting the populace at large to a concert which will include a rendering of 'Spaghetti Bolognaise on Ice'. The greengrocer has a Hallowe'en display with a verse of bad doggeral entitled 'Pumpkins are Sumkins'. The local shopkeepers are delighted to have such unusual and eye-catching attractions in their windows and the local bookshop is to sponsor a display by the class in Children's Book Week.

Martha, our most experienced staff member, stays rather aloof from all this experimental enthusiasm. She is a most competent professional, experienced and knowledgeable in all aspects of teaching at the third year level. She has a very responsible attitude to children experiencing difficulty, and provides a carefully organized remedial programme in her classroom. She admits that she is not enthused by many of the ideas with which we are working and would rather be left alone to do things in her own way. Although she makes this decision to dissociate from our endeavours, it seems clear that the drive that is being generated in the department influences her teaching in many ways. Her criticisms have a healthy influence on us all.

Some preliminary impressions

The whole experience of working together in the department forms an interesting exercise in divergent as well as convergent thinking. We all begin to think similarly about the proper goals of a literacy programme and the usefulness of the developmental model of language learning. We are all enjoying teaching and placing much greater emphasis on enjoyment by the children. But we all find scope for our own styles of doing things and are stimulated to find new and personal ways of fulfilling these commonly understood purposes. Methods as such seem less and less important. We use our ingenuity in support of healthy learning processes, creating a rich diversity in actual practice.

We find good uses for most of the materials available in the department and a proper place for the techniques we have learned from using a range of approaches. However, we no longer feel enslaved by the set provisions of any published scheme. What is emerging from new priorities and fresh insights is the concept of a well co-ordinated or balanced language programme. As we combine programmes towards serving learning rather than teaching, the diversity takes on the purposiveness of real life—we are seeing the transformation of a confused eclecticism into a powerfully purposeful and consistent body of procedures.

We were expecting a breaking down of barriers between the *language* arts because this was implied by the model we were following. What is somewhat puzzling is the natural flowering of *related* arts in most of the experimental environments. How fundamental and how necessary is this expansion of expressive activity in the developmental programme? This is a question we must explore more deeply.

What we want to move towards is a preventive programme which clarifies early confusions before they become failures, which diagnoses serious impediments to literacy learning and provides compensatory assistance as early as possible, and which succeeds in maintaining effort and optimism among slow-developing children. To what extent is it possible to avoid communicating a sense of failure to children who are temporarily confused, who are impeded by some background factor such as poor eyesight, or who are simply slow in developing literacy skill? The responsibility of the school is to provide the most effective help possible to children experiencing learning-difficulty. A sense of failure is always an *additional* impediment to learning and *the most general responsibility of the school is to minimize the development of the sense of failure in every way possible*. Sadly, the school itself tends to be the primary agent in communicating the awareness of failure. In what ways can the classroom environment be modified to minimize this tendency, and what teaching procedures are most likely to sustain children through difficulties into success without also communicating a damning personal judgement upon the learner?

Summary of major programme procedures

In combining approaches towards more balanced programmes we find a number of common procedures in our school which we all use to some extent or another. Firstly, the different approaches and materials are given coherence by a few central ideas about which we all agree:

Maintaining principles derived from the developmental model
This is achieved by giving priority to literacy activities in the normal developmental sessions, and by allowing the enthusiasms and preoccupations arising from other programmes to flow into this free activity. Playing teacher soon becomes an important part of these developmental activities and provides for massive meaningful repetition and consolidation. This more than compensates for the loss of formal repetition built into the sequential programmes—which are no longer emphasized.

Matching task difficulty to the ability of individual children
The strengths of different approaches to accomplish this match are organized in such a way that all children are working at a level of proper challenge and success. Much of the time the children determine for themselves the difficulty of the tasks they undertake and the pace at which they will carry them out.

Dismantling barriers between different aspects of language
A healthy flow of motivation is maintained between the enjoyment of literature and all aspects of the production of written language. At the same time motivations springing from expressive activity form the basis of successful and satisfying writing and reading.

Developing sound central strategies rather than unrelated peripheral skills
The emphasis of teaching is changed towards inducing the use of strategies centred around the hypothesis-test mode—a shift from the instructional style of teaching to the invitational.

Monitoring progress of actual behaviour in literacy activity
Procedures for monitoring and recording real reading and writing behaviour have been set up. Checklists are being worked out to help us interpret behaviour at different stages of development. (These considerations are taken up in chapter 9.)

Integrating the Various Approaches

We find that there are five types of approach from which we draw our major techniques:

1. The basic series of sequential readers
2. Language-experience
3. Individualized reading
4. Shared-book-experience
5. Developmental activities

1. Using the basic series

The developmental model demands that we turn away from reliance on a carefully graded series of sequential readers and adopt more natural approaches. The gains from using a tightly sequential programme are largely illusory since they are offset by so many negative factors. In particular, such systems tend to separate reading instruction from the real purposes of literacy; in spite of their central intention, they dislocate the match between ability and task difficulty; they feed negative information rapidly to failing children; they discourage self-regulation; and they tempt people with power in the hierarchy to impose false criteria for success on the classroom teacher.

However, most currently available graded series designed in the natural language style contain fine material in a pleasing format, especially at higher grade levels. It is really the uses to which such readers are put that destroys their impact for most children. We find that they fit naturally into a balanced programme and serve some puposes extremely well. They provide easy, unseen reading which is so important in developing the 'I-can-read-all-by-myself' feeling, particularly if children are able to select some of their own material. When a selection is made for children the important thing is that the reader chosen for a particular individual or group should be capable of being read at above an accuracy level of 95%. A well-designed series has that refinement of gradation which makes such careful matching possible at any particular time, but the matching is soon destroyed if a whole group of children of different abilities is forced to progress through the series, willy-nilly.

Guided reading using the basic series

Children learn best how to operate with unseen material in what has come to be known as the 'Guided Silent Reading Lesson'. In the early years, of course, children do not read silently, but they *do* read to themselves. Guided reading is a form of group instruction in which we introduce children to the techniques of reading new or unseen material for personal satisfaction and understanding. It is not an oral reading situation in which individual children take their turns reading around a group. Such a procedure has many damaging features: it over-emphasizes accuracy at the expense of understanding; it turns reading into a performance skill with great potential threat to some children; for the child doing the reading it makes the use of sound central-strategies during reading almost impossible; and it is grossly uneconomic in that only one child is reading at a time.

In guided reading all of the children read the entire unit to themselves whether they are reading aloud in the early stages or silently as competence grows. The group should be at a similar level and all capable of reading the selection with at least 95% accuracy. There are three distinct phases of a guided reading session:

1. Tune-in

A brief, lively discussion in which the teacher interests the children in the story and produces an appropriate set for reading it. This may involve the teacher—

relating the story to the children's experience

discussing the central theme or concepts

reading into the story a little to become oriented
using vocabulary *orally* that may be unfamiliar
becoming familiar with difficult proper names

It is always a good idea to leave children with one or two clear questions which will drive them into the text and serve as a continuing impulse to seek meaning as they read.

2. Reading

The children read the unit to themselves. Sometimes in the early stages, or with a long unit, the story may be broken into shorter meaning units each of which is discussed before moving on to the next with fresh questions in mind. Since rates of reading vary greatly, children should have something natural to do if they finish earlier than others. A rough sketching block is useful for faster children to draw or write about anything that has interested them in what they have been reading.

3. Follow-up

Discussion or activity arising from the reading. This may include:
answering questions raised in the introductory discussion
defending different points of view
finding evidence in the text for variant responses
discussing strategies used to determine meanings
providing instruction where difficulties have arisen
dramatizing or role-playing aspects of story
other related arts activities

A stimulating guided-reading lesson can often lead to purposeful written language. Children should often be invited during discussion to consider what may have happened if one of the characters had been different or had made a different decision; what *they* would have done under similar circumstances; or whether something similar has happened to them. They may then be motivated to write a new outcome for the story or create a similar story of their own.

Monitoring progress using the basic series

Our most important use of the basic series centres around monitoring progress. If we observe actual reading behaviour when children are using favourite books or with familiar language-experience material the contribution of memory for the text is difficult to judge accurately. When children face material that they have not read before, and when we have an accurate idea of the level of that material, we obtain a much better idea of actual reading ability.

At least once a month the teacher observes and records the actual reading behaviour of each child reading a story from the series at an appropriate level. The most satisfactory procedure for such careful monitoring is what Marie Clay has called 'keeping running records' (Clay 1972b, pp.6–8). Because our monitoring is centred on a single series, we are able to annotate an actual heat copy of the text as was described in Chapter 6. Calculation of the accuracy rate is facilitated by having a word count for each story recorded on the last page of the heat copy. We pay particular attention to the self-correction ratio—the ratio of self-corrections to total errors—since this is the best index of healthy processing, and provides a clear idea of which children are having difficulty in developing sound central-strategies (Clay 1972a, pp.118–121).

By determining the level in the series at which each child is able to process at above the 95% accuracy level (less than 1 error in 20 words), and my monitoring the development of self-corrective behaviour, we are able to keep our finger on individual progress and are alerted early to the special needs of particular children. Placed in individual folders with examples of written expression, these records constitute a valuable sequential picture of progress. After several months this cumulative picture of individual progress helps to distinguish real confusions in processing from normal, healthy approximation over time towards adequate functioning. Only where confusions persist or increase over time do we intervene to provide special instruction or deeper diagnosis of difficulties.

2. Using language-experience procedures

Although they place certain strains on teachers in preparing materials and providing a flow of engaging experiences, the techniques of language-experience provide two vital links in early literacy learning:

> the link between language and real experience especially sensory experience
> the link between spoken and written language

In making these links the teacher is given exceptional opportunities to:

> show how experience is organized and clarified by language
> stimulate the growth and clarification of concepts
> provide experience in a wide range of cognitive operations
> demonstrate how speech is transformed into writing
> induce a desire to express in writing
> keep a strong emphasis on meaning and the sentence unit
> gain intimate knowledge of the children's language and thinking

Like the basic structures of shared-book-experience procedures, language-experience techniques rest firmly on simple common sense and the teacher does not need to be a linguistic expert to handle them. Where shared-book experience is strong in providing emotional and aesthetic satisfaction, language experience has its strength in learning about the real world and channelling intellectual motivations into reading and writing. It integrates well with science and social studies and helps to turn these interests to literate use.

The *Breakthrough to Literacy* materials and rationale provide a good base for language-experience activities. As a single programme it tended to become too narrow, lacking in the driving motivations towards expression that are essential to a sound literacy programme, and decaying into a limited look-and-say programme for slower children. Charged with the energies of a lively programme mix, 'Breakthrough' has come alive again. If children come to the sentence-making procedures with a strong 'literacy set' and a small secure personal-reading vocabulary, it provides a great stimulus to written expression and to the development of insights about the conventions of written language.

Book-making and authorship through language-experience

The notion of creating books and role-playing authorship spring naturally from a lively language-experience programme in combination with shared-book-experience. By constantly demonstrating the way things are written down and stapled together into the convenient book form, the teacher displays that important aspect of literacy in an emulative way, and because what is written down is the children's own production, they readily begin to see themselves in that role. Part of the game of playing teacher then becomes making books for personal use.

Movement towards satisfying authorship, with the constant striving for better expression which it entails, may develop first in group co-operative writing with the teacher, where alternatives are discussed and the reasons for selecting this or that way of saying things are made clear. The important experience of going over a draft written some time before may also be introduced in the co-operative setting. The experience of innovating on favourite structures (we have given examples on pp.137-8) also helps children to see themselves as creators of literary products and makes it easy for them to enjoy the experience of creating something complete and worthwhile.

Topic studies are often the source of strong motivation to produce various forms of writing. Too often children lack the intensive experience, the range of related concepts and vocabulary, and the experience of other related written products, when they attempt to express themselves. The deep exploration of a topic, including much real experience, discussion, related reading and aesthetic stimulus from poems, songs, stories and dramatizations, provides the time and the conditions of saturation for individual children to express something well. By flitting from one superficial 'interest' to another we deny children the most important conditions—depth of experience and time for reflection—out of which all good written expression arises.

Concern for a responsive audience tends to increase the way written productions—or other aesthetic productions—are valued, and the effort and care which goes into their making. A class in a school tends to ignore not only the community at large as an audience, but even other classrooms in the same school. We have not found it difficult to capitalize on the audience potential both within the school and in the community.

Print as used in the modern world is often part of an exciting, colourful mixed-media display. As teachers we need to put aside the stereotype of print as the text-book—a deadly black-and-white sameness of threat to sensation. If we are adventurous with the print we ourselves create with the children in the classroom—with its colour and design and illustration—then the children soon bring all their knowledge from colour TV, magazine advertisements, and the comic-strip into their written endeavours. One of the problems of writing for young children is the difficulty in focussing all their physical and emotional energy, and all of the vocal energy they bring to speech, into the silent and dull linear symbols of print. At least print can be allowed to be colourful, gay, patterned, illustrated, decorated, embellished or in any other way made visually dynamic or even zany.

3. Using individualized reading procedures

Individualized reading is another plain common-sense programme which works better than most highly-structured sequential programmes because it is more natural and developmentally sound. Children select their own books from a very wide range and process them at their own personal pace. Additional materials may suggest activities arising from the books, and here too the children are given the opportunity to choose. When the whole class or a large group is organized to operate along these lines, as in the Scholastic Core Library programme, much sharing and corporate activity arises. Some books become great favourites and form the centre of co-operative endeavours in the related arts.

Many of the difficulties of using individualized procedures at the beginning reading stage are overcome when shared-book-experience has preceded or is combined with them. The presence of many favourite books in the available selection makes it possible for all children to participate fully, even if some are only at the emergent-reading stage. The availability of good recordings and listening post facilities makes it possible for all children to be fully engaged in reading activity for reasonable periods of time.

Individual conferences and individualizing The functional core of an individualized reading programme is the individual conference in which the teacher meets individual children in a friendly discussion of the books they have been reading (Holdaway 1972, pp.35–6). It is surprising how seldom many children have the opportunity to enjoy the full attention of that key person in their lives, especially in such a positive way. The child has a real purpose for sharing, and the teacher has a real purpose for listening and responding with that respectful interest so important to healthy growth. This type of communication is quite different from what occurs when children, clutching their 'readers', have their reading 'heard' by the teacher. Instead, the emphasis is on central meanings and on the sensitivity of the complete human response. There is still the opportunity for purposeful reading to the teacher in the conference, but this is placed in a much more natural context.

4. Using shared-book-experience procedures

These procedures, which have been discussed so fully in early sections of the book, form the natural centre of the combined programme. Through them a rich literature is made accessible to the children as they learn to read and write. They provide the basis for inducing sound central-strategies even when dealing with large numbers of children. They provide the important models for reading-like behaviour at the emergent reading stage and for other forms of literacy role-playing based on teacher behaviour. Written language reflecting the richness of the programme flows naturally from exposure and innovation.

The impact and effectiveness of other types of programme are enhanced by combination with shared-book-experience and gradually lose their exclusive pretentions. Activities in the classroom become more diverse and open, less structured, more developmental. There is a widening of materials used, teaching techniques, organizational patterns, and sheer activity, yet para-doxically there is a growing cohesion of purposes—a new sense of direction on the part of both teacher and children. Our aim to provide a more natural literacy-programme which at the same time makes proper use of professional resources seems more possible of achievement. We seem to be finding answers to the aimlessness of eclecticism.

5. Using developmental activities

The combining of programmes, the breaking down of barriers between language activities, and the bubbling enthusiasm of the children—all these lead towards a natural developmental classroom by their own momentum. And this, of course, is also our model and ideal, and so we self-consciously promote it. In addition to all the bookish activities traditionally associated with literacy we are prepared to allow into the classroom all those multifarious uses of literacy to be found in the modern world outside. There is room for only a small selec-tion of them at any time, but if they promise a functional return, and if they interest the children, we are not prepared to shut them out.[5]

However, by the children's choice it is the vigour of children's literature in story, verse, song and chant which dominates the environment. This fascina-tion, properly nurtured as it is in the activities of shared-book-experience, seems virtually universal—no child remains outside its power for long. This raises further questions about the proper motivations to literacy and the styles of adult intervention most likely to promote universal success. What is children's literature about? Why is it so compelling? What special human needs are being fulfilled? Has the fulfilment of these needs anything to do with success in learning the tedious intricacies of reading and writing? Has the failure to fulfil these mysterious needs anything to do with the frightening in-efficiency of schooling?

8
Creativity in the Literacy Undertaking

One of the guiding criteria we established in Chapter 1 was the need to consider the way in which the *total* human person engages in the language undertaking. Although we have never lost sight of this consideration completely, we have not brought it into clear focus at any time. By doing so we may clarify a number of outstanding questions and confusions. In Chapter 5 we dealt with the cognitive and perceptual aspects of reading and writing, and explored the hypothesis-test model of functioning upon which our teaching of strategies was based. At that point we noted the way in which emotional rhythms entered into the hypothesis-test strategy and provided the critical conditions for reinforcement and for fatigue-free learning. How important is the emotional component of experience in language activity and how is this related to the problem of motivation? To what extent is language learning dependent on *integrated human functioning*, and how is such functioning to be induced and maintained in young children? The literature on language use and learning is highly suggestive about these wider issues, even if research in the area is very slim.

The Functions of Language

In Chapter 1 we observed that communication is only one aspect of language and, indeed, 'that *every* human purpose or function has a linguistic correlative'. At a crude level of distinction we could point to the expressive functions of language, which often have little to do with communication. They may be personal, or even quite private, as when one deliberately inhibits the expression of personal feeling until everyone is out of earshot. Language may be private, too, in that inner discourse of verbal thought the development of which was a central interest of Piaget and Vygotsky. Language may even provide pure sensory pleasure in the enjoyment of the sound features of an unintelligible nursery rhyme. It may be multiple in function as in the appreciation of a story or poem in which thought, feeling, sound, and bodily sensation sustain each other in an integrated experience of aesthetic pleasure. We could summarize these points as follows:

Broad functions of language

Communication—Public
Expression—Private and public
Thought—Private
Sensory pleasure—Public and private
(enjoying the
sounds or the act
of articulating)

} Aesthetic satisfaction

Britton, (1970) presents an interesting scale of function in speaking about the language of children in the primary school. He notes the difficulty children experience in taking up those stances of objectivity which we associate with clear communication—their tendency to centre on self-in-the-world which gives all of their language a strong expressive component. In many ways, he points out that their expression even about mundane matters has many of the qualities of poetry. He says: 'The earliest forms of written down speech are likely for every reason to be expressive' (p.174).

Approaching the matter from a socio-linguistic point of view Halliday, (1973) in his *Explorations in the Functions of Language* delineates a number of linguistic functions and characterizes them as assuming dominance for children in a particular order. We could summarize his categories as follows:

Instrumental	The 'I want' function.	Fulfilling needs.
Regulatory	The 'Don't do that' function.	Controlling.
Interactional	The 'I love you' function.	Relating to others.
Personal	The 'This is me' function	Defining self.
Heuristic	The 'What's that?' function.	Finding out.
Imaginative	The 'Let's pretend' function.	Making-believe.
Representational	The 'This is how it is' function.	Communicating about content.

In explaining the significance of these functions Halliday says:

Language is 'defined' for the child by its uses; it is something that serves this set of needs . . . For the child, all language is doing something: in other words, it has meaning. It has meaning in a very broad sense, including here a range of functions which the adult does not normally think of as meaningful, such as the personal and the interactional and probably most of those listed above—all except the last, in fact. But it is precisely in relation to the child's conception of language that it is most vital for us to redefine our notion of meaning; not restricting it to the narrow limits of representational meaning (that is, 'content') but including within it all the functions that language has as a purposive, non-random, contextualized activity (pp.17–18).

Halliday talks of 'meaning' here in a refreshingly broad way as the fulfilment of human functions rather than in the traditionally narrow sense as representation, or communication. We can see the significance and importance of this in the oral language development of children. It becomes clear why the 'natural' developmental environment with its provision for wide language use actually works as an environment for oral language learning. It is much more difficult to see the relevance of this multi-functional view of meaning to the development of *literacy*. In what contexts is written language used to fulfil other than representational functions? If we observe the uses of print in the open society beyond the school, we will find plenty of examples. Most advertisements are instrumental and regulatory, with strong interactional overtones—very little of the representational. The roads and our institutions with their abundant signs and notices are strongly regulative. Informational books, recipes and instructions can be the answers to the impatient questioning of the heuristic mode.

Less evident is the use of literacy to serve *personal* functions, but if we respond sensitively to what children actually want to write, we see that the personal function is uppermost—particularly in the early years (Britton 1970, pp.164–180). Written language is most powerful as a vehicle for imaginative functions in the lives of children through story, drama, verse and song. In the primary, *instrumental* mode, stories themselves can become objects of want almost as important as food and toys: 'I want a story' or 'Read me a story' soon competes with 'I want a banana'.

This multi-functional view of meaning provides one of the clues as to why stories are so powerful in the early language experience of children. At their best, as seen in children's favourite literature, stories display all the functions of language in natural operation, and allow children to identify with the purposes of a recorded language. It is not only the listening to stories that is important in this sense: probably of greater importance is the way children enter into the story world *expressively* as they repeat, re-enact, read again, or live out in many expressive modes the story language which fulfils multiple functions in their experience. In Chapter 3 we observed the deep involvement of very young children in Sendak's *Where the Wild Things Are* and Eastman's *Are You My Mother?* In Halliday's terms, a major reason for this compulsive involvement can be seen to be the broadly multi-functional nature of the language of these stories. 'Then Max said, "BE STILL!"' or 'I want my mother!'. An analysis of favourite stories in these terms helps to explain the power of literature to young children and justify the central position that story, verse and song should have in the early literacy programme (Britton 1970, pp.150–157). From this multi-functional point of view the language of story embodies emotion as strongly as it embodies thought, and tends to be built from intuition rather than from logical bases alone. It is the exploratory impertinence of Goldilocks in a position of risk which gives the story its drive and satisfaction. Such logical structures as those of small, middle-sized, and large add further pleasurable dimensions, underpinning the story with current cognitive concerns and enticing the child into playing with representational modes of thinking. Rationally, the story itself is highly unlikely, but symbolically—with its "Who's been sitting in my chair?" (interactional and personal in function) and its images of father, mother, me (imaginative and personal)—it embodies essential and primitive emotions. The fact that children identify with Baby Bear *and* with Goldilocks further enriches the symbolic cargo carried by the extended metaphor of the tale. Important too is the physical language of the story, patterned and predictable, its singing repetitions inducing overt language participation from the young listener.

A great part of the power of stories, poems, songs, and chants lies in their multi-functional impact. They introduce representational modes of language sustained by all the other modes in natural relationship as children experience them in everyday life, and they thus provide ideal conditions for learning to operate confidently with representational language. A deficiency of language-experience stories is that they too often tend to be representational in a narrow sense. When developing language-experience stories with children we need to think more often of other than representational modes.

Halliday's functional analysis of meaning also helps to explain the efficiency of the developmental environment in early literacy-learning. Such an environment, openly functional by nature, expands the range of meanings and purposes available to children in the pursuit of literacy. It places language in a context of greater reality—it allows a proper place to that elusive counterpart of language, *experience*; and it stimulates the making of meanings, those links between language and experience without which the whole enterprise dooms children to failure.

Language, meaning, and the content of what is meant

We tend to think of language meanings as an integral part of language itself. But if a child wishes to report, for example, what is in front of his eyes, he will not find there, nor in his sensations, any form of linguistic marking. The forms of language are arbitrary and do not generate out of themselves the meanings with which they are associated. When someone wants to communicate something in language, his starting points are not the arbitrary elements of language. Rather, he starts from his experience—feelings, images, sensations, intuitions, thoughts, whatever. There may of course be present a linguistic content internalized from past experience, and this verbal content may play an important organizing or planning role. (Vygotsky, 1962). Thus, our speaker's task is to encode and express those non-verbal contents in linguistic form. Conversely, when someone listens to a speaker, or reads, he does not have *direct* and unmediated access to what the speaker meant—the listener himself *creates* the meanings. It follows that we cannot teach language without messing with reality—that our central concerns in teaching language, those to do with purposes, meanings, satisfactions, motivations, are largely extra-linguistic. Finally, if there is anything which the pre-verbal contents of meaning have in common, it is feeling and emotion. From the awareness of pain in the joints to an elated insight into the theory of relativity; from a vague change of mood stemming from a minute secretion of adrenalin to a crisp sensory awareness of mountains in the sun, feeling informs them all. This affective counterpart is a universal feature of all experience.[1]

Another way of putting this would be to say that language is related through meanings to the non-linguistic contents of experience. Before we even consider the problems of learning to make appropriate language associations, we need to consider the nature and organization of the personal experience with which the language is to be meaningfully associated. An essential part of efficient language-teaching must be concerned with the stimulation, enrichment, and clarification of non-verbal experience. This is the first intimation we have of why the arts generally are necessary to a language programme. We have been inclined to regard the arts in relationship to language learning as some form of motivator or attendant frill. However, the relationship is more central than this.

Language and symbolism

Let's look for a moment at the wider pattern of activities which surrounds the perception of language meanings.

And then Baby Bear said, in his little Baby Bear voice, 'And someone's been sleeping in *my* bed—and THERE SHE IS!'

The group of children on the mat 'read the words', and hear each other's voices. Nathan notices the alliterative capital 'Bs' in Baby Bear, and then remembers the feeling of being caught red-handed and the anger in the adult eyes as he glanced over his shoulder; Joanna squinches into the warmth of imagined blankets, and holds her breath. Later, Nathan has three tempera bears in burgeoning purple and yellow and black, unmistakably possessing their house. Joanna's group is dramatizing the story, and Joanna, as the intrusive adventurous Goldilocks, arranges and re-arranges the plates of porridge, the chairs, and the bedding, beyond doubt the temporary mistress of the household. After lunch, 'phys ed': the children dance towards the centre, then touch hands, retreat, spin round. Just before coming inside it's 'What's the time Mr Wolf?', and then suddenly there's the laughing pannicky flight back to the safety of the den. At home that night Nathan is momentarily aware that three people and himself sit down to dinner, baby in the high-chair, and he recollects something of the mood of that morning's story. As for Joanna: 'Mum, I want to stay up and see the *Avengers!*' 'You certainly will not, young miss, you'll go to bed at half past seven when I tell you to!' She would like to disturb that assured pattern of family order, but knows she cannot act with such impertinence. She is quiet and thoughtful.

Next day the big book is there on the trestle again.

> And the Baby Bear said, in his little Baby Bear voice,
> 'And someone's been sleeping in *my* bed—and THERE SHE IS!'

Nathan, joining in this time, is half aware of the busy abstract adult purposiveness of the bears, Joanna of endlessly embellished dreams and of fantasies of autonomy and the fear of rebuffs in the real world.

We notice the coherence between the children's awareness on the one side, and their imaginative expression on the other. We can vaguely point to the themes and pre-occupations in the children's experience: for Nathan and Joanna, they are the child's place in the world of adults, and the risks entailed in the drive towards independence and autonomy. We can see that their expressive activity in painting and drama and dance do in a sense *symbolize* these pre-occupations. We can also see that their experience of the story, and even of each other's paintings and acting, energizes these pre-occupations. We are thus led to suspect that learning to read and learning to write are instances of a far more inclusive feature of human functioning—the impulse to symbolize, and also the power of symbols to energize experience.

Of course, rather vague insights such as these turn out to be a mine-field of traps and difficulties, and if we are going to put them to work in the classroom, we need to attempt many clarifications.

Let us begin with the notion of a symbol. We all know what it is like to experience something as standing for something else, and the infinitely varied ways in which this can occur, from signs and signals in their most simple forms through to metaphors, analogies, and models. In symbolization something is isolated from experience to stand for something much more complex than itself. Often a concrete image or action will be used to represent something abstract or subjective, such as dark shadows in a painting symbolizing menace, or a lively tune symbolizing gaiety. In an important sense symbols act as an organizing centre or nucleus around which complex meanings cohere. It would seem that linguistic items, despite their initially arbitrary and unlike character, become centrally organizing symbols as they are internalized during childhood.[2]

The complex process by which verbal items become embedded symbolically within the very texture of experience remains something of a mystery, but certainly the concept of simple association is inadequate to account for it. Language takes on symbolic meanings comparable to those of an image or an artefact. However, we *can* be clear both logically and empirically about a number of essential conditions. Linguistic items can become meaningful only when experience is appropriately energized and organized. Language teaching cannot escape the central responsibility to appropriately energize and organize experience. Learning language is learning how to mean. How is this done? Clearly, by relevant dealings with the real world and by symbolizing activity in the arts. The isolation of the language arts from other modes of expression is unnatural and counter-productive. An efficient language-arts programme will also be a lively *related* arts programme because of the very nature of the language engagement and the language-learning undertaking.

During the early years of learning, the speaker's experience is right there—it is the here-and-now situation in which the utterance takes place. Most oral language is saturated in situational reality during early childhood—more of the meaning is in the situation than in the language. When baby says 'Mine!' it is clear from the situation itself what is meant. Even when the six-year-old says, 'This man he stared at me', it is clear that his mental image of the actual happening carries much of his meaning—he has not yet learned to signify all the meanings linguistically. But when the adult says, 'I was sitting opposite a very strange man in the doctor's waiting room today and he kept staring at me with sad eyes. It quite unnerved me,' we have come a long distance towards situation-free language. In expository prose we find a language which has gone the whole way. During the early years of schooling most children are less than halfway along this continuum towards the ability to separate language meanings entirely from the situation in which the language occurs.

It may be true that the process of becoming literate is also a process of learning to use language outside the informing details of a real, here-and-now situation, and that schooling in its inevitable movement towards abstraction is also a deeply de-contextualizing process (Bruner 1975). However, during the early stages of schooling, and during the period of early literacy, children need the support and confirmation of sensory experience and real situations.

Here again, it is in the deeply meaningful and emotional impact of fine stories, poems, and songs that we provide a bridge to non-situational linguistic operations. And it is through the deeply personal and emotional *expression* of young children in written modes that we approach the ability to use language objectively, descriptively and representationally. And it is through a lively related arts programme that we help children to use language in powerfully symbolic ways.

As Richard Jones (1968) puts it in his *Fantasy and Feeling in Education*:

> In schoolrooms, conditions are created which invite expression of controlled emotions for the purpose of imbuing curricular issues with personal significance. The power of emotion to generate interest and involvement in subject matters which would otherwise find children uninterested and uninvolved lies in their deep personal familiarity—such familiarity being a consequence of emotion having been integral to every phase of personal development from infancy on . . .
> This potential is carried by more than merely associative connections. The emotions are intimately interrelated with certain symbolic functions known to be central to creative thinking. (p.148).

The personal creation of meaning

If it were not for language, our entrapment in our own private world of meanings would be only too obvious. But on the other hand, among the many errors that language tempts us into is the illusion that we share *identical* meanings with others and that these meanings are transmitted intact from one language user to another. Our use of dictionaries, our arguments about what a statement *really* means, our demand in testimony for the whole truth and nothing but the truth, all serve to build this illusion that somehow the meanings are in the language alone. But in a most fundamental sense meanings partake of the personal, the unique, and the private.

The speaker and the writer must generate sentences which embody simplifications of all that is relevant in their awareness, sometimes ordering a complex present awareness into a temporal sequence of sentences. This necessarily *linear* output of language may be very different in structure from the unity of the awareness as it is experienced or meant. The speaker is likely to seek assurance from the listener that the message is getting through—he may ask, 'Do you see what I mean?' or even pepper the conversation with 'Y'know?' or 'See?'. We all know how easily we may be misinterpreted and how difficult it is to create a surface language which will fully and accurately represent our meanings.

The movement from surface language to meaning is equally personal and open to misinterpretation. Listeners or readers do not have the *meanings* poured into them—they are not conducted to them directly through the sounds in the air or from the marks on the paper; they *make* them from what is linguistically given in relationship to all that constitutes their *own* self-awareness. Thus, the interpretation of language is a creative process even when the most basic skills are being practised, as we saw in the use of central strategies in Chapter 5. Just as we must learn to 'read' faces as symbols of meaning, so we have to learn to 'read' language in such a way that the meanings we create will not be too badly mistaken.

It will have been noticed that our use of the word 'creative' does not stand for a rare ability at a polar extreme from the 'everyday', or 'ordinary', or 'objective', but refers to something essential in all communication and expression. An active creative intent is what integrates complex human functioning. In ordinary speech this creative heart of language is usually unobstrusive and taken for granted. But with those who forget the creative obligation—the gossip, the word mongerer, the jargon swinger, and the academic obfuscationist—language *does*, in fact, become an empty out-pouring of pure verbalism. 'Pure' language, that is language without any obligation to meaning, is a form of garbage—empty cans and bottles on a beach. When we teach language skills separately from the creative obligation to *mean*, we fill the classroom with just such garbage. Many workbook exercises, printing lessons, and phonic drills fall into this category.

The range of creativeness involved in language extends from the mundane, through the skilled and lively, to the brilliant or literary—but they are all forms of creative or generative intent. For example, an infant might say, 'Me clean foots', which in relationship to its semantic context or situation may mean, 'I am cleaning my feet', or 'See, my feet are clean', or with a rising intonation, 'Will I clean my feet?'. Here the child is not copying any meaningful utterance previously heard, but is applying syntactic and semantic rules to create a personal meaning. We must be ready to accept just such a generative exploration in learning to read and write. The doctrine that the learner must get the language *right* regardless of meaning, is precisely what will blight the natural growth of all language activity.

At a level of competent use a mountaineer may say, 'Give me a foot', or a worker may say, 'My feet are killing me', and nobody would be likely to note the minute creative gesture out of habit that produced the surface language. Another person may have lost the foot-feeling in 'footstep' or 'footing' but may still turn the image to use on the footie field by calling someone 'Footface', or more politely and creatively bemoan the fact that his car was out of commission by cursing his 'footbound condition'. In each case the devices of syntax and metaphor are used to squeeze a special meaning from the word which no dictionary would list. The great marvel of ordinary language is the way in which each word is sensitively interpreted according to its context—the sentence, the discourse, and the total occasion. Our task is not to teach fixed meanings but to teach how to generate unique meanings controlled by contextual agencies.

At a decidedly different level again, we could take a brilliant literary example from one of Ariel's songs in *The Tempest*:

> Foot it featly here and there,
> And let sweet sprites the burden bear.

Here, the rule-abiding power of the language is stretched to the limit in forming the verb function of 'foot' and the echoic pun on 'feet'. One is brought to a stop at the beauty of it, and begins to wonder just what processes of creation went on in Shakespeare's head as he encoded such meanings into such a surface structure. He was thinking about dancing to music, his muscles providing pleasant tingles of knowing what it was like to dance with joy, and all his synapses were crackling—perhaps, even, glandular secretions began to modify the experience. And there was a memory, an image, of that sweet time with good wine and music when his lady seemed almost immortal. His feet tingle, and—yes—he has it—'Foot it blithely my darling, here, there ---' An adverbial feel in the belly—'What a feat! Yes, of course, FEET—ha ha—featly! Foot it featly here and there . . . Wow! Or rather 'Zounds!' or whatever the Elizabethan equivalent was. 'That's got it beautifully—what a dance! What a song!'

The psycholinguists would probably be very unhappy about that clumsy attempt to seize on some of the possibilities of Shakespeare's linguistic processes, but our point is that the deep structure is a strongly semantic one, constantly organizing and reorganizing the syntactic considerations. It includes elements as disparate as organic conditions within the body, sensations, memories, images, feelings, thoughts, verbal associations and conceits. There is also the punning awareness of the surface written-form of 'feat' and the delightfully appropriate union of the two meanings ('feet' and 'feat') reflecting back on the 'Foot it'—feet, elegantly used, providing a concrete symbol for dancing.

Thus, there is a movement back and forth between deep and surface structure in the selection of appropriate linguistic forms. We could attempt to display some of these relationships in the following flow diagram:

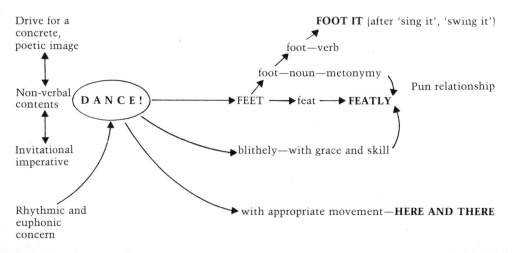

Of course, nobody can know what was Shakespeare's 'meaning' in every detail—and in terms of subconscious influences on his verbal selection, neither could he—but what we have is an artefact in language which has the power to induce the spectator to create personal meanings. Each decoding will be a unique set of meanings depending on both the experience and the verbal competence of the spectator. The surface language has the potentiality to control essential processes in the creation of meaning—for instance by placing the concrete images arising from 'foot it', 'feat', 'feet', and 'featly', into syntactically organized continuity—but the final experience will be personal and unique. And to achieve what the linguistic potentiality offers, each spectator or reader must engage in the process with *creative intent*.

The sub-structures of language

Within what framework of experience do these creative processes which link language and meaning operate? There are some relatively clear guidelines to speculation about this matter but little can be said to be 'known' about it. Just as we found that 'errors' or 'miscues' could provide a window to what goes on in the reading process, so we can gain some insights about the coding and encoding processes of spoken language through a study of mistakes and self-corrections in speech. In a fascinating article entitled *Slips of the Tongue*, Victoria Fromkin (1973) finds confirmation for the transformational notions of modern psycholinguistics in the recorded mistakes people make spontaneously in speaking. Of greatest importance are the concepts of deep and surface structure particularly as relating to grammatical operations.

For our purposes we will attempt to create a simplified schema for these operational sub-structures of language, but we need to bear in mind that the matter is so immensely complex and beyond the limits of current understanding that the model can only crudely suggest major features of the processes. Figure 4 on the following page sets out some of these relationships. (The bars connecting semantic operators are a crude representation of the importance of the interrelationships.)

Feedback is essential at every stage of the syntactic operation and between every level, whether the process is one of expression (with its movement from 'semantic awareness' towards the generation of actual words), or whether it is one of 'reading' (where a 'semantic awareness' must be created which will appropriately relate to the words). The need for feedback between every stage requires that the effective language-learning environment actively promotes self-regulation, self-correction, and self-improvement.

We should not look on the semantic operators as exclusive of each other—each may compensate for weaknesses in another, or even carry out the function of another. For instance, gesture may carry out a syntactic function as in David's shake of the head for negation in Chapter 3. An intonation may be used to create a question from a statement, or negate a positive statement by an ironic stress. The relationship between lexical and syntactic choices is very complex (Halliday 1973, pp.103–108); and in the case of idioms—locutions which break normal rules—syntactic or lexical meanings are overriden by a bonded sequence often tied together by a characteristic intonation (Cut it out!). Often weaknesses in the choices within other systems will be taken up by stronger intonational choices or by the use of italics in writing. The case of silences in speech is interesting—a significant pause or break in the flow of discourse will often change the entire meaning of the transaction.

In the terms of our earlier discussion we can say that the state of *semantic awareness*—its strength and organization—will be as important in learning any

Figure 4 Operational Sub-structures of Language

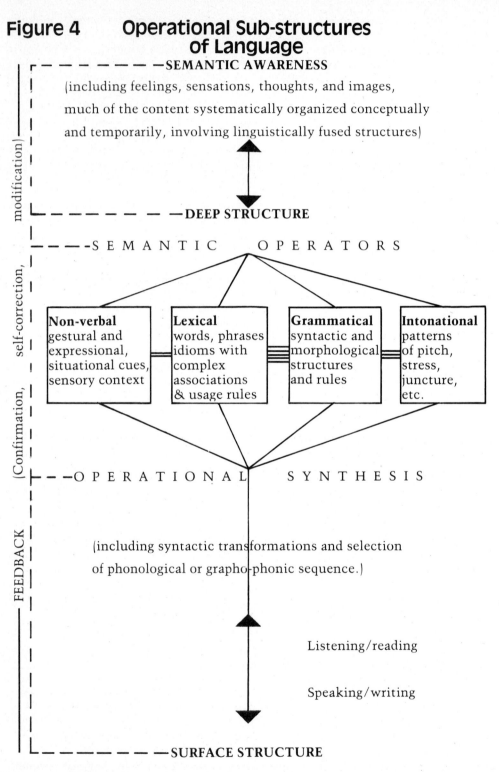

language operation as the *accuracy and appropriateness* of the surface structure. In our example of Nathan and Joanna, their semantic preoccupations concerned with family and personal autonomy are as essential to the reading of the words as is attention to the surface structure of the sentence. To some extent this is a linguistic matter, part of the semantic awareness being linguistically organized, but to some extent it is also a non-linguistic matter and must be dependent on emotion, perception, imaging, and symbolic processes in related arts. This implies that the effective language learning environment will have strong experiential and expressive components.

Young readers need the inducements to respond creatively such as are provided by a genuine literature and by interpretative activities in the related arts. 'Someone's been sleeping in MY bed' is an inducement to create personal meanings coloured by those special feelings about beds, private property, the right to a personal corner in the world, and the limits of acceptable behaviour. The impact would be very different in the form, 'Mother Bear told Father Bear that she thought that someone had been lying on her bed.' A dramatic playing out of the story also adds personal and unique feeling to the experience which is likely to be energized in a future reading of the story, or in the reading of a related story such as 'The Three Billy Goats Gruff' with its 'Who's that tripping over MY bridge?'

Finally, the model may remind us again of the deeply creative involvement which is demanded of every language user, whether he is engaged in expressive or receptive activity. There is always a transmutation of kind to be achieved—non-verbal contents into surface language or surface language into meanings. This is the real crux of the language undertaking and it is as crucial in the operation of basic skills as it is in creative writing and in the interpretation of literature.

Creativity and Basic Strategies

The process of reading is one in which personal meanings are created by a subtle interaction between the complex experience of the reader and the cues provided in the print by the author. Even in the 'decoding' of a word, the reader brings his relevant knowledge of the world to bear predictively upon the letter detail. He is assisted in this by patterns and regularities in the language as well as by semantic expectations. Traditionally, word solving has been taught with an emphasis on patterns smaller than the word (phonics) or made up by the word (configuration). Between these two are regularities of spelling pattern which are often neglected in instruction—what might be called 'clusters'—and these may sometimes be much more important and efficient features to use than letters or letter-sound relationships. Sometimes these clusters will be syllables as in 'con-tact', and sometimes not, as in 'fr-ight' or 'wind-ow'. Children should be encouraged to group and recognize in personally useful ways, and to experiment with alternative perceptual patterns (Smith 1971; Clay 1972a; Santa 1976).

Sentence patterns

However, of much greater importance are the patterns displayed at the sentence level for in these the powerful expectations derived from syntax and intonation become available. As we saw in the analysis of the hypothesis-test strategy in Chapter 5, syntax provides a predictable mapping of the verbal terrain, and developing meanings—the semantic cues—facilitate the recognition of words and reduce the number of visual features required in word solving.

Certain additional cues become available in patterned language such as that of verse, song, and rhymed story—all of which children love because of their bonuses in sensory pleasure. They should be encouraged to use the expectations based on dependable rhythm, rhyme and patterned sentence structure as *aids to decoding*, and much early reading material should be of this patterned kind. When the inner ear catches a rhythm or expects a rhyme there is something new in experience from which a creative leap can be mounted. As Bill Martin says so well in the *Teacher's Guide to the Instant Readers*, 'dependable schemes of rhyme and rhythm help children read words they didn't know they knew'. (p.24).

Patterns larger than the sentence

The power of structures larger than the sentence to arouse creative expectations and thus bear down on decoding has been greatly overlooked in teaching, although this awareness was implied by such early schemes as the Beacon Readers, and more recent collections such as Reading With Rhythm, and the E.R. Boyce Gay Way Readers. Here again, in the explicit recognition of the power of structure to aid decoding, Bill Martin had been something of a pioneer. The section, 'Figuring out how stories and poems work' in the manuals to his Sounds of Language series deserves close study by any teacher. Once the reader has caught on to the implied structure of story or poem, he has a further powerful aid in unfolding and decoding the print. Some patterns larger than the sentence are:

Story structures

Repetitive sequence	'Are You My Mother?' by P.D. Eastman
Cyclic and cumulative	'The Magic Fish' by Freya Littledale
Interlocking	'The Three Little Pigs'
Temporal sequence	'Gordon the Goat' by Munroe Leaf
Analogy	'Morris the Moose Goes to School by B. Wiseman
Logical relationships	'Stop Stop' by E.T. Hurd
Dependable nonsense	'Epaminados' by Eve Merriam

Verse structures
Rhythm and line length
Stanza form
Rhyme
Other formal devices

Logical structures

Classification	'What is Pink' by Christina G. Rossetti
Opposites	'What Good Luck, What Bad Luck' by Remy Charlip
Hierarchies	'The Old Woman and the Turnip'
Comparatives	'Three Billy Goats Gruff'
Reversible structure	'Just in Time for the King's Birthday' by E.B. Chance
Deductive structures	'One Two Three: Going to Sea' by Alain

Many stories, poems, or songs interweave several of these structures into one beautifully predictive and reliable form. 'Henny Penny', 'The Three Little Pigs' and 'Goldilocks' for instance are repetitive, cumulative and hierarchical; 'The Magic Fish' is repetitive, cumulative, deductive, with rhythmic and rhymed sequences.

All of these patterned structures introduce the notion of plot which is itself a highly predictable influence on reading. Once the ideas of problem and resolution, cause and effect, behaviour and consequence, challenge and response, and situation and dénouement, have caught on, the reader has added resources to decode even the most isolated verbal item. Only when all of these resources fail should the reader resort to the grunting cacophony of 'sounding out'.

Semantic complexities in decoding

We can see the creative complexity involved in decoding most clearly by considering the problem presented by idioms, i.e. locutions which do *not* obey normal syntactic and semantic rules. For instance, what are some of the prerequisites for understanding simple idioms like, 'Little beast, indeed. The idea of calling me a little beast!' from *Stars in the Sky*, p.35 in the Ready to Read series. It has been found that most children who have not had a wide background of oral stories fail to make sense of this literary idiom. The unreflecting adult sees little difficulty in reading such simple and flowing text, but what are the sorts of things that the learner-reader must do?

Firstly, relating to a wider context, the reader needs to know that this exclamation is being uttered by a character in a child's story. The character is an elephant who has been insulted by a tortoise who refers to him as a 'little beast'. The shock of this apparently illogical assertion by the tortoise sets up the tension of the plot in which the tortoise will prove his point in a typical fable structure embodying the principle of 'brains over brawn'.

Secondly, the words must be recognized or be capable of decoding with a degree of assurance which will withstand the feeling of dissonance or disbelief that will result from getting at a meaning.

Thirdly, the reader must have heard the idiom 'Such and such, indeed' and the idiom 'the very idea of ———' used in appropriate contexts and with appropriate intonation some time in the past. He must have understood their meaning and made a strong associational learning-link between the idiom and the special meaning of contemptuous dismissal of an impossible idea—all wrapped up in an intonation of absolute disbelief and contempt. These associations must be strong enough to override the irrelevant syntactical suggestions of both sentences and the disobedience of grammatical rule.[2]

Fourthly, he must be able to attribute appropriate grammatical meaning to the structures and determine what parts of the grammatical meaning must be laid aside on this occasion—he must apperceive the deep structure of the syntax, evaluate the surface structure as impossible of interpretation in terms of that deep structure, and yet have such strong complementary semantic responses as to deny the right of the grammatical rule to drive him into feeling that the two sentences are unintelligible.

Summarising the decoding process we could say that the reader must be prepared to:

1. Energize semantic drives from the wider context, i.e. operate from the larger meanings to the semantic detail.

2. Decode the unknown words by a hypothesis-test strategy which will relate probabilities, achieve semantic assurance, and be strong enough to deny apparent rule pressures from phonetic irregularity or from semantic and syntactic dissonance.

3. Relate to past experience both of the world and of language, creating those patterns of intonation necessary to meaning from past experience of the language.

4. Use what has been acquired through many different types of learning

from the simple associational learnings of operant conditioning, through rule abiding behaviour, to semantic problem solving.

5. Withstand dissonance at the lexical level, gaining a *total* meaning in accordance with the preceding discourse. From this meaning might be learned that the confusing item is a new word or words which mean vaguely such-and-such; or a new use of a familiar word or phrase meaning something different from the meaning of that word or phrase which he has previously learned; or a metaphorical use of the language in which the confusing item is now seen to represent something *else* symbolically.

Creative Writing

Our model of the sub-strata of language activity suggests that the most important consideration in writing will be an energized semantic intent—a feeling in experience which demands expression. It also suggests that this expression will be characterized in young children by personal and emotional content. If we are to teach five and six year olds to write, we need to take note of the self-oriented and the concrete-operational stage of their development, which places strict limitations on the extent to which they can display representational functions in their expression. In every experience that we provide for such children we need to be attentive to those features which seize personal attention whether they are logically relevant or irrelevant. The child who becomes excited about the provision of toilets on aircraft, and all the paraphernalia which accompanies such a feature, is likely to be the child who at twelve or thirteen sees the relevant features of a logical problem.

Young children attempting to control all of the intricacies of producing written language are more likely to succeed when semantic intent is clear, personal, and functional. In recalling events of high personal significance, in day-dreaming about the fulfilment of their aspirations, in displaying control of the world, or in presenting self, they will search for the accurate word and the controlling structure. As William Renehan (1977, p.124) has said in his study of the talking and writing of a sample of Australian seven-year-olds:

> 'Freedom to establish their own criteria for what is writable—not to be inhibited too much by attention to form rather than content, or by the need to puzzle about what a particular adult wants in their writing—would seem to be, if not a necessary condition, at least a most helpful circumstance for these grade 2 children in the search for what writing is about.'

Even in adult experience, if the adult is able to battle through the appalling inhibitions which have been generated by schooling, the act of writing can become the critical occasion for self-knowing. Written expression, because of its necessary deliberation and its superlative feed-back opens a potential mode of self-exploration which transcends the evanescence of speech.

If we look closely at what children want to express in writing we find two outstanding features:

1. The desire to explore self and all its meanings
2. The desire to say something memorable

Both of these desires are soon rubbed out by the pedantic concern for surface correctness in writing. Each demands a particular type of environment for written expression. The first demands a stimulating environment which is at the same time accepting and non-critical. The second demands the input of fascinating models which will be taken over by children and reproduced in creative ways.

There is something about the honesty of the very young which startles us all. It is a concern for total expression—a refusal to deny the emotional and personal honesty which abstraction and objectivity quite erroneously exclude from public language. A clinical and immaculate language may be required in science and academic life, but even for the academic, what is needed as a lifelong human resource is the opportunity to explore motive and meaning through the reflective clarity of written language. This is what the five and six year old bring to the written language engagement and we should welcome and foster it.

Taking up our second concern, that of wanting to say something memorable—to role-play as an author—it is the richness of the instructional literature that will influence and characterize the written output of the children. Once inbuilt, a literary structure becomes a resource for expression—as was illustrated in Chapters 3, 6 and 7. Let's take another example. The children have enjoyed Mercer Mayer's *What Do You Do With a Kangaroo* on a number of occasions. The repetitive structure is apparent in the following excerpt:

What do you do when you go to the bathroom
    to wash your face,
    And hanging there where your towel should be,
    brushing his teeth like he owns the place
    is an Opossum?
He says to you, "This toothpaste you use is much
    too sweet,
    and your toothbrush, I'm sorry to say,
    is all worn.
    Please get me a new one tomorrow."
What do you do?
You grab him by his skinny tail
    and carry him off, that's what you do.
    "Get out of my bathroom, you Opossum!"

The sequence goes in a predictable pattern something like this:
1. What do you do if something or other is done by an intruding animal?
2. The animal criticizes you.
3. And demands something from you.
4. You *do* something, that's what you do!
5. You give him a last reminder.
6. You get rid of him.

Here are the versions of four children from a group of thirty, all of whom produced a result which to them was memorable:

What do you do with a hairy spider
    who jumps on your head and says to you,
    "I will not move till you give me two flies and make me a
    WEB and get me a toy car so I can ride and a dolls home
    and a dolls bed and a cup of water
    and get me some pants."
What do you do?
You get him some pants BUT you
    put the pants on his head and pick
    him up and throw him out.
"Here are some pants you hairy spider!"
What do you do with a fluffy sparrow
    who sits on the bench and says to you,
    "I won't move till you give me a cup of tea
    and open the doors, it's hot in here. And why don't
    you provide fans for your guests?"

What do you do?
You give him a fan. You blow
   him right out.
"Fly away and make it snappy you fluffy sparrow!"

What do you do with a long-beaked Kiwi
   who digs in your garden and then stops and says,
"I'll never go till you clean my beak and give me a
   bath in a nice clean pool."
What do you do?
You get him by his pointed beak and throw him out,
   that's what you do.
"Get out of my garden you Kiwi!"

What do you do with a naughty hedgehog
   who jumps on your garden, eats all the flowers
   and says with his mouth full,
   "Get me more flowers and I'd like a knife and fork.
I'm very thirsty too, get me a bucket of water
and make sure it's sweet and hurry, I've been
   waiting all day."
What do you do?
You put the bucket on his head
   then he's got water!
"Get out of here you hedgehog!"

Creativity through related arts

We have seen that language is concerned with the creation of personal meanings whether through expressing semantic drives in speech and writing, or through interpreting speech or print in re-organized semantic content. Semantic content may take the form of emotions, images, ideational structures linking diverse parts of experience, physical sensations, sensory perceptions, and a variety of other non-verbal processes such as interpreting action or forming plans. Most of this content may be linguistically linked or organized but is not itself verbal. It could be said, then, that effective linguistic learning requires three conditions to be simultaneously present:

1. Strongly developed semantic content, semantic organization, and semantic drive.
2. Strong models of the surface features of related language.
3. Stimulation to relate 1. and 2. by appropriate decoding or encoding strategies.

In this chapter we have become increasingly aware of the importance of the first condition. We have found, firstly, that in the receptive processes of listening and reading, the wider and richer the non-verbal concomitants of the experience, the more personally meaningful and enjoyable is the experience likely to be. Secondly, in the expressive process of speaking and writing, the more energized the semantic drives, the more forceful, determined, precise, and creative is the encoding language likely to be. Thirdly, effective reception is likely to issue in effective related expression, and *vice versa*. Language teaching at its centre is a concern for meanings.

We have seen also that the result of energizing semantic content will be the drive towards symbolization of many kinds, displaying individual differences in personal style and current need. Some of these drives will be channelled immediately into linguistic modes of expression, others will take such non–linguistic forms as dance and music. Some of these latter may become in their turn objects for linguistic exploration. A wide range of aesthetic stimuli should be used to energize semantic content in this way, but it is not long before children *supply* such a range if proper provision is made for it in the language environment. Conversely, a lively linguistic input strong in symbolic satisfactions will produce a wide range of symbolic responses by the children both in linguistic and in non-linguistic modes. The most effective language learning takes place in an environment where the related arts are active.

Symbolic expression in other modes helps to clarify and sharpen linguistic meanings. For many children who are not primarily verbal in their modes of operating, related arts activity helps to give meaning to verbal symbolism, and those modes which combine the verbal with the non-verbal, such as drama and song, provide powerful integrating influences on the verbal development of children.

For all these reasons the effective language learning environment will be both one in which the language arts themselves flow naturally one into the other, and also one in which related arts of many kinds will flourish. It will be an environment of aesthetic excitement and satisfaction.

Often the initial stimulus will come from the literature and generate the wider activities in un-structured play, visual art of many kinds, dramatic activities, construction, dance and music. In Chapter 7 we noted how these activities flowered in the experimental classrooms quite naturally without a self-conscious effort to produce them. We now have some clear reasons why this should have been the case. Firstly, the provision of a rich literature successfully activated semantic drives in the children, drives towards the expression of meanings and insights and feelings, and these sought expression in a variety of ways. Secondly, the provision of effective procedures for the development of basic strategies which redirect language to meaning, provided proper links between surface language and semantic content and resulted in an upsurge of symbolic activity. We can therefore say with further confidence that related language and arts belong centrally in the literacy environment.

The experiences which most effectively deepen and enrich meaning include the exploration of first-hand sensory experience (the special domain of language-experience techniques), and the enjoyment of literature and the related arts (the domain of shared-book-experience). Language-learning approaches its optimum efficiency under the stimulus-to-meaning of exploring the sensory world, on the one hand, or of exploring the inner world which finds its manifold embodiments in the arts, on the other. The fact that many of these art forms are non-verbal like painting, detracts in no way from their efficiency in creating *meanings*—they are all forms of symbolization. Non-verbal expression is an integral part of the language programme.

For a variety of reasons modern schooling has tended to concentrate on the outer world of sensory experience. However, it would probably be true to say that exploration of the inner world of emotion, intention, and self-awareness has a prior and more urgent demand on our attention. Certainly it is a more difficult world to communicate about and makes special demands on language quite different from the relatively simple and objective task of labelling the outside world of the senses and describing its relationships. It is particularly in dealing with the inner world, subjective and devoid of objects as it is, that we are forced into the use of symbols which are complex in their function such as analogy and metaphor. Stories, poems and songs are usually complex symbolizations of inner concerns which have no clear and objective representation in a labelling or categorizing sense. They are usually concerned with processes rather than with things, with the dynamic rather than the static, and with the connotative rather than the denotative. They are concerned with a private and unverifiable awareness attempting to make itself public.

The symbols of art whether linguistic or non-linguistic embody meanings of that closed inner world which each of us shares directly with no other—they mediate a sense of what it is to be human, and allow us some entry into the experience of others. To do so they clothe their meanings in the concrete forms or images of the outside world by metaphorical devices which load such forms and images with special meanings which they do not have in themselves. Through imagination they imbue the structures of the outside world with foreign significances from within—the concrete images become vehicles for a cargo which could otherwise not be moved out into the public marketplace.

We have a way in our society of denigrating fantasy and the imagination as being something unreal, and we even ask young children to make the distinction between true and false, real and unreal, in such a way as to suggest that symbolic representations of inner experience are not to be taken seriously. The mistake being made is a further instance of overlooking semantic content as if what was on the *surface* of the language was what was being represented. When applied to the meanings it embodies, fantasy is usually more true and accurate than any attempt to represent the same inner reality in clinical and quasi-scientific terms.[3] One of the primary linguistic skills entails the ability to interpret symbols of the imagination in such a way as to accurately perceive the reality being represented. Furthermore, once mastered, such a skill provides rewards of a very special kind, deeply satisfying in emotional and personal terms.

One of the differences between authentic children's literature and the synthetic imitations of many instructional 'readers' lies in the nature and quality of the accompanying art. Children's books at their best present a combined symbolism in which the pictorial art transcends mere illustration to become an integral part of the symbolic message. In a programme that exploits the strength of literature and other arts the children soon respond to the deep satisfaction and aesthetic stimulation and enter into creative involvement of a remarkable kind expressed not only linguistically but in the whole range of art forms. This wide-ranging experience in creating and interpreting symbolic images generates powerful motivations towards literacy.

The related language and arts programme

We can see now the full force of the 'related' as we have used it in the 'related arts programme'. Children have deep preoccupations with human themes and problems—with their exploration of feeling and self—which form persistent patterns of interest and concern. Literature and other forms of art tend to focus and organize these patterns to form pervasive and persistent interests in surface behaviour—especially in play, in language development, and in the arts. These clusters of related concern associated with inner awareness of self and human significance generate tremendous energies towards expression of every kind. They constitute a power-house of motivation and a virtually inexhaustible reservoir of reinforcement or reward. We could call these foci of inner concern 'developmental themes' to distinguish them from the often superficial topics on which we base 'centres of interest'. 'Who Am I?' or 'Monsters Real and Imaginary' are verbal tags for centres of deep preoccupation of a rather different kind from 'The Seasons' or 'People Who Help Us'. This is not to say that superficially structured centres of interest have no value or interest, but rather to point additionally to deeper, more permanent and more powerfully fuelled areas of motivation (Holdaway 1972, pp.55–58).

Once the language programme and the skills of literacy have begun to fulfil these deep and universal human purposes, children are likely to be hooked in a way that makes it quite unnecessary to fool them with false motivations extrinsic to the actual activities of literacy. One of the saddest things about schooling has been our loss of faith in the possibility of honest and intrinsic motivation—we fool children with workbooks covered in monkeys or fairies holding up vowels walking hand in hand or waving wands over magic 'E's'. We so deeply believe that the pill of learning will be nasty that we cover it with garishly coloured and thinly applied lolly. Such deceit is not only inefficient in sustaining literacy learning, it is also both unnecessary and insulting to the human intentions and abilities of ordinary children. If we can connect with the real expressive needs of children, there is no need for jelly beans or lolly on the pill—*there is no pill*. Children need the sustenance of a healthy diet sustaining the growth of self and delight in the world. The extrinsic rewards with which we have tried to make literacy palatable embody a great lie to children about the purposes of the undertaking. Why provide jelly beans when the deep satisfactions of story and art can become *for any child* as rewarding as the comforts of a secure home?

Developmental themes

Once children have begun to be stimulated by a rich literary input through the techniques of shared-book-experience, certain persistent preoccupations tend to surface. New stories, poems, and songs—including their own innovations or variations on a theme—may sustain the interest for many weeks or months. For instance, the children's developing sense of humour, stimulated by the wealth of stories about stupidity, may generate an interest in 'What's Sensible'; songs such as 'Old MacDonald's Farm' or 'I Had a Pig and the Pig Pleased Me' may begin an interest in 'Sounds of Living'; or books about friendships may stir a deep concern for 'What's a Friend'. Each such preoccupation has generated many children's stories, poems and songs, which may be used as basic instructional material, and finally form a rich resource for personal expression and innovation through writing, drama, painting, construction, dance, and so on.

An important word here is 'preoccupation' which suggests an interest which is both deeply energized with the semantic content of experience and generates persistent attempts at self-expression. Children are seldom given the opportunity to rework an idea again and again until they get it right, as the true artist tends to do. It is surprising what happens when they are given this opportunity or are actively encouraged to persist. Elwyn Richardson (1964) in his fascinating study of a developmental expressive environment, *In the Early World*, documented startling growth in the artistic expression of children who were encouraged to rework embryonic ideas. Children should be encouraged to return to a painting for several days in succession, reworking it with a variety of media or techniques; or to return to a poem or story they are writing until they have captured something of the inner reality which they have been trying to express.[4] Sometimes, of course, they will need to begin again or come back after several days or in a different art form to the idea that is itching inside them. The long time-sweep of a developmental theme often provides both the motivation and the opportunity for such intricately reworked acts of symbolization.

Corporate art forms

A literature-fed preoccupation sustained by the familiarity of favourite stories, poems, and songs, leads naturally into corporate art. Dramatization may be a delight for very young children when the loved language has become a part of inner experience. Masks of many varieties from the simple, flat, hand-held variety to the more elaborate constructions built around cartons or modelled from *papier mache*, form an important mode of symbolization in themselves, and add greatly to the satisfaction of group drama. Puppets and the currently popular muppets provide a further enrichment to the dramatic experience. After a time children may be encouraged to create their own dramatizations, either spontaneously or as an extension of the innovation technique in which a creative blending of familiar structures with unique expression provide security for young playwrights.

Murals which are constructed over the course of several weeks may provide an opportunity for every child to contribute something to a performance of growing richness and textural excitement.[5] The children should first prepare a very simple background which may be embellished by smaller items created by groups or individuals. The addition of a lively text, written as a corporate venture by the class, keeps the importance of print in focus and provides additional material for reading and models for writing.

Chant, song, and dance, particularly in combination with other dramatic modes, satisfy very primitive needs for expression and social bonding. The common festivals of the year often provide a creative focus and have normally found some form of traditional expression which may be taken up and embellished. Festivals can be specially created to celebrate the awareness-of-being arising from developmental themes, and such festivals may be ideal occasions for involving other classes or visitors. 'Being Seven', 'Happiness is . . .', 'Modern initiation', 'Spring is Here', and 'Now We Can Read' are festival topics which have been successfully mounted. The tapes accompanying Bill Martin's *Sounds of a Pow Wow* and *Sounds After Dark* are rich in ideas for chant, song, and corporate verse.

9
Developmental Learning and Diagnostic Teaching

The consideration of children experiencing difficulty has been left to this point because the last chapter was so important from their point of view. Usually we are prepared to provide or allow an active related-arts programme for children making normal or better than average learning. But we feel that we must concentrate on more basic things for the slower children. Considering the basic nature of semantic questions in the learning of literacy, we can now see why it is necessary to provide a relevant and meaning-centred programme for the slower children. *In literacy-learning, basic equals meaningful.*

To state the obvious: learners are different and so, whatever the programme, in school learning we will always have an advanced group and a tail. What are the most striking implications of this feature of school learning? Firstly, the notion of rank which plays no part in developmental learning presents us with the most difficult problem in applying the developmental model. Competition and the constant comparison of learners feeds positive reinforcement to the advanced group and various forms of punitive feedback to the slow group, the very ones who are most in need of extrinsic reinforcement to get their own intrinsic reward systems into operation. There is simply no escape from the conclusion that an efficient early learning environment needs to be scrupulously non-competitive. There is no way in which competition, as distinct from emulation and modelling, can be retained in the system without producing a large and expensive remedial group, many of whom will not even be able to profit from the remedial intervention. What we need is a preventive system which locates children experiencing difficulty very early before accumulating failure disorders their natural learning.

The Preventive Environment

In every way the environment that we have described for normal learning would seem also to be the environment in which preventive measures may best be taken, except that it will be even more carefully developmental, non-competitive, and semantically oriented. Preventive measures entail four requirements which should in any case be present for all children:

1. Sensitive observation Monitoring of an individual and longitudinal kind which produces appropriate data and allows us to distinguish between healthy approximation and unproductive confusions.

2. Timely intervention   Most of the intervention should be a natural part of normal teaching—it should seldom require isolated one-to-one teaching, although there will be cases where this is necessary. The principles of diagnostic teaching are important here.

3. Establishing self-regulation in the learner   It will be clear from our earlier considerations that the primary objective of intervention must be to induce or restore self-regulative processes in the learner as rapidly as possible, and the main purpose of diagnosis, therefore, will be to determine how this may best be done.

4. Multi-disciplinary team work   Most early difficulties will involve inhibiting factors such as hearing loss or emotional instability which are not specific to language development. In such matters we need the help of professional expertise beyond the competence of the trained teacher, and we should use it *early* rather than wait until failure is aggravated by secondary neurosis. Let's take these matters one at a time:

Sensitive observation

The first requirement of sensitive observation is that we know what we are looking for. For this reason it is important that we have some coherent notion of what healthy development in literacy tasks really looks like. It is characteristic of developmental tasks that they display behaviour appropriate to relatively coherent stages, and that behaviour appropriate to one stage may be superseded and be inappropriate at another. Most tests, especially those of the standardized kind, do not take these differences into account, and hence provide us with highly misleading information about normal progress. For instance, what constitutes 'good reading' at one stage may be very different from what should be regarded as 'good reading' at another (Holdaway, 1974). If we take a single measure like fluency in oral reading we will find startling differences among children making healthy progress at different stages. At the emergent-reading stage of 'reading-like behaviour', oral performance is fast, fluent, and natural—but highly inaccurate at a verbal level. In early reading, fluency has necessarily been sacrificed to meticulous word-by-word checking characterized by pointing either with the finger or the voice. At the stage of fluency when most perceptual processing has become thoroughly automatic, oral reading is again fluent and natural if somewhat less smooth than in speech. In the stage of consolidation where the speed of silent reading rapidly surpasses the speed of speech, a request for oral reading is likely to produce bumbling and frustrating confusions which do not occur in silent reading, or an almost incoherent gabble which tries to keep pace with the mental operations of maturing silent reading. Finally, as flexibility develops and the reader learns the special skill of ranging the eye before the voice in audience reading, the oral performance again becomes fluent and pleasing for the listener. Each of these fluctuations is thoroughly normal and children should be confirmed in the behaviour that is appropriate to the stage.

Our best policy is to monitor actual behaviour as the child carries out the task in a meaningful situation—such as normal reading or writing within the programme—and to compare such observations with those taken *for the same child* at some previous time. Only then can we make judgements which are valid for that child. The critical distinction between healthy approximation towards final goals and debilitating confusions in processing can be made only on a longitudinal basis. It is vital that we keep records of the actual behaviour of children from time to time and that we compare these in deciding upon the need for intervention and the nature of the intervention. Exactly the same 'error' made by different children may represent healthy progress for one at an early stage of development and dangerous confusion for another at a later stage.

In our monitoring we need to be taking note of the behaviours most important to healthy development. For instance, if self-correction or self-monitoring is as vital to success in reading as our previous analysis has tended to show, we ought to be monitoring how well children are monitoring *their own performance*, and if use of a coherent strategy for relating cues characterizes success in early reading, then we ought to have some way of determining whether or not a child is using such a strategy. If the attempt to spell words by approximating to regular phonetic patterns is a sign of healthy development in the production of written language at an early stage, we need something better than error count to properly appraise the behaviour.

We have earlier introduced techniques for monitoring early literacy behaviour and will not repeat the analysis here. However, a preventive programme will be characterized by documented, longitudinal records of behaviour rather than by test results or by 'readers done'. Where the pressure of time is an impediment to keeping such records we will be particularly careful to maintain a programme of observation for slow-developing children. These records should begin at the emergent stage in the observation of 'reading-like' and 'writing-like' behaviour. (Sometimes the use of a tape-recorder may facilitate the gathering of reading records.)

As teachers we are concerned with *educational* diagnosis, and a causal or etiological explanation of failure, where it can be made, is not an excuse for educational failure but a challenge to find specifically educational solutions. More often than not the most debilitating cause of failure is the awareness of previous failure. Surprisingly, this is a relatively simple problem to solve educationally—it entails determining the level of success and adjusting the educational tasks accordingly—yet of all educational causes this is the one we least often control.

School tends to be an agency through which children find out very rapidly how they rank. This may be a useful service at the end of an educational process but it has no place in the infant room. Literacy should be regarded like oracy as a necessary human skill, and any influence which seriously vitiates the rights of individual people to become literate should be removed. The most powerful influence of this kind is the amplified feedback of failure-awareness, and it falls on those who will be most damaged educationally by it. It may be almost impossible for a school to avoid creating non-learners by this, the most direct method available, but if they are to succeed as educational agencies they must make the control of such educationally destructive forces a first priority.

In her *Diagnostic Survey* Marie Clay (1972b) suggests a systematic assessment of all children as they turn six years of age. The survey itself, currently in revision and due for republication in 1979, will be found an invaluable guide to preventive intervention in the early years of schooling.

Timely intervention

Diagnostic teaching entails a day-by-day and sometimes moment-by-moment adjustment of teaching strategy in response to sensitive observation. Much of this observation occurs through the interpretation of children's in-programme behaviour rather than through special monitoring or testing procedures. The most important adjustments will be concerned with helping individual children to select tasks at a level of success, or with actually selecting and introducing tasks of an appropriate level, bearing in mind all those devices of task control that we have at our disposal. (See pp.130–132).

We tend to think that any form of preventive or remedial action must take the form of individual tuition. The aim, however, is to achieve individual *learning* and this will often be best achieved through sensitive modifications within the programme either with groups displaying needs which can be met in similar activities or by adjusting individual questioning and discussion in handling the group. A balanced programme will also provide opportunities for natural individual interaction without withdrawal or special provisions which isolate the learner.

A critical problem of intervention arises when we 'hear' oral reading or 'help' children with spelling. The temptation is to intervene too soon, too often, too negatively. Our aim should be to maintain or re-establish healthy operation, rather than to give instruction or usurp the child's own responsibility to understand, correct, and learn from his own errors. Blocks in reading can best be overcome by questions such as, 'What do you think the problem is?' or 'Let's start from the beginning of the sentence,' or 'What do you think might be happening?' If it is clear what cues the child is overlooking, a gentle question to bring those cues to attention is preferable to correction or heavy-handed advice. If a child is puzzling over the spelling of a word which he wants *you* to spell, inducement to suggest the spelling himself or the next letter and the next is likely to be more profitable than always to write the word. Sometimes you will be able to use your knowledge of irregular or rare spellings to make a comment or comparison—'It's like such-and-such'—or having provided the irregular portion allowing the child to complete the spelling.—'The difficult part is this . . . now see if you can get the other letters.'

In certain cases it will be necessary to provide individual tuition on a short or long term basis. Wherever possible this should occur as naturally as possible in the developmentally organized parts of the programme, or in a brief session that follows, and it should provide clarification or repetition of something presented to a group. Usually the type of concern which seems to demand individual tuition will be discussed with more experienced members of staff and where necessary will entail consultation with professionals in other disciplines.

Establishing self-regulation in the learner

There is no better system to control the complexities and intricacies of each person's learning than *that person's own system* operating with genuine motivation and self-determination within reach of humane and informed help. There is no way in which any other person, however skilled, can take better control of all the factors involved simultaneously in the processes of reading or of writing than the user himself. Sometimes we are able to control one or two of the factors externally, but when we do we should be careful to do so in such a way as to allow the learner scope to control all of the others. For instance, a child often needs to choose his own pace in carrying out a guided task, or pause for moments of deliberation in finding out how our advice fits into the totality of what he is doing in word-solving or in spelling.

The first objective of observation and diagnosis, then, is to determine in what way the learner can be helped to take over control of his own processing. The question should be asked, 'In what way does this child misconstrue the nature of the task?' The answer will normally be displayed clearly in actual performance of reading and writing better than through the use of a test battery. Sometimes, especially with older children, a gently phrased direct question to the child may help to display confusions about process—'What can you do to find out what this word is?' or, after a block, 'What are you trying to work out?'

As we proceed we will study some of the typical ways in which children misconstrue literacy tasks and consider some ways of restoring sound central functioning. However, our objective must always be to make the *total* task intelligible to the child, to induce self-regulation and self-correction, and to help the child believe in his own ability to operate independently. This can be done by presenting tasks at an appropriate level of difficulty—and this is always possible within the developmental model (which demonstrates healthy stages of independent operation with books and print from infancy on). Through the Cloze procedure, problem-solving tasks may be surrounded by contextual support to the point where any child *who can talk* can solve the problem. It is then a matter of increasing the challenge by reducing the amount of oral support from the context and increasing the difficulty of the word-problems to be solved. A similar principle applies in spelling, where difficulty can be controlled by the nature of the gap-filling task required of the learner.

Multi-disciplinary team-work

We have seen that linguistic behaviour involves the whole human organism in complex activity of diverse kinds and may be impeded by a wide variety of conditions not specific to literacy learning. Every infant school should make early use of diagnostic and guidance services in an attempt to minimize initial impediments to learning. Of course, the human learner often displays remarkable ability in compensating for inhibiting factors, and we should not *expect* failure as a result of deficits. The most helpful thing to any learner is the belief by his teacher that he can learn.

If we find that a child is not making progress when considered in terms of *his own* longitudinal record, or is displaying obvious confusion despite our efforts to help him within the programme and in those limited opportunities we have for individual help, then team work *within* the school is called for. Often this will lead to calling upon services lying outside the school, particularly if there is any suspicion that inhibiting factors of a non-linguistic kind may be responsible for difficulties. Residual difficulties that a child displays in his use of oral language—in speech or in listening—will often point to the sort of difficulties which may arise in reading and writing. All such children should be considered 'at risk' as soon as their oral language problem has been identified, and every attempt should be made *very early*—in the first or early in the second year of schooling—to determine the nature of the inhibiting factors, and how best they can be overcome.

A model for functional diagnosis

We are not really concerned in this enquiry with methods of remedial teaching nor with the intricacies of diagnosis as they concern children with such deficits as would interfere with their mastery of *other* developmental tasks such as speaking or achieving social and emotional stability. We are concerned with avoiding those *unnecessary* failures which spring from educational causes. In this respect there have been a number of considerations arising in the course of our enquiry which impinge directly upon our current concerns. Among these are the need for self-regulation in the operations of literacy, the largely automatic way in which perceptual processes must operate, and the significance of the 'tension line' in maintaining fatigue-free operation (Chap. 5, pp.96–97). In an important sense these matters are so closely related as to be interdependent.

Let us see if we can bring them together and display this interrelatedness by constructing a model for perceptual control in reading and writing. This model may then be useful as a diagnostic tool in attempting to understand basic ways in which processing breaks down. Looking first at reading, we can see that in healthy perceptual processing the great majority of responses must occur at an automatic or sub-conscious level, but that a small number of critical perceptual decisions are made quite consciously and deliberately. We can refer to that point at which perceptions become consciously controlled as a *threshold* separating subconscious from deliberate attention. In healthy reading this threshold will tend to be high, allowing the majority of perceptions to be handled by automatic processes. However, if it remains high when a problem arises or when an error has been made, then the resultant meanings arising from inaccurate reading will be distorted. On the other hand, in a healthy reader what occurs at those moments when perceptual deliberation is required is that the threshold lowers and conscious attention is directed onto the problem details as if a searchlight had been thrown on them. What is it that causes the threshold to lower at just those crucial times? We remember that it is the feedback processes of confirmation, also operating automatically, which control this critical vigilance and allow the conscious mind freedom from perceptual concern for most of the time. It is only when confirmation processes are working smoothly that proper conscious attention can be given to understanding what is being read. Furthermore, active creation of developing meaning provides much of the critical feedback upon which confirmation is based, and for this reason perceptual operations cannot be properly controlled when meaning is lost or distorted. Confirmation is not completed when incompatibilities arise in the developing meaning, and this feedback, signalling a problem, lowers the threshold at the precise points where greater attention or deliberation is needed. The process will not be allowed to continue until the problem has been resolved and confirmation has finally been achieved. It is in this feedback operation that a necessary self-correction may take place, triggered by meaning and aided by greatly increased attention to visual detail *at that point.*

We could represent the process of reading as fundamentally a drive towards adequate and accurate meanings; the achievement of these meanings is made possible by a high and sensitive threshold controlled by confirmation and capable of lowering in a split second to allow deliberate study of visual detail.

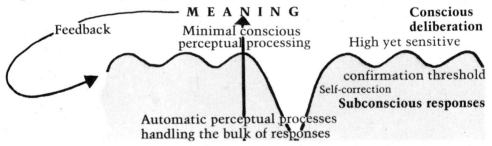

This diagram may be read as a graph, with the passage of time displayed horizontally, and the degree of conscious attention displayed vertically. The automatic and subconscious activities are placed at the foot of the diagram, and the fully conscious and deliberate activities at the top.

A further vital factor needs to be added to this model—that of prediction. The amount of detail requiring close attention either consciously or subconsciously is determined by how efficiently predictive processes operate—if strong predictions are made on the basis of syntactic and semantic expectations, less visual detail is required to achieve accurate recognitions. The amount of energy drawn off for perceptual processing is therefore greatly reduced by active prediction.

The risk entailed in predicting or guessing is covered by the processes of confirmation, and when the whole combined operation is in balance, we achieve an accurate meaning very efficiently and *safely* with a minimum expenditure of energy on perceptual tasks. We are thus able to direct conscious energy to comprehending meanings, and in doing so provide richer data to prediction (thus increasing efficiency) and to confirmation (thus increasing accuracy and maintaining a high threshold between automatic and conscious processing). We could built these features into our model in the following way:

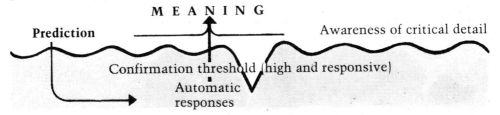

M E A N I N G

Prediction ——————— Awareness of critical detail

Confirmation threshold (high and responsive)

Automatic responses

The confirmation threshold is controlled by feedback of two kinds—the semantic coherence, or lack of it, arising from developing meanings, and expectations of visual detail arising from predictions.

An example of an actual piece of reading behaviour may help to clarify the model. Here is the record of a proficient seven-year-old reader handling a passage at the right level of difficulty.

Where the reader has mis-read, the substituted word has been printed above the textual word. Deleted substitutions mean that the error or miscue was self-corrected. Bars marked in the text represent a pause for deliberation.

Making a/mask can be fun. Do it this way. Get a
~~pisce~~   ~~you~~
large paper bag and hold it in front of your face.
~~Make~~
Mark the places for your eyes, nose and/mouth.
                the
Lay the bag on a table, and cut holes the/right

shape. When it is/finished the mask will fit right

over your head.

The miscue 'piece' was probably a rapid prediction based on the fact that 'large' and 'piece' are often paired in this way in speech, together with observation of the initial 'p'. The self-correction may have stemmed either from observation of the unexpected second 'p' (or some other letter expectation which was not fulfilled) or from the syntactic and semantic impossibility arising as he recognized 'bag' and before he articulated it. Of course, both observations may have been involved in recognizing the miscue. His rapidly corrected miscue of 'you' for 'your' could be accounted for in a similar way. The miscue 'Make' for 'Mark' has obvious featural causes amplified by its being the first word in the sentence and therefore having no clear syntactic or semantic pre-organization. Since the correction was almost instantaneous, it is likely that the observation of the 'r' contradicted the prediction of 'make' with a normal long 'a' not marked by 'r'. The miscue 'the' for 'a' is properly tolerable syntactically and semantically, and is therefore not noticed even though the letter match is so poor.

The five pauses to process problems, together with the conscious deliberation given to the three self-corrections, are in nice relationship to the large body of words processed automatically—8:48. This meant that most of the conscious attention could be directed towards comprehension, and that clear meanings provided strong predictive pressures for solution of such words as 'mouth', 'shape', and 'finished', and sensitive feedback for the self-corrections. Finally, active confirmation provided security throughout the task, moment-by-moment reinforcement, and assurance of success. The reader was in no way fatigued and could proceed in this manner for long periods.

We could add these feedback features to our model in the following way:

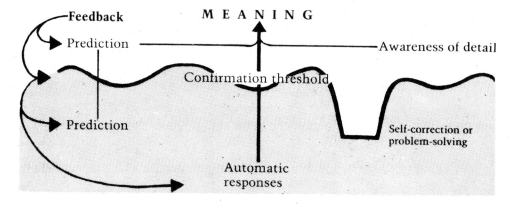

It is much more difficult for the *learner* to achieve this balanced functioning than it is for the mature reader who has autonomized most of his functioning.[1] The need to give constant conscious attention to visual detail threatens the whole process at every point—inadequate energy and 'mental room' for developing meanings not only undermine the purposes of reading but also greatly diminish prediction and starve confirmation processes of vital information. The threshold is likely to be dangerously low in order to allow deliberate processing of visual information. Reinforcement is likely to be limited, especially moment-by-moment, and the young reader becomes fatigued because there is not proper rhythm between challenge and relaxation. The 'tension line' climbs towards anxiety instead of rhythmically falling every second or two.

This set of insights explains why in so many different pieces of research, covering reading at all stages during learning, it has been found that the appropriate instructional level approximates to one error in twenty running words. The support of the nineteen automatically or easily recognized words is required to achieve meaning, sustain prediction, control self-correction, and reduce fatigue and anxiety. All the support of these combined processes can then be brought to bear on the one problem. When the level of error rises much above the 1:20 level each of these processes, and their integrity as a system, is threatened. Furthermore, the difficulty involved in solving each of the increased number of problems escalates; the distribution of available energy between comprehension and word-solving shifts at the expense of energy for comprehending; and fatigue is greatly increased. As meaning is lost, errors are likely to come in clusters and lack semantic coherence, giving the impression of much greater ineptitude or carelessness than is actually the case. The same child reading material at an *appropriate level* is likely to get the combined systems operating and make semantically coherent or 'sensible' errors.

Reading at an inappropriate level

We could illustrate reading at an inappropriate level by a further example.
Words which have been ringed were omitted in the reading. Insertions, or
words read that were not in the text, have been shown with a caret.

> Making a/mask can be fun. Do it this/way. Get a
> large (paper) bag and/hold it in/front (of) your/face.
> Mark the/places for your/eyes,/nose and/mouth.
> Lay the bag on a/table, and cut/holes the/right
> shape. When it is/finished the/mask will fit/right
>
> over your/head.

The failure on 'mask' deprives the reader of clear predictive information
which may have been all that was required to solve 'large' and 'paper'. We then
get an error cluster in line two indicating a loss of coherence. Sense begins to
return even with the miscues at 'Make the place for your eyes, nose and . . .'
and supports the self-correction of 'month'. Coherence continues until the next
error cluster where the insertion of 'in' provided an inappropriate syntactic cue
for 'right', which is artificially separated from its referant, 'shape', on the new
line. However, the miscue 'ring' has *syntactic* coherence with 'holes in the
. . .' Sufficient comprehension has been achieved from the bits and pieces
about cutting a bag on a table to make eyes, etc. to allow the reader to process
'mask' in the last line even though it had been missed in the first line.

Deliberative pauses and self-corrections total twenty—a ratio of 20:36. Yet
it is clear that this child can use healthy strategies and in material only slightly
less difficult would put the whole thing together and the error rate would fall to
an appropriate one-in-twenty. It is clear that a cyclic breakdown in the process
has occurred largely because the threshold between conscious and sub-
conscious attention to detail is too low and meaning has been starved of
attention, with the attendant losses in prediction and confirmation. We could
model this reading by a healthy reader placed on material at an inappropriate
level as follows.[2]

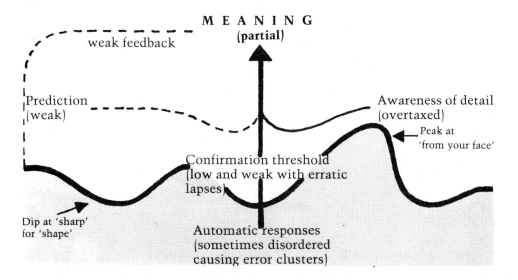

The paradox which is beginning to become clear is that too much *conscious* attention to detail leads to inaccuracy and deprives the reader of those *proper* moments of deliberative analysis of detail at well spaced critical points in the process. A high proportion of automatic responses is required to properly identify for a small proportion of critical solutions. And the suspicion is that these critical solutions, undertaken successfully with refreshed faculties and immediately rewarded by active confirmation, are the situations from which the reader *learns*. Our first reader is likely to remember 'paper' in future after self-correcting his 'piece' and making a *reinforced* observation of detail. Our second reader is likely to have learned little even from the single self-correction of 'month' to 'mouth' because intrinsic reinforcement was limited and confused.

One way of achieving a proper balance between conscious and automatic responses in the early stages of reading is through the processing of favourite books where a large proportion of the language is familiar but has not been memorized word-by-word. When decoding has been successfully accomplished the familiarity of the language helps to confirm—it sounds right. Oral Cloze procedures also have this effect of relaxing faculties so that they can turn on with powerful attention to detail at spaced intervals. This would seem to support the use of the techniques of shared-book-experience, especially for children experiencing difficulty or unable to get the integrated functions of reading operating.

Faulty processing
The under-predictive reader

When we observe the failing efforts of learning readers in terms of the model we have created, we find a number of characteristic confusions in processing. Most commonly we find the slow, deliberative puzzling of word-by-word, or letter-by-letter attention, which overloads short-term memory, crowds meaning out of conscious awareness, and raises tension to an intolerable level. Such reading is deeply fatiguing and soon cuts the reader off from proper use of the faculties and skills he has at his disposal.—it is both pointless and punitive. It is usually characterized by mindlessly flat intonation with extreme voice pointing of words. Often, this 'reading' is highly phonic with patches of accurate word-calling, but because meaning is not achieved, it cannot be called *reading* in any real sense. We could represent such 'reading' in the following way:

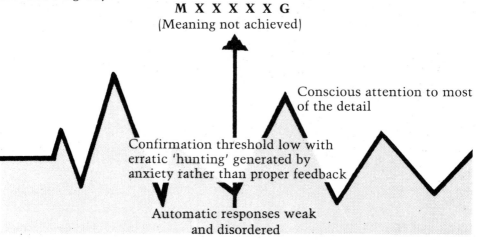

M X X X X G
(Meaning not achieved)

Conscious attention to most of the detail

Confirmation threshold low with erratic 'hunting' generated by anxiety rather than proper feedback

Automatic responses weak and disordered

Both prediction and feedback are almost absent from this sort of 'reading'. Attempts to 'sound-out' may be the main strategy and it may not be ineptitude in this skill which produces the failure—rather that the use of phonics is not sustained and shaped by prediction nor rewarded by confirmation. A single line of this reading in its extreme form will be adequate to recognize it as a common type. An underline means that those words were repeated.

> mack
> maake   mad   his
> mak   mask   by funny Did the w-ay
> Making/a mask/can/be/fun. Do/ it/this/way.

Of course, no child should be allowed to read at such a failing level, but it may still often be seen. However, even the following example displays hopelessly failing processing of the same kind:

> L-ay   ba-g   t-a-b-le   c-ut hols   rigged chap
> /Lay the/bag /on a/table,/and/cut/holes the/right /shape.

From an operational point of view we could diagnose this sort of reading as *under-predictive*.[3] Although no aspect of healthy reading is functioning properly, the spiral downwards into defeat begins in the failure to predict. For such readers our first act of diagnostic teaching will be to induce prediction. We have a number of techniques within normal programmes and suitable for individual instruction if that is required—as it very well may be in these cases:

> Oral Cloze procedures in shared-book-experience.
> Reading favourite and familiar stories, poems, and songs.
> Reading own experience stories in language-experience.
> Read-along experiences with the listening post.
> Reading material with very strong structural support for prediction.
> Development of an 'organic' personal sight vocabulary (Ashton-Warner).

Our intervention during the oral reading of the under-predictive reader would largely involve questions inducing the development of meaning and a predictive feeling, such as 'What do you think is happening?' We may also recall the meaning of the last sentence and focus this on the sentence in hand. We may provide a re-run from the beginning of the sentence or suggest that strategy.

The over-predictive reader   A second common operational confusion arises when children fail to develop appropriate strategies during the early reading stage for dealing with the visual aspects of the task. They rely more and more heavily on their oral language resources and create their own text from the barest minimum of visual information. Their reading is fast and fluent but highly inaccurate. They produce real words in schematic sentence forms with many omissions and insertions, as in the following example.[4]

> man   a lot of you know the   Go
> Making a mask can be fun. Do it   this way. Get a

> long please big man. Hdd on for
> large paper bag and hold it in front of your face.

From the point of view of operational diagnosis, the over-predictive reader fails to carry out proper confirmation, especially in terms of matching words or observing letter detail. Most of the perceptual activity is automatic and the threshold is high and static—there is no feedback to produce a conscious visual search at critical moments. The meanings that are achieved tend to be superficial, often contradictory, and seldom those of the author. We could represent this faulty processing as follows:

meaning

(not the author's)

Confirmation threshold high, static and insensitive

Prediction
largely automatic

Automatic
responses

Both feedback and conscious attention to detail are virtually absent. Such readers are often told that they are careless and should watch the words, but they may not even have developed a clear concept of what a word really is. In the early stages they may also be very confused directionally. An increase in anxiety about 'being careful' is more likely to result in new distortions being imported into the endeavour rather than to rectify the confused processing.

Our intervention in cases of this kind should attempt to induce active confirming. When attention to detail begins to provide immediate reinforcement as it does in the confirming mode, the visual features of print are likely to become increasingly significant. This can be readily achieved in the sound-to-letter confirmation during word-solving in the introduction of a new story which has been described fully in Chapter 6. Pointing and masking procedures are needed and such children should be asked to 'read with your fingers'. Every inducement should be made to interest these children in *producing* written language. They are likely to have more than usual difficulty in mastering spelling patterns and for this reason need to be encouraged to attempt their own approximations and thus give attention to the way print works at the level of detail. Their proper entry into literacy may be through writing rather than through reading. Their needs may also be met within normal aspects of a balanced programme by emphasizing the confirming aspects of the process.

In helping the over-predictive reader during individual oral reading our questions should induce confirmation from detail. We may use such questions as 'If this word is ———, how do you think it would end?' or 'Let's listen to that word. What letter would you expect to see in the middle . . . after the x . . . before the -ing?' We can read back exactly what the child has just read, perhaps pointing as we do so, and invite self-correction. When meanings become twisted, as they often do for these children, we can ask 'Does that seem sensible to you?' or 'That's a little surprising isn't it?'—all, of course, in a supportive and non-critical tone. Our aim is to induce immediate appropriate action, and such action will be inhibited by any suggestion of irritation.

Dependence and the 'performance syndrome'   Children readily get the idea that reading is a performance task like talking, rather than a receptive, thinking task like listening. This comes about because the majority of their early reading is performed orally for someone else who listens, corrects, and decides whether or not the reading is making sense. When children become confused by this performance situation their self-regulative abilities lie dormant and they fail to develop either a strong demand for meaning or an adequate self-corrective strategy. When they make a proposal for a word or come across a difficulty, they look up questioningly for help. It is as though they cannot operate unless they are plugged in to an external computer which does their correcting and problem-solving for them. In consequence they do little or no reading unless asked to do so by someone who will act as the confirming computer, and are therefore cut off from the opportunity to learn to read by reading.

Children who are tricked into this misconception of the nature of reading—and there are many of them—fail to develop the most intricate part of the reading process, i.e. the feedback or confirmation system. They are often highly motivated by extrinsic purposes of pleasing others—they are conscientious, dependent, often puzzled, and ultimately in deep trouble. We could represent this very dependent type of reading in the following way:

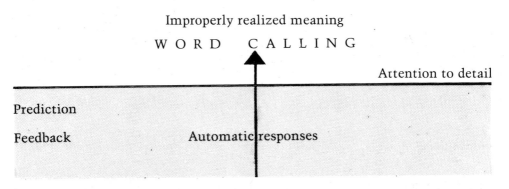

Feedback and prediction when they occur are automatic and based more on expected sequences than on meaning, and the task results in word calling—in the early stages, with intelligent children, this is often of a very accurate kind.

This is very much an 'at risk' condition because it can lead highly competent children to a serious breakdown in literacy learning later in their schooling. Because many of them *appear* to be functioning well in the infant school, they are passed on unnoticed into almost inevitable failure at a later stage. All we have said earlier about techniques for inducing self-regulative behaviour should be brought to bear early in helping these dependent, and often conscientious and competent children, towards sound central functioning.

Responding to individual confusions

There are many other patterns of confused operating which could be described using this model, but it is a model of the over-simplifying kind and more mechanical than any model we have previously discussed. Nothing can take the place of close observation of individual reading-behaviour and the use of initiative in inducing children into healthy functioning. We need to determine how each child is confusing the task—what he thinks he is supposed to be doing in relationship to what he is actually doing and in relationship to what healthy functioning entails.

One of the most difficult distinctions to make is that between healthy approximations in normal development, and faulty processing which may be potentially dangerous. This distinction can be accurately made on an individual basis only when earlier behaviour is compared with current behaviour. During the early stages confusions become damaging only if they persist or set off a spiral into cyclic failure. For instance, it is natural for children to rely heavily on their oral language patterns as they begin to relate cues in reading, but if this persists for long to the exclusion of visual processing or begins to show the characteristics of what we have called over-predictive reading, some appropriate intervention is called for. In a preventive programme backed by longtitudinal records we are alerted to such possibilities at an early stage and may take timely action.

Producing written language

Mature functioning in writing displays many of the features of mature functioning in reading. It requires the development of strong automatic processes and is characterized by self-regulation. The obvious analogy for such functioning is with speech, where we think meanings, open our mouths, and out pours a flow of language without deliberation. The flow is sometimes interrupted, redirected, or halted for self-correction, but for the most part the articulation is handled by complex, sub-conscious processes. It is probably true that few writers ever achieve this degree of automatic fluency in writing, but the principle is essentially the same. We could attempt to make a model of these factors as follows:

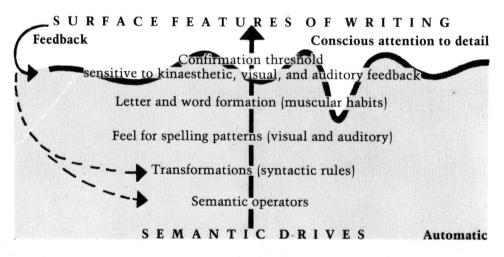

Feedback is of a much more subtle kind than in reading, depending as it does on vague intuitions that each word feels right and looks right as it leaves the pen. Self-corrective apprehensions at suitably spaced intervals cause a lowering of the confirmation threshold and directs conscious attention to significant detail. At this point some auditory or phonetic insights may be called on. Occasionally some outside resource such as a dictionary or a more competent speller may be used to obtain or check a spelling.

Here again the beginning learner is in a difficult bind since the amount of deliberate attention demanded by various mechanical aspects of the task threatens the integrity of the whole process. Because fast and fluent automatic processes have not been learned, short-term memory may become so overloaded that the writer cannot get from the beginning to the end of a sentence before semantic threads are lost or syntactic transformations have been properly accomplished. There is a need to facilitate automatic functioning as rapidly as possible. It would seem that this may best be achieved by encouraging and accepting approximations as we do with early speech behaviour, providing clarified models at a rate which will not overload current learning capacity.

A crucial aspect of the confirming process in writing seems to be the development of a vague sense of uneasiness in relationship to just those words which have been mis-spelt or most crudely mis-spelt. This vague but useful feeling may develop long before the learning writer is capable of pinpointing exactly what details cause the unease. Over-confident spellers fail to develop this sense rapidly enough to support healthy growth towards accuracy, while under-confident writers tend to be inappropriately apprehensive, even when they have made a correct response. It would seem sensible to reward children for displaying this 'error sense' rather than for correctness as such, for it is this sense which effectively controls the confirmation threshold, and lowers it at appropriate moments only. One way of doing this is to ask the children to underline those words that they are doubtful about. The teacher then has a good insight into how sensitively confirmation processes are operating and whether the responses are under-confident or over-confident. She also has the opportunity for helpful discussion about particular spellings.

Cognitive Clarity

At several points in our study we have discussed the importance of clarity in the way that we talk to children about literacy tasks and pointed to ambiguities and confusions in the terminology commonly used in teaching. This is not a question of being pedantic but of being clear. The concepts of literacy are confusing enough in themselves, and we should scrupulously avoid adding to the problem for young children. Careless ways of describing the relationship between letters and sounds can confuse children, and there is little uniformity among teachers in the vocabulary they choose—indeed, teachers themselves often seem deeply confused over such matters. In some areas children are taught to use the most common sound association of a letter as its name. One wonders what possible sense children can make of it all when they are told that the 'Tuh' in 'patient' says /sh/, or they are asked to spell the /ee/ in 'pony' with a 'yuh'. This matter was discussed in detail in Chapter 6.

There is growing evidence that cognitive confusion is a major cause of early literacy failure. Downing (1972) discusses the importance of cognitive clarity and summarizes the evidence. A number of studies document confusion during the first two years of schooling over the concepts 'word' and 'letter' (Clay 1972a, p.59; Hardy 1973, p.52). We often make unwarranted assumptions about what children have understood in instruction. In working with children who are making slow progress we need to be alert to possible confusions and attempt to clarify ambiguities immediately we become aware of them.

In her survey entitled 'Concepts About Print' Marie Clay (1972b) provides a splendid instrument for determining children's knowledge of the conventions of written language. By using this survey it is possible to pinpoint persistent confusions about basic concepts at an early stage and take appropriate action.

The positional metaphor in written language

We have noted in earlier chapters the way in which the alphabetic system rests on a serial and positional convention—the left-to-right serial positioning of letters is a spatial model for the time sequence or positioning of phonemes in words. As we all know, many children have difficulty in operating in terms of this convention. Many studies have shown a close relationship between reading and spelling difficulty on the one hand and poor auditory discrimination of speech sounds on the other. Of course, difficulty in auditory perception is normally displayed in some form of speech impairment (Clark 1970). Many children who test poorly for auditory discrimination speak well. It would seem therefore that discrimination of phonemes as used in reading and spelling and presented in typical test situations requires some additional precision not required to the same degree in learning speech. Interpretation of the research is consistent with the hypothesis that the additional difficulties arise from the need to determine the position of an abstracted phoneme in the temporal sequence of sounds, and that these difficulties are compounded when this intuition of position in a temporal sense must be re-interpreted spatially and directionally in written language. This interpretation is confirmed in the U.S.S.R. research of Elkonin (1973).

In our consideration of letter-to-sound confirmation in Chapters 5 and 6 we studied ways in which insights about position could be developed and put to rewarding uses within the hypothesis-test strategy. It may be that at a very early stage many children need help in clarifying sound sequences in relationship to letter sequences and expected position. Current methodologies tend to highlight awareness of initial sounds and letters but leave the problem of sequential positioning to the vaguenesses of 'blending'.

There are many ways in which children can be helped to make these positional insights in the early literacy programme. Most importantly the terminology we use in talking to children about the relationship between letters and sound should reflect the actual facts of the matter. It is highly confusing to talk about the sounds of letters (print is silent) or to use the sounds that letters most commonly represent as their names. Less confusing ways of talking about this matter were outlined in Chapter 6.

A simple procedure for helping children develop insights about the sequential sound structure of spoken words, and later the relationship of this structure to letter position in written words is reported by Elkonin (1973) and will be described in a slightly modified form here.[5]

A series of picture-stimulus cards is prepared with an empty grid for the phonemes drawn underneath as shown on the following page.
Spoken language sequencing   In the first stage the child is encouraged to say the word clearly and slowly and then, as he points to each square or places a counter in it, attempt to say the component sounds in sequence. The child is attempting to discriminate each phoneme in the flow of speech and assign it a position in the sequence from left to right. Note that there are sufficient boxes for the number of component phonemes—not for the number of letters as spelt in written language.

 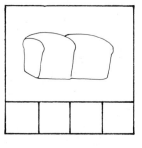 

Written letter sequencing   At a later stage the child uses alphabet cards which he places in the appropriate boxes. In work at the Newmarket Remedial Reading Clinic, Auckland, it was found that it was preferable to concentrate first on consonants, in the initial position, in the final position, and in the medial position, and then in all positions, showing vowel boxes shaded as indicating that a response was not required, or showing the actual vowel in its box.

When children are able to handle this task they have little difficulty in sound-to-letter confirmation as described in Chapters 5 and 6, with evident returns in confidence and reinforcement.

Note that we allow the child his own choice of letter where there is a variant letter-sound association. In the spoken word 'carrot' there are five phonemes, the second 'r' not being sounded. The first phoneme may be spelt in English with either a 'k' or a 'c'. In this exercise, either is correct. Note also that the speech consonants—those phonemes spelt with two letters in English—are printed on one card and fill one phoneme box, as in the 'sh' in 'shop'. A word like 'shoe' has two phonemes, /sh/ and /oo/; and a word like 'cheese' has three—/ch/, /ee/, and /z/. Words such as 'pumpkin' or 'chimney' or 'fire' may confuse many children because of the varying ways in which they are pronounced. There is no need to work through these confusing words, or indeed, all the phonemes in English: it is the positional *principle* that is being developed rather than the ability to find appropriate letters for all the sounds of English.

Finally, the children may practise the skill using the vowels and more complex consonant clusters:

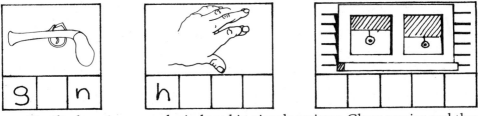

Similar learnings may be induced in simple written Cloze stories and this technique has the advantage of not being isolated from context. A simple story is reproduced leaving appropriate gaps (in the one-block-per-letter form) for children to complete. The nature of the gaps will depend on the children's level of development. The following provides examples of several tasks and levels—size of print would of course suit the level of development:

One day Chicken Licken went to the [oods]. (Initial consonant)

She sat down under a big oak [ee]. (Consonant blend)

An acorn fell on her little [ea]. (Terminal consonant)

She said, "I will go and tell the [ng] . (Consonant and vowel)

I will tell him that the sky has [a e]. (Medial consonant)

So Chicken Licken ran off until she met [f   ] [p   ] (Vowels)

This task may be simplified in two ways. By choosing a story of more or less familiarity to the children, the right degree of support may be provided. Alternatively, the story may be recorded on tape with pauses for children to complete the blocks. Generally, the density of gaps should not exceed one per sentence for the same reasons as applies to material at an appropriate level for learning.

Over-riding concerns

Inevitably it would seem that our anxiety about children experiencing difficulties takes us away from the real universals of language learning towards isolated exercises and skills—and finally to the isolation of the learner. Somehow we must resist this tendency. The universals we have determined—if they are real universals—need to be applied even more meticulously for the child experiencing difficulty than for others. Self-regulation is as important to the failing learner as to the successful learner—indeed, we are normally faced with a challenge to re-establish self-respect and to induce the setting up of a self-improving system in the slow learner. Developing healthy language strategies is an even more urgent task for those who have not done so as for those who are well on the way. Maintaining semantic drive through a lively related arts programme and through personally satisfying social interactions is a paramount need of the slow learner. Introducing literacy as a self-actualizing experience provides the most powerful motivations and systems of intrinsic reinforcement—and who needs such support more than the confused and failing child?

However we organize a preventive or support system we should not overlook the genuine universals which are always present in the context of success. We should not fool ourselves that we can obtain success without them. No teacher, however skilled, can control all the variables required for the success of a failing individual—that individual needs to know that those around him trust and support him in his attempts to gain personal control of what he is doing.

From this point of view all of our considerations throughout this enquiry must be seen to apply to the failing child. We can add something, intervening in an appropriately supportive role, but we cannot deny such a child the right to those universal facilitating conditions which cluster around success.

10
A New Conservatism

As we have applied the developmental model we have seen new light thrown on many old problems. For example, we have seen that school instruction often fails when it moves away from developmental principles—when it moves from self-regulation towards teacher and programme domination, from intrinsic motivation towards extrinsic motivation, from self-pacing towards competition, from unified activity towards isolated skills, from authentic literature towards emasculated language, and from deep meanings towards surface correctness. All of these school-based tendencies have been shown to be associated with failure for many children.

We need to enquire a little more deeply why schooling tends to move in these retrograde directions and whether or not it is possible to arrest such movements towards injustice for so many children.

We have found overwhelming evidence to support the principles of developmental learning. These are the principles we found confirmed in natural literacy-learning before school entry. They are confirmed too by our study of learning theory and the nature of effective 'instruction'. Finally, these are the principles we found confirmed by the way in which literacy processes actually operate. Although some of our conclusions seemed radical when applied to the classroom setting, they do in fact represent a more traditional and conservative approach to learning than is found in the fundamentally instruction-dominated programmes characteristic of modern schooling. The model itself, displayed most powerfully in the acquisition of speech, can hardly be called new-fangled and untried. Modern research in each of the related fields we have studied lends support to the model and helps to explain why it works so efficiently, but the model does not *arise* from these theoretical concerns nor depend on them for ratification. The model for which we have found such wide-ranging support has a venerable history and it would be hard to conceive of a more conservative approach.

To understand why this powerful model is neglected in formal education we need to consider three matters interwoven in the notion of schooling: professionalism, institutional priorities, and public attitudes. The 'Great Debate' should not be allowed to continue in the manner and spirit in which it has been conducted for several generations. Inevitably it will be children who suffer from the effects of petty factionalism. Let's begin by looking at the status of children within the school system and how this impinges upon their ability to become literate.

Professionalism and the client relationship

There are many reasons why it has been difficult to apply the principles of professionalism to the conduct of schools. Most importantly, since the rights of children are considered to be vested in their parents until they attain maturity, these rights have been traditionally vested in the school authorities when children are at school. Thus, in this case, the professional agent has all the normal rights of his child clients vested in him. The most central relationship of the professional, that between the expert and his client, is strangely twisted by this vesting of the rights of the client in the professional himself. No other professional has such power, even in the case of insane clients. Indeed, it is only in recent years, as teachers have struggled towards professionalism, that their responsibility has come to be seen as due to child clients rather than to parents, or to educational authorities or to the curriculum. Traditionally it seemed somehow unnatural to grant client status to children in their relationship with teachers.

Education in the home operates in a generally healthy and efficient way because parents, in the main, are concerned for the welfare of their children, use their knowledge to the advantage of their children, protect their children from exploitation—indeed, carry out all the responsibilities inherent in the professional-client relationship, and of course much more. It should not be surprising that the patterns of learning which have grown up naturally in the healthy home environment should display such sound features. Sometimes parents do experience difficulties as a result of their control of their children's rights and behave in a way that a responsible professional would not, but in the main they are able to support the interests of their children as developing persons.

In a professional setting the client does in a sense put himself into the hands of the professional—he delimits his own rights in a proper act of trust and in the expectation that the special knowledge of the expert will be used always to his, the client's benefit. Central to this trust is the notion of confidentiality—the client is prepared to divulge private and potentially damaging information about himself, or allow himself to be subjected to tests, in the expectation that such information will be used only in the interests of his own welfare.

Children in schools find that this proper client-relationship is breached. The school may test them and accumulate potentially harmful knowledge about them with no sense of responsibility to use this information *only* in the interests of the child. The right to confidentiality, which we regard so jealously as adult clients, is seldom acceded to children. Indeed, it is held as professionally necessary that information about the ineptitude of child clients should be widely published in order to foster competition and the motivation to strive. If the results of *our* clinical tests were displayed on the hospital notice-board, or worse, if our psychiatrist felt obliged to let the whole world know our hangups so that we would strive to be better, a number of things would happen. We would want to leave, sue, or kill our psychiatrist; we would become worse rather than better; and if we were forcibly required to continue treatment, we would resist every attempt by the psychiatrist to gain private information from us ever again.

Sadly, this is not an extreme analogy—it is an all too accurate picture of many children in school. When we breach every principle of professional responsibility towards our child clients by informing them and the whole world of every last detail of their ineptitude—through competition, published test results, and public embarrassment before their peers—we should expect exactly those results among the failing young that we winge and rail about even in the press. It is hard to understand how a society which has built up and valued professionalism to such an extent should be appalled at the outcomes of denying professionalism to children.

Difficulties in learning to become literate are as important and as *personal* to the child as the difficulties which drive us as adults to professionals of every kind. The child who has trouble in learning phonics or gets similar words confused, or is so fatigued with conscious trying that he can't make sense of what he is doing, has a personal and *private* problem equal in its importance for him to the symptoms of diabetes or a neurotic phobia. He needs expert guidance and protection of a highly professional kind, and he needs to be able to make use of that guidance without fear and without a growing sense of guilt and despair. But just as the human system has a natural tendency towards restoration of health under favourable conditions, so it has a natural tendency towards learning. The first responsibility of any professional is to set up those conditions under which the remarkable complexities of the human system restore healthy functioning autonomously. Literacy should be seen as a necessary part of self-actualizing and the most important responsibility of the professional towards child clients is to help them incorporate the challenge of becoming literate into their own self-improving systems.

Institutional priorities

It is the nature of all institutions to tend to lose sight of their original objectives and to become concerned with their own perpetuation, security, and well-being. The interests of those controlling the institution gradually take precedence over those the institution was set up to serve, and the institution is spoken about as if it were a real entity separate from and of greater importance than the individuals it serves. These may be truisms, but they must be taken into account when judging causes for educational failure. By their very scale, schools generate administrative, financial, and people-problems; this same scale offers to their staffs solutions which seem to justify the abandonment of sound educational principles. The herding of children into socially isolated age-groups, and into classes of supposedly homogeneous ability are examples of this tendency. The necessary responsibility of the teacher 'to be fair' when dealing with very large groups of childrem militates against the principles of developmental learning, where intervention is often concerned with the different and special needs of individual children.

The problems of control which arise from the first attempt to meet such institutional needs then lead in a circular fashion to further sacrifices of educational principles. The child who has responded to the fact that *his* needs are not being met must be punished so that others will tow the line.

In actual fact, towing the line is just what children always enjoy doing—it is one of the primary motivations of developmental learning: children want to be fully human *like other people*. However, this powerful motivation tends to be perverted by institutional imperatives away from the acquisition of skill, such as becoming literate, towards irrelevant types of conformity, such as being quiet, obedient, passive, and superficially careful. Efficient language learning requires the learner to be productive, risk-taking, actively questioning, and really careful—caring about the proper fulfilment of purposes.

In our classroom experiments described in Chapters 4, 6, and 7, we found no great difficulty in encouraging children to operate actively in the classroom, and because of their joy in learning and their deep respect for what they were deriving from school, they were obedient and considerate almost to a fault.

The Third Force

Most teachers understand these things very well but they face impediments to appropriate action of an almost insurmountable kind. They would be able to use a series of readers sensibly if someone in the hierarchy was not judging their whole success on what books the children were 'on'. They would gladly and intelligently accept approximation in spelling or reading if their own competence was not being judged on the accuracy of the children's 'work'. They would not over-test and rank children if the administration did not require it. They would allow a more active programme if quietness rather than good order were not such an important requirement. They would introduce new books every day if they had them. They would teach more openly if the reading schemes they had to follow did not contain such a narrow and time-wasting curriculum.

Most of these impediments arise from what might be called a Third Force lying outside the classroom and therefore lacking intimate and informed concern for the needs of individual children. The institutional, and hierarchical structure of the school and its own place in a similarly institutional and hierarchical system, tend to generate spurious motives and direct strange pressures onto the classroom—strange at least in developmental terms. It is from these sources that notions of force and demand, so foreign to developmental learning, are often unintentionally brought into the atmosphere of the classroom, with deeply destructive results.

Proper authority *need not* express itself through these concepts. For instance, there is no lack of authority as such in the bed-time story situation, which we took as one model of developmental learning. The parents, by bringing such pleasure and security through their skill, gain in real authority to the extend that the babies wish to emulate them and go about doing so. We found the same dynamics operating in the developmental classroom. When youngsters emulate the skill and performance of adults, these adults find themselves en-haloed with an almost embarrassing pervasiveness of authority.

Those in the Third Force tend to argue for discipline, control, and hard work, but they fail to make important distinctions which would remove the false injunctions they place on teachers and children. We agree that discipline, control, and hard work are crucial to efficient learning but there is no better example of disciplined, controlled and conscientious activity than the learning of such developmental tasks as walking and speaking. What the institutonal authority figure is usually talking about when he uses those words is 'externally enforced discipline', 'extrinsic control' and 'routine but fully-occupying busy-ness'. In place of these institutional distortions we would suggest a return to the original ideals, and in good schooling these are seen as 'self-discipline', 'intrinsic control', and 'motivated activity'.[1]

There is no word we use more readily to describe school learning than the word 'work'. 'Get on with your work', 'Are you working?', 'Get out your work', 'Work hard', 'That's nice work', 'This is your homework', 'Works well but lacks basics', and so on. It is another highly abstract term which can allow us to talk about learning without talking about content or process. It forms a convenient imperative or injunction and can nicely shift the responsibility for motivation from the teacher over to the children. Naturally, the word reflects the middle-class puritan origins of modern schooling, but in the way that it is often used in the schools it does so in a peculiarly dishonest way. The notion of work belongs with the notion of wages—industriousness in our society, however dehumanizing the labour, is dignified by the right to be paid. When we impose the ideal on children as an equivalent of learning we distort the obligation in several ways. We then deny children the right to genuine purposes, suggesting that they will not find the practice of the skill rewarding, and we suggest that the skill should be practised in a mindless way.

Public attitudes

Falling literacy standards, illusory or otherwise, are good for a bitter public debate and a back-to-basics campaign every decade or so. There are few topics carrying such an emotional charge, and few that can be so readily distorted or turned to political advantage. Everyone has been schooled and therefore feels competent to hold dogmatic views about the matter. In actual fact few can remember the actual experiences of learning to read, and they recall dictums from a rather later stage of schooling than from the first three years. Many play the age-old game of 'It wasn't like that in our day', or 'Aren't the young going to the dogs?'—from which men and women have derived immense consolation since time immemorial. Others operate out of genuine concern and try to think the matter through from the beginning, making the old logical mistakes of analysis and simplification all over again—'Words are made up of letters, letters have sounds, therefore teach the sounds and blend them into words'.

It is astonishing that the same parents who supported their child's learning of speech with such good sense so often act in a completely opposite and destructive manner when the child begins to have difficulties in reading and writing. Of course, we must accept that they learned to act in such a way from their own schooling, and that probably, as teachers, much of what *we* do in teaching stems from the same sources. Because *we* learnt to read and write we are inclined to say, 'Such-and-such worked for me, why shouldn't it work for them?' Yet we forget the many children who were taught with us but failed. And we don't really know what it was that worked for us—as we have seen earlier, the relationship between instructional shibboleths and what the learner really does is very tenuous.

Parents should be encouraged to look closely at the *successful* learning in which their children engage with them, and to remember their approach and attitude when their children were learning to walk and talk. They then need to be encouraged to delight in the early stages of literacy learning and support them in the same manner as they supported the early stumblings of walking and the early bumblings of talking. The acquisition of literacy needs to be demystified for them by taking them back to a clear recognition of the principles of developmental learning which form a natural part of their recent experience with their children. The principles are simple, natural, and familiar to us all.

The factious and political elements in the society at large present a rather more difficult problem, dangerous to children in many ways. Militant pressures demanding another return to mindless drudgery must be met by professional confidence and sanity. Schools would have made much more consistent advances if it were not for the influences of public faction, but the sober fact remains that every system for teaching literacy over the past century has produced very similar results in success and failure, and the general flight of the adult community from literate pursuits after leaving school is the most serious indictment of all. In every way possible the 'Third Force' and the public at large need to be educated to face some of the sobering conclusions that our enquiry has led us to. Let's summarize those of our conclusions which bear on the conditions demanded to achieve anything near universal literacy within the school setting.

Competition and reinforcement   Any system which relies on competition, the ranking of children, and public labelling in terms of attainment in the early years *must* produce a large, recalcitrant group of failing children, many of them disturbed to the point of neurosis; and an even larger body of 'normal' children who will see no need to use their literate skills actively in ordinary life.[2] A hundred years of such schooling has exhibited such a result. It is also completely concordant with all versions of learning-theory—in an ascending scale from basic operant conditioning to the theories of cognitive learning and self-actualization (Chapters 1 and 9).

The dismembering of the literacy processes   The traditional attempt to simplify learning by dividing the literacy processes into an ever-increasing list of minor skills is self-defeating. Unless they function in concert and are taught largely within meaningful contexts, the so-called 'basic skills' constitute a parody of reading and writing. What in the abstract seems *logically* sound—the breaking of complex wholes into parts—turns out to be quite *illogical* in the classroom, especially when the crucial learnings are concerned with the inter-relationship of parts within organic functioning (Chapters 2, 5, and 8).

Automatic functioning   Reading and writing are largely automatic processes which operate—and can only operate properly—at speeds well beyond the capacity of the deliberative human brain. Children must be taught in a way which allows *largely* automatic functioning and encourages the rapid development of efficient processing in reading and writing. This applies most importantly to the slow or confused learners, for whom exactly the opposite provisions are normally made (Chapters 1, 5, 8, and 9).

Self-regulation   All language tasks are largely self-regulated and require an intricate feedback system under the control of the learner and user. Emphasis on extrinsic correction and reward denies children the opportunity to develop this self-regulation, the most complex and vulnerable part of the functioning language system. From the earliest stages—from infancy, as we noted in Chapters 1 and 3—self-regulation, self-correction, and the development of a self-improving system characterize efficient language learning. Self-regulation is also crucial to smooth and reliable automatic functioning (Chapters 1, 3, 5, 6, and 9).

Approximation   Such complex developmental tasks as reading and writing, which take many years to master, are characterized by gradual approximation towards 'correct' performance. The crude division of responses into right and wrong, which is so deeply set in the practices of schooling, flouts this crucial principle, which may be seen in the efficient learning of any developmental task. Provision for appropriate approximating necessarily imples longitudinal monitoring and recording of actual behaviour rather than the results of isolated exercises or 'right/wrong' tasks (Chapters 1, 3, 8, and 9).

The client relationship   Although many teachers do regard each of their children as clients and protect that relationship, this has never been a general feature of schooling. A rather special and unique relationship with children is set up in schooling, one dependent more on the principle of *in loco parentis* than on the principles of true professionalism. This view of the relationship is held particularly by what we have called the 'third force'. There would seem to be little possibility of meeting the needs of failing children unless all the implications of the client relationship are realized within the school system (Chapters 9 and 10).

Authentic literature   The demands of instruction for increasing simplification and control in the teaching of literacy have gradually eroded the quality of reading materials used in the early years of schooling. Children should experience all the rich and special powers of the written word. If this is witheld from them they will not develop and sustain the deep motivations required to persevere for years with a task which may appear to them peripheral to the concerns of modern life. More than ever before there is a need to introduce children to a satisfying literature, to use such materials at the centre of instruction, and to develop methods of teaching which bring to children the sustained and special joy from the written word that they can experience from no other activity. The purposes for which they are induced to produce written language should, in the same way, fulfil special and deeply satisfying goals suited to the personal, expressive and concrete modes of operating at that early age (Chapters 1 and 8).

Individual learning   We have seen that the search for THE way in which children should be taught is a falsifying exercise. Children approach literacy by many different paths in the same way as they approach learning to talk by many different paths. All the paths that they do follow successfully are purposeful and meaning-oriented, winding through the terrain and around the obstacles in intelligent and personal ways. The terrain is different for each learner. Whether or not your temperament, your dialect, your cultural background, your inherited difficulties, your mother, your father, your teacher, or your intelligence forms the largest obstacle you must pass—always the learning is a personal thing. Any approach to literacy must allow the individual learners to pick their own way—always in the company of guiding and sustaining friends (Chapters 5, 8, and 9).

These are some of the conditions necessary to any substantial improvement in the school's power to develop basic literacy for all children. Taken together these conditions may at first sight appear impracticable in our society. However, in the practical aspects of our enquiry we found that there were already ways of following many of these principles in the modern classroom: determination and ingenuity will find many others (Chapters 4, 6, 7, and 9. The most important implications were summed up in Chapter 6).

An Authentic Conservatism

We have noted on a number of occasions the way in which abstraction and sweeping generalization become dissociated from concrete detail in the real world and, lacking specificity, become a cover for illicit moralizing. An example of this is the use made of the term 'work' in relationship to the learning situation. In our enquiry we have attempted to avoid such generalizations and developed in detail the abstractions we have considered, giving concrete examples which display both our denotations and our connotations to open criticism. 'Back to basics' is another abstract generalization with high-sounding and apparently impeccable connotations. In fact, it is vague, manipulative, and fundamentally dishonest when used without specific examples of its reference or denotation.

In the course of our enquiry it has been necessary to define what *is* basic to literacy in great detail and with many examples—we did not find it a simple concept. As for going back to anything, we have again and again found it necessary to go back beyond formal schooling or instruction to the wisdom and efficiency of developmental learning. We have found it necessary to be conservative in a much more fundamental way than is suggested by the slippery imprecision of those who use the back-to-basics slogan. Such strong-arm abstractions have all the crudeness of the sword and none of the refinement or precision of the pen. They are in an aggressive way out of contact with reality.

When speaking about complex issues, if our ideas depart from what the real world is like, we are then prone to turn on reality and try to force it to be like our ideas. Strange and terrible things may then happen; we do violence to the real world—and it may be violent to us in return; or the toughness of the real world resists our efforts to manipulate it and we become frustrated, disheartened or cynical; or we become engaged in wasteful and often bitter argument with those around us who are in better contact with things as they are.

There is no more prevalent and damaging fallacy than this tragic dislocation of thought from the world—it is the characteristic mistake of our Western intellectual tradition (Holt, 1974). Because schools play a central role in that tradition, it is not surprising that they have had this fallacy forced upon them more strongly and more persistently than any other institution in our society.

No other environment has been so manipulated by ideas disembodied from reality. And no other group of people more than teachers has been so exploited, threatened, and injured by ideas which have lost contact with reality—what teachers call in defence 'airy-fairy ideas'. Only determined vigilance and a humble honesty before the facts can extricate our teaching from the effects of this fallacy. We must demand that ideas conform to reality and oppose those who would have us deform the world into the shape of their ideas.

One answer to this problem of the inherent danger of abstraction lies in the type of research which is developmental and descriptive. In this mode of research the actual behaviour of children is observed and described with as few preconceptions as possible. An accurate picture of total behaviour in the activity being studied is built up before a model is suggested and before parts of the behaviour are separated off for detailed study. We owe our most reliable and useful insights about the learning of spoken and written language to research of this kind. Among the advantages of this type of research is the assurance that what is being described is what actually happens; the focus is on learning rather than on teaching; and total processes are studied first so that later analysis of special features of the behaviour can always be clearly linked back to their functional or organic place in the whole. Wherever our continuing enquiry takes us, it should not take us towards conclusions which are not supported by descriptive, developmental research of this kind.

The term 'basics' as used in the factional spirit makes illicit pretensions to being concerned with fundamental issues in conservative ways. This is not the place for a thorough analysis of social questions even as they affect the school, but at least the point must be made that the 'back to basics' generalization is ambiguous, inconsistent and plainly shoddy. It involves an abuse of language in that the words have no clear reference to anything in the *real world*.

Culture and the school

Most Western societies are now multi-cultural due to emigration, the increase in birthrate of indigenous people, and, insofar as rural societies can be said to represent a distinct sub-culture, the great migration from the land into the cities. Schools have experienced great difficulties in adjusting to this movement, especially in abandoning their own narrow cultural goals and prejudices. The inner city school has become a special type of multi-ethnic community challenging all the verities of middle-class education and facing the system with problems that, despite the intelligent commitment of many teachers, remains largely unsolved. It is one thing to respect the rights of ethnic minorities through equality of opportunity; it is another thing to provide open opportunities for literacy, both for the ethnic minorities and the socially impoverished.

All of the concerns of our enquiry bear down on this complex of problems centering around the more extreme human differences in race, culture, and class. The traditional school with its narrow culture entrenched in the values of dominance and conformity professes the provision of equal rights while committed in action to the production of an elite. Among its primary functions are the ranking and labelling of people and the preparation of people to accept their assigned rank. It uses and teaches a language which can be readily understood only by a minority and even in the field of manners and customs values a very convergent set of standards. Unfortunately, it does not leave these functions to the last few years of schooling—it begins the great enterprise in Year One. It rapidly sets up an environment of social inequality.

Not that equality is any longer a very useful idea—it is certainly not a fruitful notion in considering the needs of very different people. Equality has become another of our high-level abstractions which finds little contact with the world as it is. The problems we face in providing a just education in a culturally divergent society require insights flowing from the notion of fraternity rather than from those of liberty or equality. Fraternity is *also* an ancient and respectable ideal which took its proud place alongside liberty and equality as the era of the modern school began, but it is an ideal which has been sadly neglected in thought, in research, and in action. We know very little about it and would find great difficulty in locating recent authorative references to underpin our exposition by scholarly sanction. It would be our claim, however, that this is a basic and a conservative notion, and the one most likely to lead towards proper solutions to the current problems of function within the school system.[3]

Fraternity and the multi-ethnic school

There are, of course, special provisions and techniques appropriate to teaching English as a second language, teaching ethnic languages, and meeting the needs of children in the second generation of migrant families. Such matters are not the concern of our present enquiry, but promoting general literacy despite people differences is very much our concern. Most of the experimenting in classrooms lying behind the theses of this book took place in multiethnic, inner city, or new-suburban classrooms, and were self-consciously directed to the needs of children displaying a rich diversity of culture. The first consideration that we would like to establish is that the developmental approach which we have examined so carefully has a natural multi-ethnic dimension. The concerns of each chapter need to be thought through in that light and with an adaptive ingenuity.

Central to our thesis has been the need to teach literacy through the medium of a wide and authentic literature. Because it is concerned with the deepest human preoccupations common to all peoples, literature may transcend cultural differences and thus provide deep satisfaction for all. An open literature, through translation and cross-cultural transmission, also presents the universal human condition from a great variety of cultural standpoints. It is always possible to select from the great wealth of material available literature which will be culturally meaningful to different groups represented in our classrooms. It is more than ever necessary when we teach in an environment of cultural diversity to free ourselves from the limitations of serial readers designed to take the middle cultural way.[4]

Because reading to children during infancy and providing opportunities to experiment with writing is not a general cultural feature of pre-school experience, the development of a strong literacy set during the first year at school is vital to all early literacy programmes. Shared-book-experience is particularly suited to this vital undertaking and, indeed, the techniques were especially designed to meet the needs of multi-cultural classrooms. Many children from other ethnic groups than the Anglo-Saxon bring a rich oral tradition to school. This should be mined for stimulating and relevant material suited to language-experience techniques. Children of all ethnic groups are likely to be enriched by sharing the cultural tradition of other children in the class (Chapters 3 and 4).

Children who are not thoroughly familiar with the syntactic patterns, idioms, and tunes of written English are likely to experience more difficulty in developing sound central strategies than those who are. This is not a reason for limiting their reading materials to the most fundamental English or to the patterns of simple spoken English, except in the very early stages: they require the joyful repetition of a rich literature through the ear and across the tongue even more than those children who have enjoyed this experience in their own homes and in their own vernacular. Only when the patterns and tunes of written English are running through the automatic language system of a child can he profit fully from the facilitation of prediction and confirmation in applying the central hypothesis-test strategy (Chapters 5 and 6).

Language-experience procedures have a special place in programmes for culturally diverse groups—their needs lie in familarity with oral as well as with written language. The support of here-and-now situations meets their needs for clarity in their struggle to find relevance in the written dialect of English. For them, the additional motivation and drive springing from active related arts not only facilitates the creation of linguistic meanings but also sustains their confidence and feeling of belonging during the period when the less familiar meanings of English language leave them with a certain sense of alienation (Chapters 7 and 8).

The more distant children's dialect may be from the favoured formal dialect of the school the more at risk they are likely to be in mastering literacy.[5] If they come to fear the language used in school as something which leaves them with a sense of confusion, and is often making demands for action in a way that leaves them in doubt about what is actually required of them, they are likely to feel the same insecurity when the rhythms of written English impinge on their attention. This linguistic gulf needs to be bridged from both sides: on one side the oral language used in the classroom must take the needs of culturally different children into consideration and acceptingly go out to their dialects, while from the other side, the lively language of books, verse, and song must enter their experience and become both meaningful and automatic (Chapters 8 and 9).

Finally, children from different strata in society, or from different ethnic groups, experience much greater difficulty in identifying with their teachers as mother or father substitutes. The parent substitute view of early schooling has been common during past periods when schools were more socially homogeneous—it is a natural extension in caring feeling from the principle of *in loco parentis*. The culturally different child may mistake the 'mother-figure' role played by many infant teachers to their culturally consanguinous charges as favouritism, and deeply resent his own inability to share in that flow of feeling. The true client relationship has much to offer children who feel culturally disoriented in the school. When they find that their personhood is respected and that they are protected from any form of exploitation or ridicule, they will readily respond in trust to the professionals who serve them in this manner. As the universal values of a wide literature touch their spirits, however, all the deeper feelings of warm fostering gradually open to them, and they *too* may share in the strong family feeling of a healthy classroom. The starting point, however, is fraternal rather than maternal—once they respond to a genuine mood of fraternity around them they will find that their rights to liberty and equality in that society are theirs to enjoy.

Sharing a shared experience with a multi-ethnic group

One of the third-year classes described in Chapter 7 had strong multi-ethnic dimensions both in composition and in programme. At least five distinct ethnic groups were represented, typical of the new suburban Auckland school—a large contingent of Polynesian children from all round the Pacific, many New Zealand Maori children, and several children from mid-European countries. It was not difficult to include in the literature stories, poems, and songs from the different cultures, some in the original language, and these proved most successful, especially on occasions when parents participated. However, we found that matters of common feeling embodied in the language were of greater importance than a *particular* cultural flavour. The literature of the American negro culture seemed to evoke a deep and genuine response from all of the children, and negro spirituals were among the most deeply loved songs—and of course, through shared-book-experience they became deeply loved instructional reading material.

One sequence of related activities in language and the arts stimulated activity for several weeks and we have chosen this as a final example of all the things we have discussed in this study of literacy. The stimulus was an old negro story in dialect which seemed to 'energize semantic drive' in ways that we would not attempt to analyse. We will not discuss how the story was introduced—each reader should make a personal response. However, there was great problem-solving excitement in decoding dialect words. In unstated ways, the tale itself may symbolize many of the complex issues we have discussed throughout this adventure into literacy. All of the children produced art and written expression of a powerful and personal kind. Some of the art is illustrated in the colour section of this book; examples of written work follow the story.

Tailypo[6]

Once upon a time, way down in de big woods of Tennessee, dere lived a man all by hisself. His house didn't hab but one room in it, an dat room was his parlor, his settin room, his bedroom, his dinin room, an his kitchen, too. In one end ob de room was a great, big, fiarplace, an dat's where de man cooked an et his suppar. An one night artter he had cooked an et his suppar, dere crep in troo de cracks ob de logs de curiestes creetur dat you ebber did see, an it had a great, big, long tail.

Jis as soon as dat man see dat varmit, he reached fur his hatchet, an wid one lick, he cut dat thing's tail off. De creetur crep out troo de cracks ob de logs an run away, an de man, fool like, he took an cooked dat tail, he did, an et it. Den he went ter bed, an artter a while, he went ter sleep.

He hadn't been sleep berry long, till he waked up, an heerd sumpin climbin up de side ob his cabin. It sounded jis like a cat, an he could heer it scratch, scratch, scratch, an by-an-by he heerd it say, "Tailypo, tailypo, all I want's my tailypo."

Now dis yeer man had tree dogs. An when he heerd dat thing he called his dawgs, huh! huh! huh! an dem dawgs cum bilin out frum under de floo an dey chased dat thing way down in de big woods. An de man went back ter bed an went ter sleep.

Well, way long in de middle ob de night, he waked up an he heerd sumpin right above his cabin door, tryin ter git in. He listened, an he could heer it scratch, scratch, scratch, an den he heerd it say, "Tailypo, tailypo: all I want's my tailypo." An he sot up in bed and called his dawgs, huh! huh! huh! an dem dawgs cum bustin round de corner ob de house an dey catched up wid dat thing at de gate an dey jis tore de whole fence down, tryin ter git at it. An dat time, dey chased it way down in de big swamp. An de man went back ter bed agin an went ter sleep.

Way long toward mornin he waked up, and he heerd sumpin down in de big swamp. He listened, an he heerd it say, "You know, I know; all I want's my tailypo." An dat man sot up in bed an called his dawgs, huh! huh! huh! an you know dat time dem dawgs didn cum. Dat thing had carried em way off down in de big swamp an killed em, or los em. An de man went back ter bed an went ter sleep agin.

Well, jis befo daylight, he waked up an he heerd sumpin in his room, an it sounded like a cat, climbin up de civers at de foot ob his bed. He listened an he could heer it scratch, scratch, scratch, an he looked ober de foot ob his bed an he saw two little pinted ears, an in a minute, he saw two big, roun, fiery eyes lookin at him. He wanted to call his dawgs, but he too skeered ter holler. Dat thing kep creepin up until by-an-by it wuz right on top ob dat man, an den it said in a low voice, "Tailypo, tailypo; all I want's my tailypo." An all at once dat man got his voice an he said, "I hain't got yo tailypo." An dat thing said, "Yes, you has, an *I'm gonna git it.*"

The group of seven and eight year-olds had a rich experience of story and the functions of fantasy. The story looks remarkably difficult and mature especially with its dialect and non-standard spellings. The choice was right for current preoccupations which had been stimulated by some of the more gentle yet bitter-sweet negro stories and songs such as Kum Ba Yah, and Swanee River. In an important way the non-standard dialect seemed to have an emancipating effect on many of the children, enriching their feeling for the power of language and confirming the propriety of their own spelling approximations.

As the story began to unfold the children were captured in their different ways by the rich texture of the language and the simmering tensions just below the surface. The images they were creating tallied with nothing within their actual experience of the outside world but, transformed by imagination, symbolized inner realities. The children's own written creations best explain these matters of personal meaning. The small selection reproduced here represents first attempts by the children concerned. They were later edited for a class booklet. The structure of the story, moving towards a satisfying climax, sustained the children's endeavours into extensive writing. Some of their art is reproduced in the colour section of the book, and this too reminds us that comprehension is a highly personal matter.

Earypo

Long Long ago there was a Big Scary
forest and in the Scary forest was a mushroom
and in the mushroom lived a fairy and
in that mushroom there wasn't But one
room and that room was her bedroom,
her dining room and her Bathroom
and one night after the fairy had ate her tea
and gone To bed, Creeping through the floor
came a BIG BIG thing and it had a
BIG BIG ear. The fairy cut off
The BIG BIG ear and the thing ran
away and the fairy went to Sleep.
later on the fairy heard
a "SSSS SSSS" noise and she sat up in bed
and she heard it say "Eary Po, earypo
all I wants my earypo". The fairy
called her lady bird, "wh---i---s---tLwe
and the lady bird chased the BIG
BIG thing way down in the trees and
the fairy went back to sleep. Later
on the fairy woke up and heard

S-S- S- S- S- S-S--S---S." a voice
said " Earypos earypos all I wants
earypo". The fairy called her lady
bird " wh---i---s----tl---e." and the
lady bird chased the B I G BIG thing
way down in a big haunted house.
and the fairy went back to sleep. She
woke up again because she heard
ssssss--s---s. and a voice "you
know all I want's my earypo. The
fairy called her lady bird,
wh---i---s---t---le. but the thing had
ate or lost it. The BIG thing
Started to climb up her bed and
it crawled more and more and
the fairy saw two big black eyes
looking up at her and she heard
ssss--s--s---- Gimme my
earypo back." and the fairy said "I
haven't got your earypo. The thing said
"oh yes you has. chuckle chuckle
and I gonna get it.

BIG FOOT

Once upon a time in a

dark forest a dwarf lived under a mushroom. One night a big dragon with one leg longer than the other came limping through the forest The dwarf cut down a tree to stop the dragon because he was making too much noise. The tree fell on the dragon's foot and cut it off so that now his legs were both the same size. The dwarf eat the foot for supper and went to sleep. Later he woke up and he could hear, Dra-ag, dra-ag, dra-ag and a voice said," Big foot. "Big foot all I want's my big foot." So the dwarf called his four brother. "Here, Here. Here Here" and they came running from under the toadstool and chased him away to the beach. Then the dwarf went to sleep again. He woke up soon. He could hear Dro-ag dra-ag, dra-ag and a voice," Big foot big foot, give me my big foot." And the dwarf called his four brothers. ".Here, Here. Here. Here. They chased the dragon down to the beach again. And the dwarf went back to sleep. The third time he woke up and he could hear Dra-ag, dra-ag dra-ag and the voice said,"you know, I know all I want is my big foot."The dwarf

called his "brothers "Here, Here, Here, Here." But his four brothers didn't come because the ( ) dragon might have killed them. The dwarf saw the draggon coming at the foot of his bed. "Give me back ( ) my big foot." But the dwarf said, "I haven't got it." "yes you have and I'm going to get it."

Come, Come, Come.

Once upon a time in the nice woods a furry bear lived in a tent. allof a sudden a poisonus spider with a longlong leg came jumping into the tent. The bear piked up a little knife and cut the Leg off. The spider suttled away and the bear went off to sleep. Later he woke up and heard, Thump, thump thump and a voice said I want my long leg back. The bear called his budgie. cheep cheep. 'Come, come, come.' and the budgie chased that spider into a spiderweb. Nearly asleep the bear heard again the loud noise. Thump thump thump and a voice said I want My leg back again and the bear called his budgie. "Come, come, Come." But it did not come because the spider had poisoned him and the spider climbed up on the bears head and said "I want my long leg back

and the bear said, I ate your
leg. The spider looked at the bear
with a mad face and said "Well
I want it and I'm going to GET IT!"

Hairypo

Once upon a time a goblin lived
under the ground in a little room and
that room was his bed room and his sitting room
and his Kitchen too. one day something
came knocking on his door and it had Long
Long hair and that goblin made the Things hair
disappear and the thing ran away. The goblin
went to bed. Half way to moring he could
hear some Thing was Knocking on the door and he
could hear it say "hairypo hairypo all I want is
my hairypo. This goblin had one ugly angry ape
and the ape ran after the thing. so The goblin
went to bed. Near morning he could hear a some thing climbing
up the chair and he could hear It. Howl! Howl!
Howl! He [—] looked on the chair and he saw
a great big hairless monster. It still was climbing
up the chair till it was on the table and it
jumped on the goblin. It said in a whispery voice.
hairypo hairypo all I wants my hairypo. "I
haven't got your hairypo [——] my ape
-ate it." The thing said, "Your ape did not eat my
hairypo you put it in the swamp."
"Oh no I didn't" Oh yes you did
and I'm going to get it

The Problem of Eclecticism

Much of the controversy about teaching reading and writing has been concerned with competing methods, each expressing an over-simplification and demanding a spurious choice. It would be irresponsible to suggest that everyone was right and all methods should be used haphazardly without a coherent and ratifiable basis—that is the mistake of eclecticism. However, we have moved far enough in our enquiry to see the shape of a coherent theory of language-learning and to avoid the pitfalls of factionalism and eclecticism with sound foundations in reason and research.

There is much yet to be researched about the mastery of language and the ability of the ordinary learner to engage in such diverse learning styles as to encompass all our theories and much more.[7] The notion of language strategies takes us a step closer to explaining this inclusive complexity of language learning.

Our enquiry has identified crucial mistakes in the way we have traditionally presented the tasks of literacy to children and has indicated where dead ends need to be closed off—however unlikely it is that they will be. But the enquiry must go on.

While we argue, the ordinary child moves readily from one level of learning to another, from one type of word recognition to another, and combines these many styles of perception in naturally concerted action towards meaningful ends. Just as children move freely up and down the analytic-synthetic dimension in learning spoken language, so they must do so in mastering literacy from the earliest stages. Helping children to identify and clarify the conventions of print in specific terms is as necessary as helping them to depend on meaning and the larger structures of language to develop efficient self-improving processes. There is a place for planned instruction, but such instruction will be emulative and invitational rather than prescriptive. It will support and not supplant the learning system of each learner, and will express itself in respect and trust for the divergent ways in which children teach themselves the tasks they wish to master.

And what about those who do *not* want to master literacy? *That* is the central responsibility and challenge of the school and of a common-sense community. It can never be shifted onto the shoulders of failing children. The major causes of failure in the great literacy undertaking are not to be found in the incompetence of children but in the departure from sound educational principles as represented in developmental learning. In this sense Western schooling has always been too radical—logically arrogant, patronizing and sentimental to children, moralistic, and destructively factionalist. Our enquiry would suggest a return to properly conservative principles in a new spirit of fraternity—to principles attested to by the millions of children who have learned to speak their native tongues since time immemorial.

Notes

Notes to Chapter 1

1. An exception must be made for research of the developmental kind such as that of Clay (1972a, 1972b, and 1975) and Goodman (1968, 1973a, and 1973b) which is fundamentally descriptive in nature—and, of course, to the germinal work of Piaget and Vygotsky.

2. Most directly we would cite the work of Halliday (1973, and 1975a), and for detailed consideration of teaching implications, Britton (1970), Doughty, Pearce, and Thornton (1972), and Jones (1968). For a more philosophical approach to the fundamental issues see Bruner (1975) and the germinal work of Langer (1942) which may lead on for the persistent reader to Langer (1962, 1967, and 1972). Those interested in the poetic uses of language will find a scholarly yet stimulating consideration of the basic questions in Burnshaw (1970).

3. An over-riding consideration must be in the concept of developmental stages as represented in the work of Piaget. There could be no more serious mistake than to forget that the children we are concerned with are at the level of 'concrete operational thinking'—with all that that implies in terms of limited ability to abstract, to generalize, and to apply abstract rules.
A useful summary of the characteristics of developmental learning may be found in Lefrancois (1975, pp. 188-197) and a more detailed consideration in Mussen (1973).

4. The use of the term 'learning theory' in this chapter is, of course, greatly simplified and refers mainly to the principles of operant conditioning. However, it will become clear as we proceed that we need to consider the learning of reading and writing as displaying *all* forms of learning from the most simple to the most complex. In this sense we are using the term 'learning theory' in the way in which it applies to many levels of learning such as are described in Gagne (1970), who distinguishes eight types: signal learning, stimulus-response learning, chaining, verbal association, discrimination learning, concept learning, rule learning and problem-solving. Our analysis of literacy strategies in Chapters 5 and 8 implies that reading and writing entail *discovery learning* at the centre of normal operation (Bruner, 1961), although the principles of such learning are more usually applied to content learning than to process learning such as we are concerned with here. In the end, the position we are forced to take up by the evidence favours cognitive theories of learning (Smith, 1978a and 1978b), although in Chapter 8 we note the deficiencies in *all* theories in accounting for the emotional content of meaning and experience (Langer, 1967). In our final chapter we also consider the importance of that type of learning which might be called 'self-discovery' (Rogers, 1969). An excellent summary of the views of the self-actualizing school has been made by Lefrancois (1975, pp. 137-153). See also under Note 6, Chapter 10, *The Philosophical Method of this Text*.

5. 'Punishment' is being used here to mean the opposite of reinforcement. We can distinguish four 'response conditions', or states that may be associated with a response and thus influence learning:
Positive reinforcement:
   the effect of adding a rewarding or pleasant stimulus to a response situation, such as praise or a smile.
Negative reinforcement:
   the effect of the removal of a painful or unpleasant stimulus from a response situation, such as being let out of school early.

Punishment (direct):
>the effect of adding a painful or unpleasant stimulus to a response situation. (The aim is to produce aversion to the response but the effect is usually wider and less predictable than this.)

Punishment (indirect):
>the effect of the removal of a pleasant or rewarding stimulus from a response situation, e.g. the effect of being sent to bed without supper, or of being detained in school. (In the form of solitary confinement or denial of sleep, indirect punishment may be even more powerful than direct punishment in the form of torture, as Solzhenitsyn's *Gulag Archipelago* makes clear.)
>A clear exposition for the lay reader may be found in Lefrancois (1975, pp. 50–54).

6. J.S. Bruner (1974, pp.10–11). The Bernsteinian explication of the problem in terms of language codes seems to leave us as trapped behind solid brick walls as we were by the concept of the intelligence quotient, i.e. we have an *explanation* of educational failure rather than a *diagnosis* upon which effective remediation may be planned.

7. The term 'models' is being used in its widest application to refer to any complex metaphor or image used to explore structure or process. 'Theoretical models' conveys a much more narrow idea of model-making, normally arising from factor analysis or some other mathematical approach. Such models tend to display all the problems associated with abstraction and division into parts—especially in obscuring the crucial matters of process and function.

8. Although in the last ten years grave doubts have been thrown upon the notion of language acquisition as an innate human competence, the idea is still very influential (Smith 1975; Bruner 1975, pp. 61–80). The debate between Skinner (1957) and Chomsky (1959) could be cited as a high level instance of the type of harmful factionalism which has plagued thinking about the teaching of reading for a century—both points of view must be encompassed in any adequate theory of language learning.

9. Only one important aspect of learning is considered here. See note 4.

10. For a more detailed exposition of language acquisition covering aspects not touched on here, such as the development of syntax, see Britton (1970, pp. 33–96), Slobin (1971, pp. 41–66) and Smith (1975, pp. 168–179), and for a detailed account McNeil (1970) or Menyuk (1971).

11. The non-mentalist emphasis of modern psychology makes the learning theorist rather timid about the concepts of 'intrinsic reinforcement' and 'motivation'. However, there is no way of understanding developmental learning without acknowledging the power of what might be called personal desires and rewards, which are more effective in promoting learning than forces extrinsic to the learner. We could distinguish two types of intrinsic rewards:
    1. Those stemming from the results of acting on the outside world. Examples here would be the learning of muscular control by an infant through moving a rattle and being rewarded by the sound; or by a beginning reader hearing his own voice as he reads.
    2. Those stemming from the awareness or knowledge of success. Examples here would be the pleasure felt by a child in understanding a story he is reading, or by anyone in gaining insight into a problem.

There is increasing evidence to show that intrinsic rewards are more powerful than extrinsic, and that extrinsic rewards may be damaging in supporting the learning of skills for which natural motivation has not been fostered—such skills tend not to be practised when the rewards are withdrawn. See Donaldson (1978 pp. 115–120) and for a detailed and persuasive study, Deci (1975).

Notes to Chapter 2.

1. The alphabetic method as it was used in the early part of the century, and is described here, is not used today. However, there has been a resurgence of interest since the

sixties following many research reports of early alphabetic knowledge being found to be an accurate predictor of later success in reading. A useful account of this matter and of methods as they occur in the current practice of reading teaching in the United Kingdom is given by Elizabeth Goodacre (1972).

2. Working in the twenties and thirties, the Gestalt-psychologists amassed a formidable experimental basis for their view that we perceive form before we perceive detail, and that we perceive whole forms when the detail incompletely displays it. An important concept here is that of *closure*: in perception we tend to complete unfinished or open figures, fill in gaps, detect order in chaos, and rearrange detail into meaningful wholes. This concept will become very important in our later consideration of 'Cloze procedures' in teaching. See also the following note.

   The concept of closure is important in reading not only in the sense in which it was applied to the perception of whole words during the forties and fifties, but also in terms of the predictive, gap-filling drive that characterizes listening and reading. If a gap or uncertainty occurs in the flow of a meaningful sentence, we compulsively fill it with an appropriate place holder.

3. It is significant *features* rather than configurations which seem to characterize visual perception in reading, and features become significant for a variety of reasons, including the bearing down of the developing meaning of what is being read on the visual detail. For a brief account of feature analysis see Deborah Lott Holmes, 'The Independence of Letter, Word, and Meaning Identification in Reading' in Frank Smith (1973 pp.99–149). For a detailed account of feature analysis see Smith (1978 pp.81–184).

4. For a simple account of language-experience principles see R.D. Walshe, 'What is the Language Experience Approach', in Walshe (1977b, pp.39–43). A detailed account by one of the most experienced exponents will be found in Nora Goddard (1974).

5. William S. Gray. e.g. (1960) *On Their In Own Reading*. 2nd ed.
   Chicago: Scott, Foresman and Company
   Paul McKee. e.g. (1966) *The Teaching of Reading in the Elementary School*. Boston: Houghton-Mifflin.
   David H. Russell. e.g. (1961) *Children Learn to Read*. 2nd ed.
   Boston: Ginn and Company
   Edward Dolch. e.g. (1960) *Teaching Primary Reading*. Champaign, Illinois: Garrard.
   Marion Monroe. e.g. with Bernice Rogers (1964) *Foundations for Reading. Informal Pre-reading Procedures*. Glenview, Illinois: Scott, Foresman and Company.

6. It is typical historically for a back-to-basics reaction to destroy healthy movements long before they are properly implemented in classrooms. This happened to the work of Huey, Thorndike, and Dewey in the United States, and to Beeby in New Zealand, and is now happening to the work of the Goodman's, Frank Smith and others. Hopefully, the same thing will not happen to the current work of Clay in New Zealand.

   The problem is that before reforms are brought about at the school and classroom levels they are blamed for declining standards. There has never been a time when our Western system of schooling could be said to have operated in an efficient, humane, and rational way. James Britton in his preface to *Teaching for Literacy: Reflections on the Bullock Report* (Davis and Parker 1978) says:

   > I do not believe that 'enlightened education' (meaning, in its true sense, 'progressive education') is part of any bandwagon, or fashion cycle, or pendulum swing; it is a slowly growing movement with philosophical roots way back in the past and pragmatic roots deep in the intuitive wisdom of the most successful teachers today. It has not been tried and found wanting: as the Bullock Committee Survey was able to indicate, it has as yet barely achieved a foothold in the schools of this country. I doubt whether there was ever a time when it was more important, or more difficult, than it is today to keep these ideas alive.

These matters are taken up in Chapter 10.

7. Apart from the work of Jeannette Veatch to which reference has already been made, a brief account of individualized reading procedures will be found in Holdaway (1972).

8. For a brief account of the modality question see Wepman (1971), and Robinson (1972a and 1972b), and for a survey of the literature, J.P. Jones (1972).

Notes to Chapter 3

1. The following data and conclusions arose from a number of studies conducted between 1969 and 1974 in Auckland, New Zealand. These movements were first reported in Holdaway (1976b). A very brief account of these matters is given in the Preface to the present volume.

2. All case studies in this chapter are selected transcripts of extant tape recordings.

3. Detailed longitudinal studies are not available. This would be a fruitful area for further research. In a very recent article Moira McKenzie (1978) reports on very similar behaviour during the emergent reading stage following school entry and develops the implications for beginning reading teaching in an incisive way.

4. Marie Clay reports in several places on the necessary slowing down of reading as children begin to match cues in the early reading stage. This is accompanied by pointing behaviour with the finger or by voice intonation as a visual check is made of each passing word. (Clay, 1967 p.16, and 1972a pp.56–57 and 71–73)

5. See in particular Hawkins (1969); Hasan (1973); and Slobin (1971, pp.112–113).

6. Our society tends to devalue fantasy as fundamentally unreal or untrue. However, the work of the imagination is often more real, true, accurate, detailed, and objective than literal descriptions or even photographs. The camera has a lot to answer for in distorting our view of living processes by presenting them as static, dead segments rather than as acts with functional meaning. Works of the imagination have the potential of representing processes with much greater verisimilitude than literal and analytical descriptions. See also notes 1 and 4 to Chapter 8.

7. It would appear that the crucial factors in reading readiness so far determined develop from actual experience with language, with print, and with text. They include such factors as letter recognition and naming, awareness of fundamental conventions of print, auditory discrimination of the language, familiarity with written dialect forms including the special vocabulary of books, etc. (Hardy 1973; Clay 1967 and 1972a; Robinson, 1972; Downing and Thackray 1975)

8. Perhaps the culture of TV and radio, including pop songs, advertisements, and popular children's features is the nearest equivalent in our society to an oral culture. Certainly children learn from these sources at a very early age and feel socially coherent in a peer group because of a common oral code. Playground games, of course, continue to contribute deeply to the development of special language codes. (Opie 1959)

Notes to Chapter 4

1. The account of applying the developmental model to the classroom given in this chapter, and in Chapters 6 and 7, derive from an amalgam of experiences over the course of some ten years in various projects within Auckland schools. A brief history of these activities is given in the Preface to this volume. The procedures introduced in these chapters have now undergone extensive trialling and full implementation by hundreds of teachers in New Zealand schools and form an important part of the national curriculum in junior language. (A fine booklet and supporting tape recordings for parents has been prepared by the Department of Education in New Zealand. The booklet by Jo Horton, *On the Way to Reading*, may be obtained from the new Zealand Government Printer, or from The Principal, Correspondence School, Department of Education, Private Bag, Wellington. The tape recordings may be obtained by sending two blank C60 cassettes to The National Film Library, P.O. Box 9583, Wellington, New Zealand.)

2. It is strange that the materials which most fascinate young children are not used as

the most central core of the instructional programme, or that in 'storytime' the children's requests for repetition of favourite stories are seldom met. This quite general feature of our schools indicates how adult assumptions blind us to common sense action along developmental lines. Even when attempts have been made to devise experimental programmes for pre-schoolers, the natural developmental inclinations of children seem to have been over-ruled in this way. For example, Durkin (1974) in her fine study of very early instruction in reading emphasises the importance of storytime following her earlier studies of spontaneous reading before school (Durkin 1966). However, the instructional programme for the four and five year olds made no explicit use of favourite stories but relied on extant basal reading programmes and language-experience techniques.

In an exceptional project involving a structured pre-school programme for Maori three and four year olds in Hamilton, New Zealand, Nancy Gerrand (1977) used favourite books as the centre of the language programme. The results fully vindicated the hypothesis that the 'favourite-book-syndrome' as described in the last chapter can be set in operation within a preschool framework and that literacy skills develop naturally in such a setting.

3. Carol Chomsky (1976) reports on a highly successful study in which the tape-recorder was used to make large amounts of textual material available with a high level of repetition. Later in this study it may become more apparent why the 'read-along' situation proves so effective in promoting literacy-learning without instruction.

4. Favourite stories, poems, and songs reflect the current cognitive concerns of children at each stage of development and provide models for organizing experience. For instance, such conceptual structures as opposites, comparatives, and hierarchies, and such logical structures as hypothetical and causal relationships play a dominant part in children's favourite literature. More complex acts of the imagination such as figurative and symbolic thinking are also induced by the literature. Margaret Donaldson (1978, pp.86–95) in her outstanding study of children's thinking, *Children's Minds*, comments on the significance of this literature-induced cognitive learning.

5. Detailed suggestions for innovating on literary structure are provided in Chapter 6. See also Bill Martin and Peggy Brogan (1972) or the Teacher's Edition of any of their *Sounds of Language* series.

6. A more detailed discussion of the use of graded materials is provided in Chapters 6 and 7.

7. In a recent study of beginning reading Moira McKenzie (1978) describes a very similar developmental transition into literacy as we have considered in the last two chapters. She develops the following implications:

> The teacher using language and story experience operates from a different understanding of reading. She can offer the child better reading material, real stories, because she anticipates that he will work on the text to get at the meaning in his own way. She does not expect him to begin by getting all the words right. The stories he is asked to tackle provide motivation and satisfaction on his own terms. Because they have a very clear story structure and appropriate language which, although simple, is real language, these stories are actually easier to read than the 'primerese' of many beginning-reading books. The learner begins reading with an expectation that it will make sense and sound like the language of stories. From the beginning he engages in dialogue about what he is reading; he actively processes the text, responds to it, increasingly draws closer to the author's language, and gradually gets to know about the visual aspects of print. (p.50)

Kenneth Hoskisson (1974 and 1975) in his development of the concept of 'assisted reading' makes very similar points and suggests a very similar set of procedures as we have done in this chapter and in Chapters 6 and 7.

A series of enlarged texts, with supporting materials, has been published by Ashton Scholastic, Sydney and Auckland. Entitled the *Read-It-Again Series*, these materials are edited by Libby Handy and Don Holdaway. Teachers Manuals to the series provide simple guidelines for shared-book-experience teaching.

Notes to Chapter 5

1. The conditions necessary for learning from mistakes are explored in Chapter 9. See also Clay (1972a, pp.124–126) and Donaldson (1978, pp.114–115).

2. There is no real problem here. Most of the basic concepts of any discipline prove impossible to define because our understanding of the definition depends on experience and understanding of the basic concept itself—if the definition uses the concept, then it is tautological; if it avoids the concept, it is unintelligible. We come across the same problem when we talk of such basic concepts in reading as 'comprehension' or 'learning'—we understand what they are and can talk about them quite intelligibly, but cannot adequately define them. This is why no attempt has been made in this book to define 'reading' or 'written expression'.

3. As Carol Chomsky (1973) has pointed out, our spelling patterns reflect the morphology (morpheme relationships) of the language rather than the phonology. This is extremely important in word recognition where the immediacy of meaningful perception is facilitated by familiarity with the base word, or morpheme, and by the way in which bound morphemes in the form of affixes bond into the spelling pattern of different words—e.g. *face, facial, facet, facade, facetious, surface,* where the phonetic value of the 'a' in the base morpheme takes three quite distinct forms, while the spelling retains the configuration. Regular phonetic spelling would destroy this vital source of recognition cues. In traditional teaching of reading, the skill involved in perceiving these morphological relationships has been called *structural analysis*.

4. The concept of deep and surface structure has tremendous explanatory power, although, like any powerful idea, it may be put to strangely stressed speculative uses. Tied to the notion of syntax rather than to the wider notion of semantics (of which syntax is a vital part) it has led to an over-emphasis on syntactical questions in language to the exclusion of other important semantic questions such as those of intonation, idiom, and metaphor. This may be harmless within the academic exclusiveness of the discipline of grammar—and even lead to breakthroughs in that discipline—but it can be deeply distorting when applied rigidly to the complex interdisciplinary problems of learning to read and write. The matter is taken up in greater detail in Chapter 8. For a splendidly lucid discussion of transformational, generative grammar, and of generative semantics, see Smith (1975, pp.96–106, or 1978a, pp.212–219, or 1978b, pp.70–77).

5. There has been little attention in research to this question of automaticity, perhaps because it has not been recognised as a crucial question. To some extent the question resolves itself into a restatement of the problems centering around the over-loading of short-term memory and the use of redundancy in such synthetic tasks as letter-by-letter processing, phonic blending, and the recognition of words isolated from context. (Smith 1975, pp.67–69; 1978b, pp.27–42; or 1978a, pp.43–54). In regard to syllabification see Canney and Schreiner (1977). This set of problems remains unanswerable from a decoding-to-speech model of reading. The major study by LaBerge and Samuels (1976) based on a sub-skills view of reading makes difficult, convoluted, and unconvincing reading. An alternative thesis is developed in this chapter, and the practical implications are worked out in the diagnostic model presented in Chapter 9.

   The linguists use the term *redundancy* to refer to those factors in language which reduce uncertainty and therefore limit the amount of sensory information needed to solve a problem. Redundant features are of many different kinds—semantic, syntactic, and grapho-phonic—increasing always with more familiar and predictable text. The value of redundancy decreases as attention is given more exclusively to the visual detail of isolated words in reading, and increases as experience of the language and awareness of the developing meanings of a text are brought to bear on the visual detail. Both prediction and confirmation operate out of redundancies in the language. They reduce the number of features which must be attended to in order to achieve an assured recognition. Stated in these terms, it can be said that a proper degree of automaticity in language-learning depends on strategies for making use of the redundant features—especially syntactic and semantic redundancies.

We have avoided approaching the hypothesis-test strategy in terms of redundancy for two reasons:

 a. It is a difficult and abstract concept used in a highly specialized and technical way for which there are alternative—if less elegant and economic—locutions.

 b. The term itself has ambiguous associations likely to be brought over from its use in ordinary language. People find it very difficult to understand how the most important factors to attend to in achieving fluency and ease are the redundant ones!

However, the concept has tremendous explanatory power and is worth tussling with. For a scholarly treatment see Smith (1978a).

6. For those who wish to gain some experience of miscue analysis see Kenneth Goodman (1973a) and Yetta Goodman and Carolyn Burke (1972).

7. This use of a denuded alphabet was first devised by the author in 1963 in a paper entitled *Facing the Alphabet* which has been in circulation in New Zealand in various formats for many years. The initial purpose was to find a less time-consuming exercise than that provided by Paul McKee in his delightful *Primer for Parents* (1968)

8. This way of looking at reading as first of all an inside-out process rather than as an exclusively outside-in process is developed by Goodman (1976) and by Frank Smith in several places (1975, pp.83–107, 1978a, pp.4–7 and 25–42, and 1978b, pp.12–35). A simple and humorous introduction to the psycholinguistic point of view will be found in Anne Pulvertaft, (1978); *Carry on Reading*, Ashton Scholastic.

9. A number of important psychological ideas do not render down well into academic jargon and hence centre themselves on common-place yet complex colloquial idioms (Eric Berne, e.g. 1972, the originator of transactional analysis, used this principle to astounding academic effect—would that we could all be a little less jargonistic and a little more colloquial). The term the *Aha response* has this characteristic of experiential clarity—we don't need to define it because we all *know* under what conditions we expostulate 'Aha'.

10. The importance of *reactive inhibition* on perceptual processes in reading and writing has not been studied as the important issue it would seem to be, e.g. Eysenck (1965). Inhibition and fatigue in the context of anxiety are among the most common features of failure or difficulty in learning literate tasks. Together with the notions of overload of short-term memory, lack of self-regulation, and under-development of automaticity, they constitute the central complex of problems facing the beginning learner and the retarded learner. However, almost all methods of beginning reading and of remediation based on sub-skills research of the currently dominant kind, as represented by e.g. Gough (1976), greatly *increase* the effects of this central set of problems. Workable answers can be found only in the facilitation of meaningful processing of genuine text supported by strong rhythms of intrinsic reinforcement. This alternative point of view is worked out more fully in Chapter 9.

11. In a forceful article Merritt (1972) argues that the problems of reading failure can be better understood in terms of *neurosis* than in terms of neurological dysfunction. Certainly many of the conditions known to produce neurotic symptoms are present in the environment of children failing in literacy, and many neurotic symptoms are almost indistinguishable from neurological dysfunction—or, perhaps more accurately, *bring about* neurological dysfunction. Unlike implied neurological deficits within the learner, neurosis-producing factors in the environment lie under our control, and we should first remove these factors before engaging in those loose and irresponsible postulations of neurological impairment which lead to prophesies of failure or organic pessimism.

Notes to Chapter 6

1. For a thorough survey of the research, see the germinal work of Frank Smith (Smith 1978a, pp.99–131). Clay (1972a, pp.133–163) documents the highly complex and

personal ways in which beginning readers process the visual information from print. The matter of what visual features are most useful to the brains of young learners remains largely a mystery, and we therefore have little hard information upon which to base any sequential programme of word recognition. Rather, the evidence that we *do* have suggests that only the complex mental equipment of the individual learner, in control of his or her own attention, can be trusted to formulate a personally effective programme for him or her self—and then, provided only that the opportunities are available for purposeful functioning with *real* text. See Dilena (1977a and 1977b). It is almost certainly the case that by modelling how we read and write, and by pointing to a variety of different features as we help children to process or produce text, we may facilitate these acts of personal perception and help develop that *range* of personal styles of feature-awareness which support the reading and writing of individuals. However, we should not fool ourselves that a progressive system of letter and word identification can pattern in any adequate way the immensely complicated processes by which the individual learner builds his or her repertoire of recognition skills. Unless he or she suffers from some rare and extreme debilitating condition, any child who as a baby has sorted out the baffling complexities in the discrimination of speech sounds to become a listener and a talker has the ability—within a similarly functional and accepting environment—to sort out a working repertoire of strategies for handling print. In calling this particular strategy of feature-sorting the *compare strategy* we are deliberately using a very broad, inclusive, and invitational term—*compare* in any way that is personally meaningful.

2. Teaching children the 'abaca' as a set of names for both the sounds and the letter shapes is not only highly confusing (because sounds and shapes are quite different phenomena), but it is also systematically misinforming them. How can we justify lying to children about what we are teaching them? Margaret Donaldson (1978, pp.103–105) makes some interesting points from the cognitive point of view on this question and comes out in favour of an early explanation to beginning readers that letter-sound relationships are a set of *options* rather than a one-to-one correspondence. Downing (1977, p.28) also supports clarity and honesty in this matter in order to avoid cognitive confusion.

   Young children under suitable developmental motivation become highly interested in letters and numbers. The sooner they learn the culturally acceptable names for these shapes, the sooner they will make sense of normal talk and instruction about them—and be able, critically, to talk and *question* about them themselves. How ridiculous it would be to insist that until the age of seven all children should refer to dogs as *woof-woofs* and never be permitted to use the term in cultural currency, namely *dog*, even though this was the term being used by older people all around them. There was no collapse of literacy standards in New Zealand schools after the 'abaca' was abandoned by most teachers several years ago.

   Of critical concern to the thesis of this enquiry is the need to be able to induce visual images of letters in children's minds by naming the letters. Only in this process of *imaging* expected letter forms can confirming strategies develop.

3. Since the pioneering work of MacKinnon (1959) in Canada there has been a wealth of research indicating that children find great satisfaction in puzzling out the problems of interpreting print. Mastering the techniques of any task, even if the task is cognitive, can be manifestly exciting and rewarding in and for itself. Watch three-year-olds trying to get their tongues around something like *windscreen-wiper*; or seven-year-olds concentrate on manipulating a muppet; or beginning adults becoming aware of the relationship between snow conditions, slope, speed, and angle-of-ski in mastering how to perform a snow-plough turn. The striving is only equalled by the glow of satisfaction in *getting the idea or intuiting the principle*. Why shouldn't the fascinating puzzles of print, with all their rewards in comprehension and in expression, produce equal thrills? In the right *learning environment*, with the right *text*, they do.

Notes to Chapter 7

1. Even those writers who have expressed insights about the importance of memory-for-text within the 'favourite book syndrome' remain timid about the distinction between memory and *real* reading. (Hoskisson 1974; Carol Chomsky 1976; McKenzie 1978). Note that in Chapter 3 we referred to the children's retrieval of stories in reading-like behaviour as a *re-enactment* simply because it was a reconstruction from deep semantic sources rather than recall of the surface language of the books. In any case, *real* reading is *always* largely a matter of memory—bringing what is already in the mind to what is on the page.

   To some extent repeating loved language is a matter of shifting whole language sequences from short-term into long-term memory. (Smith 1975, pp.64–85). Having been reposited in long-term memory, the meanings, rhythms, and language-sequences of favourite stories, poems, and songs can be retrieved for a variety of purposes helpful to reading and to written expression. However, such retrieval is not an easy matter of rote recall; it requires triggering from an organizational or meaningful base. (See Smith 1975, p.69). This is why children seldom recall all of the *exact words* of the favourite book—and therefore must use visual cues to 'decode' a proportion of the text. As they do so, they are properly assisted by appropriate semantic expectations and then gain *immediate confirmation* because the repository of language deep in long-term memory has been effectively triggered by the larger structure—when they decode what they cannot remember with verbal accuracy, bells ring. In this way they are induced into using a facilitated hypothesis/test strategy in all its phases.

   In the read-along situation where the children follow a text as they listen to a story, language expectations induce them from time to time to *precede* the spoken voice by a fraction of a second in recognizing some words. They then receive *immediate* confirmation as the reader's voice enunciates what they have just recognised independently. The same process occurs in unison reading of a favourite story. (Place neck microphones on individual children and monitor their responses in turn against the unison output. You will find that the responses and the strategies are characteristically different depending on each child's developmental level in reading.) It is probably for reasons such as this that the read-along and unison situations—provided the material is fascinating—*promote learning without direct instruction*. In combination with Cloze techniques these situations may be used to induce a wide range of reading and writing skills. Detailed research in such areas as this could be far more fruitful than complex studies of non-reading tasks such as recognizing words out of context or learning to read nonsense words by different procedures.

   An exemplary study of genuine reading tasks using Cloze procedures by Neville and Pugh (1976) advances our understanding of how children solve difficulties in real text, and is therefore suggestive of what might be done to aid poorer readers. A replication of studies such as this using *familiar* text may assist in clarifying the nature of the support provided by favourite books in mastering basic strategies at the beginning reading stage.

2. See Note 1 above re other features of unison response. A close study such as that by Southgate, Arnold and Johnson (1978) of the *actual* use made of teacher's and children's time in reading instruction provides insight into the gross inefficiency of ordinary classrooms as language-learning environments. They say, for instance:

   > The high work output of teachers was not always mirrored by high task-orientation in their pupils. In fact, in certain lessons, particularly when the teacher was engaged in listening to individual children's oral reading or, in a writing lesson, helping them individually with spellings, there were indications that with certain children an adverse effect took over. High teacher output was then related to low pupil output. (p.130)

   See also Clay (1967, pp.18–19, and 1972a pp.102–103) in terms of the difference in quantity read during the first year of instruction between the high and low progress quartiles of her study (20,000 words versus 5,000 words). The *quantity* of language processed can be massively increased by those techniques of shared-book-experience which induce meaningful unison participation, by read-along techniques, and by the repetitive individual processing of favourite books—and other high-impact forms of print such as signs, labels, and TV advertisements.

3. The inordinate amount of time spent *on* a particular book (up to nine weeks as the norm for the lower quartile on Red Book 1 (Clay 1967, pp.13–17) suggests that:

  a. Many children are forced into *boring* repetition from their earliest contact with print.

  b. Slower children are being induced to memorize non-memorable books in the harmful *rote* sense rather than in the healthy familiarization sense in the self-sought repetition of favourite books.

  c. Whole stories are being broken up into meaningless page-lots during the long period of instruction on a particular book.

Even the wide use of related supplementary readers does not fully overcome these difficulties. Compare the approach of Bill Martin and Peggy Brogan (1972) as embodied in the *Instant Readers* designed for whole-book success from the first day at school.

4. A note of caution is suggested here by such studies as that of Neville and Pugh (1976). Forward reference into the text has been shown to be a special feature of healthy reading strategies (indicated by the *Read-on* minor strategy introduced in Chapter 6). When using techniques of progressive exposure, the teacher should sometimes say such things as, 'Let's take a look ahead to see what we can find out about what this word might be.' A *variety* of minor strategies should be modelled in a balanced way. For instance, in the *Red Fox and his Canoe* strategy-lesson in Chapter 6 using a progressive exposure mask, the Read-on strategy was modelled twice, along with the other minor strategies.

5. Kohl (1973, pp.174–190) lists a fascinating range of functional print sources (although I would be cautious and judicious about some other of the techniques suggested by Kohl in this book).

Notes to Chapter 8

1. Susanne Langer (1967, p.4) says:

  Feeling, in the broad sense of whatever is felt in any way, as sensory stimulus or inward tension, pain, emotion or intent, is the mark of mentality. In its most primitive forms it is the forerunner of the phenomena that constitute the subject matter of psychology. Organic activity is not "psychological" unless it terminates, however remotely or indirectly, in something felt. Physiology is different from psychology, not because it deals with different events—the overlapping of the two fields is patent—but because it is not oriented toward the aspects of sensibility, awareness, excitement, gratification or suffering which belong to those events.

Imagination is the human faculty which transcends the dryly cognitive in such a way as to include intellect *and* feeling. As Burnshaw (1970, p.176) puts it:

  What Karl Popper observed of science—that it is cosmology, the problem of understanding the world, ourselves, and our knowledge as part of it—holds equally for all the arts. And the imagination is the only instrument available to a mind with this primary concern. In the arts obviously, but also in "the purest and driest parts of science, imagination is as necessary as in lyric poetry" (Russell). There is indeed no logical path leading to the universal laws which give a picture of the world, as Einstein stated three decades ago: "They can be reached only by intuition, and this intuition is based on an intellectual love of the objects of experience." One thinks of Rilke's earlier declaration about works of art: that "only love can grasp and hold them." By now, to be sure, the essential identity among all approaches to "cosmology, the problem of understanding the world and ourselves" is no longer questioned. "The pioneer scientist," says Planck, "must have a vivid intuitive imagination for new ideas, ideas not generated by deduction, but by *artistically* creative imagination." The dedication of a recent book on *Scientific Uncertainty and Information* affirms that "An artist's inspiration or a scientist's theory, reveal the

unpredictable power of human imagination."
And Langer again (1972, p.342):

> As fast as objective impingements strike our senses they become emotionally tinged and subjectified; and in a symbol-making brain like ours, every internal feeling tends to issue in a symbol which gives it an objective status, even if only transiently. This is the hominid specialty that makes the gulf between man and beast, without any unbiological addition, and probably goes back as far as any possible division between our kind and other primates.

Stories, songs, and poems are teachers of imaginative processes. As such they represent reality in its cognitive/affective/organic wholeness and provide the centre of relevance, the major spring of motivation, and the chief source of reward in the literacy programme.

The affective domain has been tragically overlooked in literacy instruction, especially since, in an effort to achieve narrowly educational ends, the priorities of readability and a host of text controls have taken precedence over literary worth and memorableness in the creation of instructional materials. For a brief consideration of some aspects of the affective dimension in reading instruction, see Carter (1977), and for a deeper consideration of theoretical questions and problems, see Mathewson (1976).

2. Even in such a complex account as this of some processes involved in the interpretation of written language, the matter has been grossly oversimplified. For a lively and readable exploration of some further complexities in the interpretation of ordinary written language, see Dilena (1977a and 1977b).

3. As Angela Ridsdale (1972, p.13) says so well:

> The great fantacists often express truths too subtle for the intellect alone. In tales of witches and goblins, and princesses and animals and dolls, there are judgements passed on reality, ideas presented which the child may not consciously remember, but which he absorbs along with the luminous tissue of the tale itself.

And Langer, again, in her own luminous style (1972, p.342):

> Certainly in our history, presumably for long ages—eons, lasting into present times—the human world has been filled more with creatures of fantasy than of flesh and blood. Every perceived object, scene, and especially every expectation is imbued with fantasy elements, and those phantasms really have a stronger tendency to form systematic patterns, largely of a dramatic character, than factual impressions.

Two fine recent articles are Alexander (1978) and L'Engle (1978). See also again the important study by R.M. Jones (1972), *Fantasy and Feeling in Education*.

4. The reproductions of children's art on the 'Tailypo' theme in the coloured section of this book represent work performed in this unhurried time-space that any expressive artist requires. Note also how the teacher valued the children's creations in the care with which they were preserved during perhaps several days of working and in their careful display.

5. See the coloured section of the book again for examples of corporate mural activity. The language-learning environment should be one of aesthetic pleasure and excitement created by the children under the influence of a moving literature and the fostering model of a teacher who also responds deeply to the themes of the literature.

Notes to Chapter 9

1. The question may be asked, 'How can *beginning* readers possibly operate in this way?' The answer to this question has been explored at many different points of our enquiry. Three important aids to fluency and automatic processing in the early stages are:

   a. Reading one's own language-experience stories.
   b. Reading familiar, loved material.
   c. Reading predictable material.

A more technical way of discussing this matter of having difficulties spread through the task in comfortable proportion to the support of readily recognised items would be through the linguistic concept of *redundancy*. From this point of view, we need to place the beginning reader in a situation of high redundancy—where there is a wealth of supportive cues limiting possibilities and reducing uncertainty. See also Note 5 to Chapter 5.

Clay (1972a, pp.72–76) notes the importance of developing meticulous match and check strategies at the early stages. In later reading children are likely to bring these strategies into operation again when they face a difficulty, a confusion, or the need for self-correction. It is as though, to use her own graphic term, the reader in difficulties 'drops into a lower gear'. Compare this notion to that of a lowering threshold between automatic and conscious attention developed in this chapter. The notion of flexible strategies including *both* the meticulous, serial processing of visual detail *and* the facilitating support of prediction would seem to be important from the earliest stages. The important study by Terry (1977) may be interpreted in this way, rather than in the extreme sense that beginning readers may operate in an exclusively serial manner in comparison with fluent readers. The evidence would certainly suggest that beginning readers *must* operate more often in a meticulous serial fashion than fluent readers, and that the strategies they master stand by them (as 'lower gears') in later reading, but there is no evidence to suggest that they must do so exclusively. It would seem that the peculiar problems of attention and memory-overload during early reading can best be met by a judicious interaction between serial processing and what we might call predictive processing (what Terry refers to as 'parallel processing').

2. The distinction between healthy processing at an inappropriate level and genuinely *faulty* processing is of the first importance. No other remedial action than the provision of motivating material at an appropriate level is required for the reader displaying the sort of symptoms described here. See also Chapter 7 on the controlling of task difficulty.

3. In terms of the 'top-down or bottom-up' controversy about reading (Adams, Anderson, and Durkin 1978), this under-predictive type of misfunctioning can be seen as the lack of top-down processing and an exclusive reliance on bottom-up processing. Goodman (1976) and Smith (1975) use the terms 'inside-out' processing versus 'outside-in' processing. In these terms, the under-predictive reader is a heavily outside-in processer.

4. The over-predictive reader operates in an almost exclusively 'top-down' or 'inside-out' manner. The fact that this kind of misfunctioning is quite common (although nowhere near as common as under-predictive reading) provides strong evidence that this peculiarly modern controversy is factionalist and misleading in the same way as more traditional controversies over method. The healthy reader moves readily in *both* directions as the task demands. However, because reading has been traditionally taught as a bottom-up, outside-in process, the urgent reforms lie mainly in the development of techniques for top-down, inside-out strategies. But this is required to rectify a gross imbalance, *not* to supercede all bottom-up teaching.

5. My first exposure to this procedure of ordinal phoneme placement was during the sixties through the Practice Books of the fine series of remedial books, *The Jim Forest Readers* by Margaret Moreau. The procedure worked so efficiently in helping children with the classic directional and auditory problems of the seriously retarded reader that I developed a range of such materials for use in the clinical setting. Once the learner has 'caught on' to the *idea* of the temporal-positional convention, the insight should be immediately applied to the prediction-confirmation strategy in real reading, and isolated practice then serves no further purpose.

Notes to Chapter 10

1. This criticism of the influence of the 'third force' raises the whole issue of accountability. We need *better* accountability for our practices in literacy teaching rather than *more* accountability. In this respect the following points need to be made:

   a. Effective processes of accountability need to be developed for the 'third force' itself—processes which will not permit improper pressures to be passed down onto the classroom teacher and to children. These processes would include a more specific and professional definition of the responsibilities of people in positions of power within the system to children first, to classroom teachers second, to parents third, and to administrative and institutional priorities last. The first responsibility for removing the invidious pressures of ranking and competition, and for protecting the client confidentiality of children, lies squarely on power figures within the educational system.

b. Individual, longitudinal records such as have been described at several points in the text should replace, or at least minimise the frequency in the use of standardized tests, which rank and compare children yet provide almost useless information for instructional action, and break all the principles of identifying changing developmental stages in the mastery of complex skills. It would be difficult to justify the use of standardized tests of competence more than once a year—and then under the strictest rules of professional confidentiality. Much of the in-institution discussion about children can be termed little other than irresponsible gossip. For fully adequate alternative procedures, see Clay (1972b and 1978).

c. Literacy is a process—it has no content. Progress in literacy should, therefore, be evaluated from the point of view of process, with strong emphasis on monitoring the development of *self*-regulative behaviour in reading and written-language tasks. The keeping of what Marie Clay has termed 'Running Records' (perhaps in the simplified format used in Chapter 9), or the use of miscue analysis techniques, provides for this type of process-analysis. Various forms of Cloze analysis are likely to become available to fulfil similar purposes, especially for silent reading processes, in the near future. For instance, research being carried out at Riverina College, New South Wales, by Drs Peter Rousch and Brian Cambourne is moving rapidly in this direction.

2. It is an all too manifest fact that many children and adults who have learned to read and write do not *use* their competence to any extent. Although the causes for this 'practical illiteracy' are certainly complex, such an outcome is predictable from our instructional methods on the thesis of extinction. Where learners receive little or no reinforcement, intrinsic or extrinsic, the learning is unlikely to be practised spontaneously, and may in fact decline or be lost. The most serious lack in this respect lies in the area of intrinsic rewards. If the meanings and satisfactions arising from reading and writing lack significance, literacy is unlikely to be practised. There are two ways in which intrinsic reinforcement becomes available to the learner—through *process* and through *ends*. As processes, reading and writing are intrinsically satisfying, moment-by-moment, when the learner operates in a self-regulative manner and confirmation feeds constant knowledge of success back into the system. As purposeful activities, reading and writing are rewarding when the language meanings are worthy of achievement or when the act of expression adequately embodies important, personal meanings. The approaches to literacy-learning outlined in this text are important not only in sustaining efficient learning, but also in sustaining on-going *use* of the resulting competence.

3. This way of diagnosing our modern needs in terms of a lack of fraternity has been a recent educational talking-point in New Zealand. I am not certain of the origins of the discussion but believe it to have been stimulated by various statements of the Director of Education, Mr Bill Renwick. Considering the various theses of this book, it is not surprising that I endorse this diagnosis of our educational needs. Taken genuinely, as a value of the first priority, the notion of fraternity could facilitate the solution of our most intransigent educational problems. There is no reason why it should not become a major area of research. At the most practical level we should look at any range of educational options—especially when the issues are complex and lacking in a ratifiably correct solution—with a view to choosing the *fraternal* solution. Such a policy is more likely to result in sound educational outcomes than any other. A claim of such generality can be argued in the most objective terms on the basis of developmental, cultural, and educational verities.

At least until some devastating crisis destroys the viability of modern schooling as

Illich predicts (Macklin 1976), the de-schooling facton present an unconvincingly vague manifesto: and in the actual event of such a crisis, the knowledgeable practice of fraternity would still constitute our most fundamental need (Illich's 'convivial society'). However, this book has been written in a spirit of informed optimism after observing many divergently fraternal classroom environments set up within the modern school.

4. In her delightful study, *Reading and Loving*, Leila Berg (1977), exposes the cultural insipidness of many of our materials and methods.

5. We should note here the complexity of the problems centering around different dialects and codes, and the significant effect that levels of oracy have on beginning reading and writing. We have been able to explore only a few dimensions of this problem—especially that concerned with gaining aural-oral mastery over the dialects of written language. For a penetrating developmental study of the oral language dimension, see Tough (1976 and 1977).

6. This slightly simplified version was prepared from:
Cox, John Harrington (1934). 'Negro Tales of West Virginia';
in *The Journal of Americal Folk-Lore*, Vol. XLVII (October-December),
No. CLXXXVI, pp.341–342.
   There is a note: 'Learned by the Editor from Mr Richard Wyche, Honorary President of the Story-Tellers' League, Washington, D.C. Printed by his permission. A quite different version of this story is printed in Harris, *Uncle Remus Returns*, pp. 52-78.—J.H.C.'
   A finely illustrated version, 'Pitchers and Lettern by Ray Barber', may be found in Bill Martin and Peggy Brogan (1972), *Sounds of a Young Hunter*, pp.96–99. New York: Holt, Rinehart and Winston.

7. *In learning literate tasks healthy operation demands constant two-way processing under the control of a self-regulating and comprehending mind.* From this point of view every competing faction, both traditional and current, embodies a dangerous over-simplification. As we have seen, the language user operates both from top-to-bottom and from bottom-to-top; from inside-out and from outside-in; from wholes-to-parts and from parts-to-wholes. However, the cognitive psychologist is closer to the truth than the behaviourist because of the third part of our definition of healthy functioning—the need for a controlling and comprehending mind. Such a mind is likely to learn from experience and instruction of many kinds, but the most significant learning will arise from the purposeful exercise of the task being learned. Furthermore, there is no known way in which the specifics of such learning can be programmed or sequenced by anyone but the learner—let alone for learners generally, however they are grouped.
   Some sane thoughts may be found in Adams, Anderson, and Durkin (1978); Clay (1978); and Dilena (1977a and 1977b). For the ordinary committed reader, Frank Smith's recent non-technical exposition (Smith 1978b) may provide vital insights from a fresh perspective.
   All theories or models of language-learning undervalue emotional involvement—largely, perhaps, because it is difficult to research or talk about emotional issues. Both in moment-by-moment functioning and in the final achievement of adequate outcomes, the emotions sustain literate operations. Works of the imagination, whether linguistic or non-linguistic, embody meanings which properly encompass both the emotions and those sensations which are subtle reminders of the organic functions which permeate all we do. For this reason, children's literature should constitute the central core of instructional programmes, although we need to use a wide range of other materials. The oft-quoted work of Bill Martin and Peggy Brogan provides detailed suggestions for teaching in a balanced way from this central body of literary material.

The Philosophical Method of this Text

The inclusive way in which different theories and models which have often been considered contradictory have been brought together in this text represents sound and respectable method in the history of thought. When one model subsumes or explains the features of another, it does not so much contradict as *include* the lower level model. Our treatment of learning theory, for instance, as we have moved through the enquiry, represents a scale of increasing inclusiveness in which the cruder behavioural models have been encompassed within wider theories of higher explanatory power. Universal features such as reinforcement or approximation have not been contradicted in the movement towards more adequate models, while at the same time the dangerous simplifications of the lower order models have been both contradicted and corrected.

This is not the place for an essay in epistemology; however, for those interested in these questions and in the methodology lying behind the thinking in this book, the following represent major influences. The notion of a *scale of models* (or *forms* as he calls them) I have taken from the great Oxford philosopher, R.G. Collingwood (1933), in his germinal work, *An Essay on Philosophical Method*. A more recent influence has come from the philosophy of science, and especially the essays by several leading thinkers in *Criticism and the Growth of Knowledge*, edited by Imre Lakatos and Alan Musgrave (1970). The influence of Susanne Langer I have acknowledged on several occasions earlier in these Notes. A recent helpful article on the use of models for language acquisition is Ingram (1971).

References

Adams, M.J., Anderson, R.C., and Durkin, D. (1978) 'Beginning Reading: Theory and Practice'. *Language Arts*, Vol. 55, No. 1, pp.19–25.
Alexander, Lloyd. (1978) 'Fantasy as Images: A Literary View'. *Language Arts*, Vol. 55, No. 4, pp.440–446.
Arvidson, G. (1963) *Learning to Spell*. London: Wheaton.
Ashton-Warner, Sylvia. (1958) *Spinster*. London: Secker and Warburg.
——(1965) *Teacher*. New York: Simon & Schuster.
Athey, Jane. (1976) 'Reading, Research and the Affective Domain'. In *Theoretical Models and Processes of Reading*, eds Harry Singer and Robert B. Ruddell, pp.352–380. Newark, Delaware: International Reading Association.

Beeby, C.E. (1973) 'Why Reading? Why Books?'. In *Reading is Everybody's Business*, ed. W.B. Elley, pp.1–19. Wellington: International Reading Association.
Berg, Leila. (1977) *Reading and Loving*. London: Routledge and Kegan Paul.
Berne, Eric. (1972) *What Do You Say After You Say Hullo?* Paperback edn. 1975 London: Corgi Books.
Britton, James. (1970) *Language and Learning*. Harmondsworth: Penguin Books.
——(1978) Forward in *Teaching for Literacy: Reflections on the Bullock Report*, eds F.R.A. Davis and R.P. Parker, pp.vii–xiii. London: Ward Lock Educational.
Bruner, Jerome S. (1961) *The Process of Education*. Cambridge: Harvard University Press.
——(1974) *The Relevance of Education*. Repr. ed. Harmondsworth: Penguin Books.
——(1975) 'Language as an Instrument of Thought'. In *Problems of Language and Learning*, ed. Alan Davies, pp.61–81. London: Heinemann.
Burnshaw, Stanley. (1970) *The Seamless Web: Language-Thinking, Creature-Knowledge, Art-Experience*. London: Allen Lane, The Penguin Press.

Canney, George, and Schreiner, Robert. (1977) 'A Study of the Effectiveness of Selected Syllabification Rules and Phonogram Patterns for Word Attack'. *Reading Research Quarterly* Vol. 12, No. 2, pp.102–124.
Carter, Garry C. (1977) "Assessing and Improving the Affective Dimensions of Reading". In *Literacy for Life*, eds. A. Ridsdale and J. Horan. Melbourne: Australian Reading Association.
Chall, Jeanne. (1967) *Learning to Read: The Great Debate*. New York: McGraw Hill.
Chomsky, Carol. (1971) 'Invented Spelling in the Open Classroom.' *Word*, Vol. 27, pp.499–518.
——(1973) 'Reading, Writing, and Phonology.' In *Psycholinguistics and Reading*, ed. Frank Smith, pp.91–104. New York: Holt, Rinehart and Winston.
——(1976) 'After Decoding: What?' *Language Arts*, Vol. 53, No. 3, pp.288–296, 314.
Chomsky, Noam. (1957) *Syntactic Structures*. The Hague: Mouton.
——(1959) 'Review of Skinner's *Verbal Behaviour*'. In *The Psychology of Language, Thought, and Instruction*. ed. John P. De Cecco, pp.325–339. London: Holt, Rinehart and Winston, 1970.
(1965) *Aspects of the Theory of Syntax*. Cambridge, Mass.: M.I.T. Press.
Clark, Margaret M. (1970) *Reading Difficulties in Schools*. Harmondsworth: Penguin Books.
——(1975) 'Language and Reading—A Study of Early Reading.' In *The Road to Effective Reading*, ed. William Latham, pp.17–26. London: Ward Lock Educational.
——(1976) *Young Fluent Readers: What Can They Teach Us?* London: Heinemann Educational Books.

Clay, Marie M. (1967) 'The Reading Behaviour of Five Year Old Children: A Research Report.' *New Zealand Journal of Educational Studies*, Vol. 2, No. 1, pp.11–31.
——(1972a) *Reading: The Patterning of Complex Behaviour*. Auckland: Heinemann Educational Books.
——(1972b) *The Early Detection of Reading Difficulties: A Diagnostic Survey*. Auckland. Heinemann Educational Books.
——(1975) *What Did I Write?* Auckland: Heinemann Educational Books.
——(1977) *"Write Now, Read Later": An Evaluation*. Auckland: International Reading Association.
——(1978) 'Reading Acquisition: Do You Get What You Plan For?' In *Literacy for Life*, eds A.M. Ridsdale, D. Ryan, and J. Horan. pp.1–12. Melbourne: Australian Reading Association.
Collingwood, R.G. (1933) *An Essay on Philosophical Method*. Oxford: Clarendon Press.
Conrad, R. (1972) 'Speech and Reading', In *Language by Ear and Eye*, eds J.F. Kavanah and G. Mattingly, pp.203–240. Cambridge Mass.: M.I.T. Press.
Cox, John Harrington. 'Negro Tales from West Virginia'. In *The Journal of American Folk-Lore* Vol. XLVII (October-December, 1934), No. CLXXXVI.

Deci, E.L. (1975) *Intrinsic Motivation*. New York: Plenum Press.
Dilena, Mike. (1977a) 'Computer Models of Language Understanding and the Implications for Teaching Reading Comprehension.' In *Perspectives on Reading* eds R. Levi, G. Forrest, A. Watson, and B. Bishop, pp.121–133. Sydney: Ashton Scholastic.
——(1977b) 'Reading as Understanding—Or Beyond the Way of All Flesch?' In *Literacy for Life: Proceedings of the Third Australian Reading Conference*, eds A.M. Ridsdale, D. Ryan, and J. Horan, pp.39–46. Melbourne: Australian Reading Association.
Doake, David B. (1976) 'Comprehension and Teaching Strategies.' In *New Horizons in Reading*, ed. John E. Merritt, pp.125–140. Newark, Delaware: International Reading Association.
Dolch, Edward. (1960) *Teaching Primary Reading*. Champaign, Illinois: Garrard.
Doman, Glenn. (1964) *Teach Your Baby to Read: The Gentle Revolution*. Repr. ed. London: Pan Books, 1975.
Donaldson, Margaret. (1978) *Children's Minds*. Glasgow: Fontana/Collins.
Doughty, Peter; Pearce, John; and Thornton, Geoffrey. (1972) *Exploring Language*, London: Edward Arnold.
Doughty, Peter, and Thornton, Geoffrey. (1973) *Language Study, the Teacher and the Learner*. London: Edward Arnold.
Downing, John. (1967) *Evaluating the Initial Teaching Alphabet*, London: Cassell.
(1972) 'The Cognitive Clarity Theory of Learning to Read.' In *Literacy at All Levels*, ed. Vera Southgate. pp.63–70. London: Ward Lock Educational.
——(1975) 'The Child's Concept of Language.' In *The Road to Effective Reading*, ed. William Latham, pp.27–33. London: Ward Lock Educational.
——(1977) 'Learning to Read with Understanding.' In *Perspectives on Reading*, eds R. Levi, G. Forrest, A. Watson, and B. Bishop, pp.21–34. Sydney: Ashton Scholastic.
Durkin, Dolores. (1966) *Children Who Read Early: Two Longitudinal Studies*. New York: Teachers College Press.
——(1974) 'A Six Year Study of Children Who Learned to Read in School at the Age of Four.' *Reading Research Quarterly*. Vol. 10, No. 1. pp.9–61.

Edfeldt, A.E. (1960) *Silent Speech and Silent Reading*. Chicago: Chicago University Press.
Elkonin, D.B. (1971) 'USSR'. In *Comparative Reading*, ed. J. Downing, pp.551–580. New York: Macmillan.
Ewing, James M. (1978) 'The Place of Attitudes in the Reading Curriculum.' In *Reading: Implementing the Bullock Report*, ed. Elizabeth Hunter-Grundin and Hans Grundin. London: Ward Lock Educational.
Eysenck, H.J. (1965) *Fact and Fiction in Psychology*. Repr. ed. Harmondsworth: Penguin Books.

Fernald, Grace M. (1943) *Remedial Techniques in Basic School Subjects*. New York: McGraw Hill.

Fromkin, Victoria. (1973) 'Slips of the Tongue.' *Scientific American*, Vol. 229, No. 6, (Dec. 1973), pp.110–117.

Gagne, Robert M. (1970) *The Conditions of Learning*, 2nd ed. London: Holt, Rinehart & Winston.

Gerrand, Nancy. (1977) Unpublished Working Papers, Te Kohanga Preschool Project. Centre for Maori Studies and Research, University of Waikato, Hamilton, New Zealand.

Geyer, John J., and Kilers, Paul A. (1976) 'Some Aspects of the First Stage of Reading.' In *Theoretical Models and Processes of Reading*, eds Harry Singer and Robert B. Ruddell, pp.217–241. Newark: International Reading Association.

Gillooly, William B. (1973) 'The Influence of Writing Charateristics on Learning to Read'. *Reading Research Quarterly*, Vol. VII, No. 2. Winter 1973, pp.167–198.

Goddard, Nora. (1974) *Literacy: Language-Experience Approaches*. London: Macmillan.

Goodacre, Elizabeth J. (1971) 'Methods of Teaching Reading.' In *The Reading Curriculum*, eds Amelia Melnik and John Merritt, pp.114–128. London: University of London Press, 1972.

Goodman, Kenneth S. (1968) 'The Psycholinguistic Nature of the Reading Process.' In *The Psycholinguistic Nature of the Reading Process* ed. Kenneth S. Goodman, pp.13–26. Detroit: Wayne State University Press.

——(1973a) 'Analysis of Oral Miscues: Applied Psycholinguistics.' In *Psycholinguistics and Reading*, ed. Frank Smith, pp.158–176. New York: Holt, Rinehart and Winston.

——(1973b) 'Psycholinguistic Universals in the Reading Process.' In *Psycholinguistics and Reading*, ed. Frank Smith. New York: Holt, Rinhart and Winston.

——(1976a) 'Behind the Eye: What Happens in Reading.' In *Theoretical Models and Processes of Reading*, eds Harry Singer and Robert B. Ruddell, pp.470–508. Newark: International Reading Association.

——(1976b) 'Reading: A Psycholinguistic Guessing Game.' In *Theoretical Models and Processes of Reading*, eds Harry Singer and Robert B. Ruddell, pp.497–508. Newark: International Reading Association.

Goodman, Yetta M., and Burke, Carolyn. (1972) *Reading Miscue Inventory*. New York: Macmillan.

——(1978) 'Reading for Life: The Psycholinguistic Base.' In *Reading: Implementing the Bullock Report*, eds Elizabeth Hunter-Grundin and Hans U. Grundin. London: Ward Lock Educational.

Gough, Philip B. (1976) 'One Second of Reading.' In *Theoretical Models and Processes of Reading*, Second edition, eds H. Singer and R.B. Ruddell. pp.509–535. Newark, Delaware: International Reading Association.

Gray, William S. (1960) *On Their Own In Reading*, 2nd ed. Chicago: Scott, Foresman and Company.

Great Britain, Department of Education and Science. (1975) *A Language for Life*. The 'Bullock Report.' London: H.M.S.O.

Halliday, M.A.K. (1973) *Explorations in the Functions of Language*. London: Edward Arnold.

——(1975a) *Learning How to Mean: Explorations in the Development of Language*. London: Edward Arnold.

——(1975b) 'Talking One's Way In: A Sociological Perspective on Language and Learning.' In *Problems of Language and Learning*, ed. Alan Davies. New Jersey: Humanities.

Hardy, Madeline T. (1973) 'The Development of Beginning Reading Skills: Recent Findings.' In *Reading and Related Skills*, eds Margaret M. Clark and Alistair Milne, pp.46–56. London: Ward Lock Educational.

Hasan R. (1973) 'Code, Register and Social Dialect'. In *Class, Codes and Control. Applied Studies Towards a Sociology of Language*, Vol. 2, ed. Basil Bernstein, pp.253–292. London: Routledge and Kegan Paul.

Hawkins, P.R. (1969) 'Social Class, the Nominal Group and Reference.' In *Class, Codes and Control. Applied Studies Towards a Sociology of Language*, Vol. 2, pp.81–92. ed. Basil Bernstein. London: Routledge and Kegan Paul, 1973.

Holdaway, Don. (1972) *Independence in Reading: A Handbook on Individualized Procedures.* Auckland: Ashton Educational.

——(1976a) 'Self Evaluation and Reading Development.' In *New Horizons in Reading*, ed. John E. Merritt, pp.181–192. Newark, Delaware: International Reading Association.

——(1976b) 'The Oral Dimensions of Literacy.' In *New Directions for Reading Teaching*, eds David B. Doake and Brian T. O'Rourke, pp.83–101. Wellington: New Zealand Educational Institute.

Holmes, Deborah Lott. (1973) "The Independence of Letter, Word, and Meaning Identification in Reading." In *Psycholinguistics and Reading*, ed. F. Smith. New York: Holt, Rinehart and Winston.

Holt, John. (1975) *Escape from Childhood: The Needs and Rights of Children.* Repr ed. Harmondsworth: Penguin Books, 1974

——(1976) *Instead of Education: Ways to Help People Do Things Better.* Repr. ed. Harmondsworth: Penguin Books, 1977.

Hopkins, Harold R. (1977) *From Talkers to Readers the Natural Way.* Sydney: Ashton Scholastic.

Horton, Jo. (1978) *On The Way to Reading.* Wellington. Department of Education.

Hoskisson, Kenneth, and Krohm, Bernadette. (1974) 'Reading by Immersion: Assisted Reading,' *Elementary English*, September, 1974, Vol. 51, No. 6, pp.832-836.

——(1975) 'The Many Facets of Assisted Reading' *Elementary English*, Vol. 52, No. 3, pp.312-315.

Huey, E.B. (1908) *The Psychology and Pedagogy of Reading.* Cambridge, Mass.: M.I.T. Press.

Ingram, Elizabeth. (1971) 'The Requirements of Model Users.' In *Language Acquisition: Models and Methods*, eds R. Huxley and E. Ingram, pp.147–160. London: Academic Press.

Jones, John P. (1972). *Intersensory Transfer, Perceptual Shifting, Modal Preference, and Reading.* Newark, Deleware: International Reading Association.

Jones, Richard M. (1968) *Fantasy and Feeling in Education.* Repr. ed. Harmondsworth: Penguin Books, 1972.

——(1973) *Involving Fantasies and Feelings.* In *Facts and Feelings in the Classroom*, ed. L. J. Rubin. London: Ward Lock Educational, 1974.

Kohl, Herbert. (1973) *Reading, How To.* New York: E.P. Dutton and Company Inc.

Kolers, P. A. (1970) 'Three Stages of Reading'. In *Basic Studies on Reading*, eds. H. Levin and J. P. Williams. New York: Basic Books.

LaBerge, David and Samuels, S. Jay. (1976) 'Toward a Theory of Automatic Information Processing in Reading.' In *Theoretical Models and Processes of Reading*, second edition, eds. Harry Singer and Robert B. Ruddell, pp.548–579. Newark: International Reading Association.

Lakatos, Imre and Musgrave, Alan, eds. (1970) *Criticism and the Growth of Knowledge.* London: Cambridge University Press.

Langer, Susanne K. (1942) *Philosophy in a New Key: A Study of the Symbolism of Reason, Rite, and Art.* Repr. ed. New York: The New American Library, A Mentor Book, 1959.

——(1962) *Philosophical Sketches.* Baltimore: John Hopkins Press.

——(1967) *Mind: An Essay on Human Feeling.* Vol. 1. Paperback ed. Baltimore: John Hopkins University Press, 1975.

——(1972) *Mind: An Essay on Human Feeling.* Vol. 2. Paperback ed. Baltimore: John Hopkins University Press, 1974.

Lefrancois, Guy R. (1975) *Psychology for Teaching.* 2nd ed. Belmont: Wadsworth.

L'Engle, Madeleine. (1978) 'What is Real?' *Language Arts*, Vol. 55, No. 4, pp.447-451.

Luria, A.R., and Yudovich, F. Ia. (1956) *Speech and the Development of Mental Processes in the Child.* Ed. and translated by Joan Simon, repr. ed. Harmondsworth: Penguin Books.

Lynskey, Alan. (1974) *Children and Themes.* London: Oxford University Press.

McGinitie, Walter. (1977) 'The 'Merican Methods Madness.' In *Perspectives on Reading*, eds R. Levi, G. Forrest, A. Watson, and B. Bishop, pp.9–20. Sydney: Ashton Scholastic.

Mackay, D.; Thompson, B.; and Schaub, P. (1970) *Breakthrough to Literacy: Programme in Linguistics and English Teaching*. London: Schools Council/Longman.

McKee, Paul. (1966) *The Teaching of Reading in the Elementary School*. Boston: Houghton-Mifflin.

——(1968) *A Primer for Parents*. Boston: Houghton-Mifflin.

McKenzie, Moira. (1978) 'Learning to Read Through Reading.' In *Reading: Implementing the Bullock Report*, eds Elizabeth Hunter-Grundin and Hans U. Grundin. London: Ward Lock Educational.

MacKinnon, A.R. (1959) *How DO Children Learn to Read?* Vancouver: Copp Clark.

Macklin, Michael. (1976) *When Schools Are Gone: A Projection of the Thought of Ivan Illich*. Queensland: University of Queensland Press.

McNeill, David. (1970) *The Acquisition of Language: The Study of Developmental Psycholinguistics*. New York: Harper & Row.

Martin, Bill, and Brogan, Peggy. (1972) *Teacher's Guide, Instant Readers*. New York: Holt, Rinehart and Winston.

Mathewson, Grover C. (1976) 'The Function of Attitude in the Reading Process.' In *Theoretical Models and Processes of Reading*, second edition, eds H. Singer and R.B. Ruddell, pp.665–676. Newark, Delaware: International Reading Association.

Menyuk, Paula. (1971) *The Acquisition and Development of Language*. Englewood Cliffs, N.J.: Prentice-Hall.

Merritt, John E. (1972) 'Reading Failure: A Re-examination.' In *Literacy at All Levels*, ed. Vera Southgate, pp.175–184. London: Ward Lock Educational.

——(1978) 'Learning to Read and Reading to Learn: Developing Effective Reading.' In *Reading: Implementing the Bullock Report*, eds E. Hunter-Grundin and H.A. Grundin, pp.92–106. London: Ward Lock Educational.

Monroe, Marion, and Rogers, Bernice. (1964) *Foundations for Reading: Informal Pre-reading Procedures*. Glenview, Illinois: Scott, Foresman and Company.

Moreau, Margaret. (1960) Practice Books for *Jim Forrest Readers* by John and Nancy Rambeau. Harr Wagner Pub. Co.

Mussen, Paul. (1973) *The Psychological Development of the Child*. 2nd ed. Englewood Cliffs: Prentice-Hall.

Neville, Mary H. and Pugh, A.K. (1976) 'Context in Reading and Listening: Variations in Approach to Cloze Tasks.' *Reading Research Quarterly*, Vol. 12, No. 1, pp.13–31.

Opie, Iona and Peter (1959) *The Lore and Language of School Children*. London: O.U.P.

——(1969) *Children's Games in Street and Playground*. London O.U.P.

Peters, M. (1967) *Spelling: Caught or Taught*. London, Routledge and Kegan Paul.

Pines, Maya. (1967) *Revolution in Learning: The Years from Birth to Five*. Repr. ed. London: Allen Lane, The Penguin Press.

Pulvertaft, Anne. (1978) *Carry on Reading*. Sydney: Ashton Scholastic.

Reid, Jessie F. (1973) 'Towards a Theory of Literacy.' In *Reading and Related Skills*, eds Margaret M. Clark and Alastair Milne, pp.28–36. London: Ward Lock Educational.

Renehan, William. (1977) *Seven-year-olds: Talking and Writing*. Victoria: Australian Council for Educational Research.

Richardson, Elwyn S. (1964) *In the Early World*. Wellington: New Zealand Council of Educational Research.

Ridsdale, Angela. (1972) 'Children and Books.' In *Reading, Books and Children*, ed C.S. Brockett, pp.8–19. Auckland: International Reading Association.

Robinson, Helen M. (1972a) 'Visual and Auditory Modalities Related to Methods for Beginning Reading.' *Reading Research Quarterly*, Vol. VIII, No. 1, Fall 1972, pp.7–39.

——(1972b) 'Perceptual Training—Does it Result in Reading Improvement.' In *Some Persistent Questions on Beginning Reading*, ed. R.C. Aukerman, pp.135–150. Newark, Delaware: International Reading Association.

Robinson, Susan (1973) 'Predicting Early Reading Progress.' Unpublished thesis, University of Auckland.

Rogers, C.R. (1969) *Freedom to Learn*. Columbus, Ohio: Merrill.

Russell, David H. (1961) *Children Learn to Read*. 2nd ed. Boston: Ginn and Co.

Ryan, D. J. (1975) *The Reading Process*. Melbourne: Access Skills Project Team.

Santa, Carol Minnick. (1976) 'Spelling Patterns and the Development of Flexible Word Recognition Strategies.' *Reading Research Quarterly*, Vol. 12, No. 2, pp.125–144.

Schonell, F. (1932) *Essentials in Teaching and Testing Spelling*. London: Macmillan & Co.

Skinner, B.F. (1957) 'A Functional Analysis of Verbal Behaviour. In *The Psychology of Language, Thought, and Instruction*, ed. John P. de Cecco, pp.318–325. London: Holt, Rinehart and Winston, 1970.

Slobin, Dan I. (1971) *Psycholinguistics*. Glenview: Scott, Foresman and Company.

Smith, Frank. (1971) *Understanding Reading: A Psycholinguistic Analysis of Reading and Learning to Read*. New York: Holt, Rinehart and Winston.

——(1973) 'Twelve Easy Ways to Make Learning to Read Difficult.' In *Psycholinguistics and Reading*, ed. Frank Smith, pp.183–196. New York: Holt, Rinehart and Winston.

——(1975) *Comprehension and Learning: A Conceptual Framework for Teachers*. New York: Holt, Rinehart and Winston.

——(1978a) *Understanding Reading: A Psycholinguistic Analysis of Reading and Learning to Read*, 2nd edition. New York: Holt, Rinehart and Winston.

——(1978b) *Reading*. Cambridge: Cambridge University Press.

Southgate, Vera; Arnold, Helen; and Johnson, Sandra. (1978) 'The Use of Teacher's and Children's Time in Extending Beginning Reading.' In *Reading: Implementing the Bullock Report*, eds Elizabeth Hunter-Grundin and Hans. U. Grundin, pp.120–132. London: Ward Lock Educational.

Terry, Pamela R. (1976) 'The Effect of Orthographic Transformations upon Speed and Accuracy of Semantic Categorizations (Abstracted Report).' *Reading Research Quarterly*, Vol. 12, No. 2, pp.166–175.

Torrey, Jane. (1973) 'Learning to Read Without a Teacher: A Case Study.' In *Psycholinguistics and Reading*, ed. Frank Smith, pp.146–157. New York: Holt, Rinehart and Winston.

Tough, Joan.(1976) *Listening to Children Talking: A Guide to the Appraisal of Children's Use of Language*. London: Ward Lock.

—— (1977) *Talking and Learning*. London: Ward Lock Educational.

U.S.A., Association for Supervision and Curriculum Development. (1962) *Perceiving, Behaving, Becoming*. Washington: ASCD.

Veatch, Jeanette. (1959) *Individualizing Your Reading Programme*. New York: Putnam's Sons.

——(1966) *Reading in the Elementary School*. New York: Ronald Press.

——(1968) *How to Teach Reading with Children's Books*. New York: Citation Press.

Vygotsky, L.S. (1962a, transl. Hanfmann and Vakar) *Thought and Language*. Cambridge, Mass.: M.I.T. Press.

——(1962b, transl.) 'Language and Thought: The Problem and the Approach.' In *The Psychology of Language, Thought, and Instruction*, ed. John P. de Cecco, pp.56–60. London: Holt, Rinehart and Winston, 1967.

Walshe, R.D. (1977a) 'Reading Needs Writing!' In *Literacy for Life*, eds A. Ridsdale, D. Ryan, and J. Horan, pp.55–62. Melbourne: Australian Reading Association.

——(1977b) 'What is the Language Experience Approach.' In *Better Reading/Writing— Now!* ed. R.D. Walshe, pp.40–43. Sydney: Primary English Teachers Association.

Wepman, Joseph M. (1971) 'Modalities and Learning.' In *Coordinating Reading Instruction*, ed. Helen M. Robinson, pp.55–60. Glenview: Scott, Foresman and Company.

Whitehall, H. (1951) *Structural Essentials of English*. London: Longmans Green.

References to Children's Books

Ainsworth, Ruth, and Ridout, Ronald. *House of Hay, Come and Play*, and *A Name of My Own*. Purnell Books, Maidenhead.
Alain. *One Two Three Going to Sea*. Scholastic Book Services.
Benchley, Nathaniel. *Red Fox and His Canoe*. Scholastic Book Services.
Berenstain, S. & J. *Bears in the Night*. William Collins & Sons Ltd.
Blair, Susan. *The Three Billy Goats Gruff*. Scholastic Book Services.
Bonne, Rose, and Graboff, Abner. *I Know an Old Lady*. Scholastic Book Services.
Carle, Eric. *The Very Hungry Caterpillar*. Hamish Hamilton Ltd. London.
Chance, E.B. *Just in Time for the King's Birthday*. Scholastic Book Services.
Charlip, R. *What Good Luck, What Bad Luck*. Scholastic Book Services.
Clarke, Mollie. *The Three Little Kittens*. Wheaton & Co.
Cole, Joanna. *Fun on Wheels*. Scholastic Book Services.
Cook, Bernadine. *The Little Fish That Got Away*. Scholastic Book Services.
Eastman, P.D. *Are You My Mother?* William Collins & Sons Ltd.
Emberley, Barbara. *One Wide River to Cross*. Scholastic Book Services.
Emberley, Barbara, and Emberley E. *Drummer Hoff*. The Bodley Head.
Freeman, Don. *Corduroy*. Viking. Also published in *Systems* by Scott, Foresman.
Galdone, Paul. *The Three Bears*. World's Work.
Guilfoile, Elizabeth. *Nobody Listens to Andrew*. Follett Pub. Co.
Heilbroner, Joan. *This is the House Where Jack Lived*. World's Work.
Hulbert, Elizabeth. *Out and In*. Scholastic Book Services.
Hurd, E.T. *Stop, Stop*. Scholastic Book Services.
Keats, Ezra Jack. *Apartment 3*, and *Over in the Meadow*. Hamish Hamilton Ltd.
Leaf, Munroe. *Gordon the Goat*. Scholastic Book Services.
Littledale, Freya. *The Magic Fish*. Scholastic Book Services.
McGowen, Tom. *Dragon Stew*. Harper & Row.
Martin, Bill, Jr. *Brown Bear, Brown Bear, What do you See?*
——*David Was Mad, The Haunted House, Old Mother Middle Muddle*.
——*When it Rains . . It Rains*. Holt, Rinehart & Winston.
Merriam, Eve. *Epaminados*. Scholastic Book Services.
Meyer, Mercer. *What Do You Do With a Kangaroo?* Scholastic Book Services.
Rose, Gerald. *Trouble in the Ark*. Penguin.
Rossetti, Christinas G. *What is Pink*. Macmillam Publishing Co.
Sendak, Maurice. *Chicken Soup With Rice*. Williams Collins & Sons Ltd.
——*Where the Wild Things Are*. Harper & Row.
Seuss, Dr. *Dr. Seuss's ABC, Green Eggs and Ham*. William Collins & Sons Ltd.
Slobodkina, Esphyr. *Caps for Sale*. Addison Wesley. Inc.
Wiseman, E.B. *Morris the Moose Goes to School*. Scholastic Book Services.

References to Instructional Materials

A Book for Me to Read. Ruth Ainsworth and Ronald Ridout. Purnell Books.
Beacon Readers. J.H. Fassett. Ginn and Co. London.
Gay Colour Books. Alice Williamson. E.J. Arnold & Sons.
Instant Readers. Compiled by Bill Martin, Jr. and Peggy Brogan. Holt, Rinehart and Winston, New York.
Jim Forest Readers. John and Nancy Rambeau. Harr Wagner.
Nippers Series. ed. Leila Berg. Macmillan.
Read-It-Again Series. eds Libby Handy and Don Holdaway. Ashton Scholastic.
Reading with Rhythm. Jenny Taylor & Terry Ingleby. Longman.
Ready-to-Read Series. Compiled by Myrtle Simpson. Methuen Education, London.
S.R.A. Reading Laboratories. Gen. ed. Don Parker. S.R.A.
Scholastic Core Libraries. Gen. ed. Don Holdaway. Ashton Scholastic.
Sounds of Language Series. Compiled by Bill Martin, Jr. and Peggy Brogan. Holt, Rinehart and Winston.
Systems, Scott, Foresman & Co.

Indices

Name Index

Adams, M.J. 214:3, 216:7
Ainsworth, Ruth. 51, 69
Alain, 111, 158
Alexander, Lloyd. 213:3
Anderson, R.C. 214:3, 216:7
Arnold, Helen. 211:2
Arvidson, G. 35
Ashton-Warner, Sylvia. 7, 31, 69, 78, 114
Beeby, C.E. 7, 205:6
Benchley, Nathaniel. 121
Berenstain, S. & J. 68
Berg, Leila. 216:4
Berne, Eric. 209:9
Bernstein, Basil. 204:6
Bonne, Rose. 67
Boyce, E.R. 158
Britton, James. 13, 148, 149, 203:2, 204:10, 205:6
Brogan, Peggy. 71, 207:5, 212:3, 216:6, 216:7
Bruner, Jerome S. 152, 203:2, 203:4, 204:6, 204:8
Burke, Carolyn. 209:6
Burnshaw, Stanley. 203:2, 212:1
Cambourne, Brian. 215:1
Canney, George. 208:5
Carle, Eric. 66
Carter, Gary. 212:1
Chall, Jeanne. 15, 26
Chance, E.B. 158
Charlip, Remy. 158
Chomsky, Carol. 35, 47-9, 93, 207:3, 208:3, 211:1
Chomsky, Noam. 81, 204:4
Clark, Margaret M. 38, 39, 48, 60, 110
Clarke, Mollie. 50-1
Clay, Marie M. 7, 34, 35, 38, 39, 47, 49, 52, 56, 70, 75, 88, 89, 90, 107, 109, 124, 127, 132, 143, 157, 169, 181, 203:1, 205:6, 206:4, 206:7, 208:1, 209:1, 211:2, 212:3, 213:1, 215:1, 216:7

Cole, Joanna. 74, 118
Collingwood, R.G. 217:7
Cook, Bernadine. 112
Cox, John Harrington. 216:6
Deci, E.L. 204:11
Dewey, John. 205:6
Dilena, Mike. 221:1, 213:2, 216:7
Dolch, Edward. 30, 205:5
Doman, Glenn. 59
Donaldson, Margaret. 204:11, 207:4, 208:1, 210:2
Doughty, Peter. 203:2
Downing, John. 32, 181, 206:7, 210:2
Durkin, Dolores. 38, 60, 110, 207:2, 214:3, 216:7
Eastman, P.D. 41-46, 149, 158
Edfelt, A.E. 85
Elkonin, D.B. 35, 90, 182
Emberley, Barbara. 68
Eysenck, H.J. 209:10
Fernald, Grace M. 31, 35
Freeman, Don. 111
Fromkin, Victoria. 155
Gagne, Robert M. 203:4
Galdone, Paul. 68
Gates, Arthur. 26
Gerrand, Nancy. 207:1
Goddard, Nora. 205:4
Goodacre, Elizabeth J. 205:1
Goodman, Kenneth S. 7, 84, 87, 95, 203:1, 205:6, 209:6, 209:7, 214:3
Goodman, Yetta M. 205:6, 209:6
Gough, Philip B. 209:10
Graboff, Abner. 67
Gray, William S. 30, 205:5
Guilfoile, Elizabeth. 67
Halliday, Michael A.K. 14, 148, 149, 155, 203:2
Handy, Libby. 207:7
Hardy, Madeline T. 181, 206:7
Heilbroner, Joan. 111

Subject Index

and neurological dysfunction 16, 96–8
and neurosis 16, 96–8, 209:11
omissions 175–9
oral 142–3, 168, 170
over-predictive 177–8, 214:4
performance syndrome in 28, 179
pre-reading 39, 56, 206:7
pre-school (before institutional contact)
  58–60
quantity read 207:3, 211:2
readiness 39, 47, 49, 52–6, 206:7
records 124–5, 143, 169, 214:1
  see also Monitoring progress
running records 124, 143, 215:1
  see also Monitoring progress
silent 142–3, 215:1
strategies 109–146
  see also major entry
substitutions 173–9
under-predictive 176–7
unseen text 124
whole-book success 212:13
and word-calling 13, 179–80
see also Basic skills, Cloze procedures;
  Developmental stages; Directionality;
  Feature analysis; Language, spoken—
  relationship to written; Language,
  writing and reading; Letter-sound
  relationships; Phonics; Print;
  Reinforcement; Sight vocabulary;
  Sound-to-letter confirmation;
  Structural analysis; Unison response;
  Visual discrimination
Reading-like behaviour 40–62, 70–1, 132, 149,
  210:1
Read-on strategy 99, 109, 212:4
Records, longitudinal 124–5, 143, 168,
  214:1
Reduction of uncertainty 87, 95, 99, 208:5
Redundancy 208:5, 213:1
Reinforcement 15–16, 20, 22, 59, 174, 190
  cyclic 22, 96–8, 204:11
  extrinsic 60, 164, 167, 204:11
  intrinsic 15, 22, 164, 167, 204:11, 215:2
  positive/negative 203:5
Repetition *see* Learning, repetition in
Re-run strategy 52, 99, 109
Rhyme 158
Rhythm 57, 115, 158
  in complex behaviour 96–7
Role-playing
  as reader 40, 61, 64, 67, 68, 70, 73
  as teacher 68, 70, 73, 133–4
  as writer/author 47–8, 61, 64, 78, 116,
  134, 144, 161
Rote-learning 41, 44, 127–9, 211:1, 212:3

Scholastic Core Libraries 132, 139, 145, 225

Schooling 22, 26, 103, 107, 125, 163, 167,
  169, 185–9, 202, 214:1
Second-year programmes 135–8
Self correction 31, 38, 40, 44, 53, 59, 91,
  93, 127–9, 136, 143, 169
  ratio 175
Self-evaluation 31–2, 169, 209:1
Self-expression 160, 165
Self-improving system 89, 136, 160, 170,
  202, 210:1
Self-regulation 15, 22, 60, 61, 72, 80, 86–8,
  88–9, 91, 136, 155, 168, 170–1, 187,
  210:1, 216:7
Self-selection 23, 31–2, 59,
  see also Individualized reading
Semantic
  awareness 156, 162
  coherence 159–60, 173
  cues 88, 91–5, 159
  drive 150, 159–62
  operators 156–7
Semantics 13, 82–8, 147–55, 207:4, 208:4
Sensitive observation *see* Evaluation;
  Monitoring
Sentimentality 39, 103
Shared-book-experience 7–8, 64–80, 126–46,
  163–76, 207:7, 211:2
  objectives of 71–2
Short-term memory 99, 180, 208:5, 211:1
Sight vocabulary 28, 31, 69, 91–2, 98, 113:6
  basic 114
  organic 31, 114:5
Song and chant 57–8, 66, 78, 157–8, 163–5
  see also Art, related
Sounding out *see* Blending
Sound-to-letter confirmation 93–100, 120
  see also Confirmation
Spelling 26, 33–4, 35–6, 94, 101, 123, 170
  approximation in 34, 123, 181
  healthy processing 180–1
  over-confident 181
  patterns 208:3
  pre-school 47–9
  under-confident 181
S.R.A. Reading Laboratories 132, 139, 225
Story 39, 149, 152, 158–9, 163–4
  Goldilocks 53, 149, 150–1, 156, 158
  plot 49, 158–9
  structures 158–9
  see also Favourite books
Strategies 32, 56, 91–7, 134–8, 141, 157,
  211:1
  minor 109–23, 163, 212:4
Structural analysis 69, 93, 94, 121, 208:3
  see also Configuration; Feature analysis
Surface structure 84, 153, 162, 180, 208:4
Syllabification 27, 98, 103, 157, 208:5
Symbolism 55, 114, 116, 149, 150–60,
  212:1